AT DEATH'S DOOR

AT DEATH'S DOOR

End of Life Stories from the Bedside

Sebastian Sepulveda

and Gini Graham Scott

ROWMAN & LITTLEFIELD
Lanham • Boulder • New York • London

Published by Rowman & Littlefield
A wholly owned subsidary of The Rowman & Littlefield Publishing Group, Inc.
4501 Forbes Boulevard, Suite 200, Lanham, Maryland 20706
www.rowman.com

Unit A, Whitacre Mews, 26-34 Stannary Street, London SE11 4AB

This book is not intended as a medical manual, and the data presented here are meant to assist the reader in making informed choices regarding wellness. This book is not a replacement for treatment(s) that the reader's personal physician may have suggested. If the reader believes he or she is experiencing a medical issue, professional medical help is recommended. Mention of particular products, companies, or authorities in this book does not entail endorsement by the publisher or author.

British Library Cataloguing in Publication Information Available

Library of Congress Cataloging-in-Publication Data

Names: Sepulveda, Sebastian, 1960- author.
Title: At death's door : End of life stories from the bedside / Sebastian Sepulveda and Gini Graham Scott.
Description: Lanham : Rowman & Littlefield, 2017. | Includes bibliographical references and index.
Identifiers: LCCN 2016032742 (print) | LCCN 2016034056 (ebook) | ISBN 9781442273344 (cloth : alkaline paper) | ISBN 9781442273351 (electronic)
Subjects: LCSH: Right to die--Popular works. | Terminal Care--Popular works. | Medical ethics--Popular works. | Death--Planning--Popular works.
Classification: LCC R726 .S448 2017 (print) | LCC R726 (ebook) | DDC 362.17/5--dc23
LC record available at https://lccn.loc.gov/2016032742

♾ ™ The paper used in this publication meets the minimum requirements of American National Standard for Information Sciences Permanence of Paper for Printed Library Materials, ANSI/NISO Z39.48-1992.

Printed in the United States of America

CONTENTS

INTRODUCTION

As a doctor specializing in hospital inpatients and in my own private practice, I have encountered many patients and families who approach death in very different ways. Their attitude and decision as to whether or not to choose a DNR (do not resuscitate) or DNI (do not intubate) order affects the kind of treatment they get at the end. Another factor that influences their treatment is the view of family members when patients can no longer make these end-of-life treatment decisions, such as if a patient has slipped into a coma or has a serious stroke or other mental disability so he or she can't think logically or even talk. Then, someone else has to decide. In some cases, patients have given clear instructions to their doctor and family on what to do at the end; but often they don't, which can make determining what to do difficult.

As the doctor who has cared for these patients in their final days, I can only provide advice on what to do, if they can understand, or advise their family and sometimes their personal physician if the patients can't understand themselves. However, I often find that their physician has withdrawn and turned their end-of-life care to the hospital. So I often have to sort out these decisions with the patient, family, or sometimes both, where the family still consults with the patient.

Whatever the case, being a doctor at the end of a patient's life has its special challenges, especially today because the advances of modern medicine make it technologically possible to do much more to prolong a patient's life. But complicating the situation is the concern of both the patient and family about the difficulties at the end of life, most notably the increasing deterioration of the body and mind, along with the increasing pain.

While a doctor's long-standing ethical commitment is to provide the best possible care and maintain life, this commitment is challenged by changing attitudes about whether to alleviate pain as possible or provide medication that may end the patient's suffering by ending life. In almost all states today except for five of them, providing any treatment to end the patient's life is still illegal. However, the notion of assisted suicide in the face of a terminal illness seems to be growing in acceptance, as reflected in the case of Brittany Maynard. She went to Oregon, which permits such suicides under its Death with Dignity Law, and on November 1, 2014, she took a lethal dose of drugs prescribed by her doctor to end her suffering. She stated that "death with dignity was the best option for me and my family."[1] At the time of her death, only three states had passed such death with dignity laws, but another seven states have introduced such laws, and California passed an End of Life Option Act, signed into law by Governor Brown on October 5, 2015.[2]

Yet despite these changing laws and public attitudes, as a doctor I am still committed to preserving life as long as possible, while relieving suffering. In that spirit I have approached end-of-life care to work with each patient as long as I can, as well as with any family members who are present at the end.

At Death's Door has been written from this perspective to provide an inside look at how a doctor deals with dying patients and their families. As it illustrates, every patient is different, because they vary so greatly in the condition that has led them to this end-of-life dying process, in the support they receive from family members and friends, and in their own attitude toward what is happening—ranging from anger and denial to acceptance and even humor. While some patients feel the love around them, which helps them feel better physically, emotionally, mentally, and spiritually, others experience dying alone, which may contribute to their resistance and denial. I even had one patient who, though morbidly obese and without any family or friends to visit, found the humor in his situation and made jokes about what he was experiencing. Perhaps this humor was his way to distance himself from an otherwise painful and hard-to-accept reality. Eventually, toward the end, he finally accepted the truth of his condition and two days later, he died.

I

CARING FOR END-OF-LIFE PATIENTS

In writing this work, I have described my everyday experiences in dealing with patients in their last days of life, and with family members, relatives, and medical professionals involved in their care. At times, these interactions have included religious leaders, such as ministers, priests, and rabbis, who provided guidance and support for some patients in their last difficult days.

To fully understand what happens in caring for patients, it is also important to understand the hospital system and the other organizations and companies providing end-of-life care and services. Now that individuals are living longer and healthier lives, end-of-life care has gotten increasing attention, and a growing new profession of doctors and other medical care providers has emerged to deal with these patients. I am one of the thousands of such professionals, although the newness of this profession means that the vast majority of people in the United States haven't heard of us.

Accordingly, in this chapter, I want to describe this growing system in which we operate, so readers can better understand how everyone in it works to provide this care as best as possible, within the legal restrictions and guidelines which influence what we can do. For example, in most states, if someone wants a doctor's assistance in terminating their life, we can't do this. But if someone wants to end his or her life with minimal suffering in his or her last days and opts to not have any resuscitation procedures, we can provide comfort and compassion to reduce or elimi-

nate any pain while stopping any treatment, so the patient can die naturally, without any active assistance.

The following sections describe the major elements of the system,
which include:

- the doctors providing end-of-life care
- the hospital intensive care unit
- other hospital units providing end-of-life care
- services providing palliative care
- hospices that care for dying patients
- nursing homes that include end-of-life services
- other professionals assisting with end-of-life patients

THE HOSPITALIST: DOCTORS WHO PROVIDE IN-HOUSE AND END-OF-LIFE CARE

In the last few years, hospitals have become the center for a new type of
doctor called a "hospitalist," who specializes in inpatient medical care,
which includes caring for patients with an end-of-life care status. Being a
hospitalist is not yet a formal specialty, and some doctors combine this
practice with other types of medical practice, as I do.

While doctors of all ages have been drawn into this specialty, for the
most part these doctors are very young, right out of medical school training. Most of them have finished their training, but they have not set up a
private practice or developed long-term relationships with patients, since
they are so new in the field. While some hospitalists have acquired the
needed skills to work effectively and compassionately with individual
patients and their families, as well as coordinate with other medical professionals who help provide the necessary care, for many doctors end-of-
life care is just a job. They regularly go on rounds and interact with the
patients, families, and medical professionals, but they don't necessarily
have the experience to provide patients and their families with the support
they need to deal with the many issues that come up at the end of one's
life.

Rather, as this book illustrates, it takes some time to develop a prognosis of a patient's condition and determine the best approach to deal with
that patient. Although such knowledge may initially seem unnecessary,

because all patients facing the end of life will be dead in a matter of days, perhaps a week or two, sometimes a few months, there are great differences in how to care for such patients. Also, death is not always the outcome, at least in that admission. For example, some patients clearly have an irreversible terminal condition and can be expected to die in a few hours to a few days, such as one patient who was experiencing a rapid organ and system shutdown, with no way to revive him. So the demise of such patients is readily expected. By contrast, some patients rally, even though everything looks very bad and there seems to be no hope. But somehow, against all odds, doctors are able to stop the shutdown or reverse the course of a deadly disease, so the patients survive or last longer than anticipated.

A doctor treating such patients can help them to better understand their prognosis and chances for recovery or not. Then the outcome can depend, to some extent, on the patient's will to fight the disease or injury. However, when the patient's system is already ravaged past the point of no return, there is in general no coming back, regardless of what the patient does. In turn, the role of the doctor providing end-of-life care is to advise and support a patient, and either encourage the fight or help the patient come to terms with impending death and make the best possible choices for end-of-life care. Preferably the patient should early on choose the comfort-and-compassion option with limited or no pain and suffering, rather than trying to get revived, only to feel great agony until he or she finally dies.

The Role of the ICU

One of the key services in the hospital that plays a role in end-of-life care is the intensive care unit, or ICU. While it treats many patients who are suffering great trauma from an injury or have a potentially life-threatening illness but are expected to pull through, the ICU provides much of the end-of-life care to patients who are expected to die within a few hours, days, or weeks.

The unit is set up to provide more intensive, round-the-clock care than is possible by the services provided on a regular hospital floor, and it usually has even one-to-one nursing care when needed. For example, the ICU has all the resuscitation and intubation equipment that is used in helping a patient survive. It has a medical team which is available to respond quickly to any change in the patient's status, in the event that he or she needs to be quickly resuscitated or intubated. The ICU also has the monitoring equipment to track the patient's status by the minute and note any changes. However, because of the intensity of care required in this unit, the ICU serves patients during an immediate crisis only and sends them back to a regular floor when they become stable where they can be in regular beds, or to intermediate care or a step-down unit, which is relatively similar to the ICU, but the patients in general are a bit more stable or out of crisis.

The Hospital–Doctor Relationship

The relationship between a patient's doctor and the hospital that provides end-of-life care is another element in the system for treating a dying patient. In some cases, doctors have a relationship with a hospital and continue to provide care once the patient is admitted, which is what I do. More often, though, a primary care doctor can lose touch with a dying patient, when a doctor within the hospital specializing in inpatient services and end-of-life care takes over the patient's treatment. While I treat all of my patients who are spending their last days at the hospital, most of my patients in the hospital are no longer being seen as inpatients regularly by their own primary doctors, though some doctors drop by from time to time. Mainly, these patients are now under the care of a doctor like myself who is assigned to provide their end-of-life care and coordinate their treatment with other medical professionals in the hospital. However, as more doctors become trained in end-of-life care, it is likely that primary physicians will increasingly be less involved in caring for their patients in these last days.

The point at which a primary care physician can turn over a patient to an in-house doctor specializing in end-of-life care can vary greatly. For example, some primary-care doctor–patient relationships can go back ten or twenty years. But no matter how long the doctor–patient relationship, at some point the patient will get sick enough to need to go to the hospital for treatment, leading to a recovery in some cases, though usually death in others.

This shift from primary care to care by an in-hospital doctor commonly occurs as the patient ages, because with age, the patient suffers from a growing combination of illnesses that lead to organ damage. At some point, these organs can no longer be repaired—or an extended hospital stay is needed for a recovery. For example, a mild chronic anemia or a slight difficulty in breathing can respond more readily to treatments when a patient is younger, but over time, these conditions can become more serious and complications can develop, such as a heart attack or complex pulmonary illness. Or an initial numbness and tingling of the extremities can lead a patient to get wobbly or experience pain while walking, which can affect the person's posture, resulting in further aches, pains, and a decreased ability to move the joints and limbs. Moreover, should an older person experience an accident, such as in a car crash or ski collision, or contract any sort of disease, from a common cold to a more severe condition such as bronchitis or pneumonia, he or she will take longer to heal or may be less likely to recover at all.

Thus, with age, patients are more likely to end up as an end-of-life patient. The situation is comparable to what happens to a car as a driver puts more miles on it. More and more can go wrong with the car, since the tires wear down, the radiator is more prone to leaks or to break down in the heat, and the engine might be more likely to lose fluid. Eventually, so much is wrong with the car that it's not capable of being repaired and it has reached the end of its life.

Ideally, a primary care doctor can help a patient with a terminal condition deal with end-of-life issues, since this doctor is already familiar with the patient and can better recognize the best strategies to deal with the patient's current problems or deal with these issues. But once the patient is admitted to the hospital, the new doctor, sometimes called the "hospitalist," takes over the patient's treatment. And often this hospitalist will require extra tests or consultations to learn about the patient in order to decide what to do and deal with the many questions that patients and their families have about what comes next and what they should do. Unfortunately, many of these tests are expensive as well as uncomfortable for the patient, though they could be completely unnecessary according to a primary physician who already knows the patient. Plus, a new doctor may not be aware of how the patient responded to different treatments on previous admissions, since this information is often not included in the medical record that follows each patient.

At one time, just a few years ago, primary care physicians used to go to the hospital and remain at their patient's bedside and later follow-up at their office if the patient was released. But now hospital-based doctors are increasingly taking over this end-of-life care while the primary physician is pulling back. This situation is much like the way more and more medical treatment is provided by different types of medical care specialists, in part because of the increasing use of high-tech medical equipment in treating patients for different conditions.

However, this lack of specific information about a patient with a life-threatening condition can mean the difference between life and death, since typically the medical chart provided to the in-hospital physician only contains the highlights of the person's past diseases and injuries. But the chart doesn't contain specifics of the previous treatments given to that patient with what results. Fortunately, as medical records are increasingly centralized in the hospital's data collection system, this information is becoming more available, although if the patient went to a different hospital, there would be no access to that information, unless that hospital received a request for a formal release of selected records.

Unfortunately, developments in the medical profession have led to this growing split between primary care physicians, who see their patients outside of the hospital, and hospital physicians or hospitalists, who are assigned patients to see in the hospital. One reason for this split between what the two types of doctors do are that changes in medical technology have made it more economically efficient for primary care doctors not to visit their patients in the hospital, since it is very inefficient to see one or two patients there, when these doctors see almost all of their other patients in their office. As a result, the hospital doctors have been increasingly taking over the practices of primary doctors for inpatients at the end of their life.

At the same time, a shrinking number of primary care physicians are learning how to become hospitalists, too, whereby they see both their own patients in the hospital along with other new patients, which is what I have done. This kind of scenario has also lent itself to providing the patient with a second opinion on his or her prognosis and best course of treatment, with one opinion provided by the patient's primary care physician, who is regularly seeing other patients in the hospital, and by the hospital doctor. In this situation, the patient becomes basically a dual patient, in having a primary care doctor to provide preventive care and treatment for conditions that occur while the patient is an outpatient. It's a scenario that frequently occurs for diseases where the patient goes in and out of the hospital as the disease becomes worse or gets better for a time, such as with COPD (chronic obstructive pulmonary disease). When the patient is out of the hospital, the primary doctor provides the care, but when the patient is sick and in the hospital, a hospital doctor takes over as the lead doctor. This is an evolving form of end-of-life care that is ideal in that the patient has two doctors taking the lead in providing some personalized care. While one doctor understands the patient based on a long-term relationship, the other understands how to deal with the high-risk and acute or near end-of-life issues that confront patients and their families, as well as negotiate the relationships with other medical care professionals involved in end-of-life care. In some cases, a doctor may be able to play both roles, which is what I do.

The only caveat to this arrangement is that most inpatient services have a large number of hospitalists who take turns dealing with patients, so it is highly unlikely that a patient will get the same doctor each time. Thus, in general, this dual-doctor arrangement results in one primary care doctor caring for the outpatient's problems, while a relatively large number of inpatient doctors provide services in the hospital. As a result, every time a new hospitalist takes over the care of a patient, it is as if there is a brand new patient–doctor relationship. The only way to resolve this problem is to have a dedicated inpatient hospitalist who can be there for the patient, whenever needed, which is what I do. However, this is a very rare situation, because most hospitalists work only every other week.

A further problem, in my view, with this approach is that these tend to be new doctors only recently out of medical school with little specific training in dealing with dying patients and their families, so they may end up making decisions and guiding the team in ways that are different from a doctor who has more personal experience with that patient. For example, they may try to get a patient who has previously expressed a clear desire not to be aggressively treated or resuscitated to agree to an intensive treatment regimen to fix a problem, when previous arrangements may have been made. They may seek to push this aggressive treatment on the patient, because that's what doctors do—treat patients. But they may only prolong the patient's misery for a short time rather than withholding treatment and providing only comfort and care, as the patient may have previously requested.

Conversely, this second type of team may decide to be less aggressive in providing care for some patients who otherwise believe in their recovery by only providing only care and comfort. For instance, I have seen doctors deem a patient irreversibly terminal and withdraw care instead of fighting for an individual who is going through a very difficult time, but with some appropriate care and support did heal and become engaged in life again.

Working with Palliative Care Teams

The growth of end-of-life care, due in part to the aging population, has led to the growth of palliative care teams. A palliative care team is a group of individuals led by a medical doctor who specializes in end-of-life issues and knows how to deal with these situations. The team is able to dispel false hopes and is familiar with the use of end-of-life narcotics and sedatives that relieve pain. Some team members also spend time with the patient and relatives to help them feel more comfortable with what is happening at a time when nurses and doctors at hospitals don't have the time to provide extended personal care. Generally, the primary medical team at the hospital asks the palliative care team to meet with the patient and family and provide a second opinion on whether the case is terminal, and if so, how to proceed to provide the dying patient with social support and pain control to make his last days ones of care and comfort. Generally, a patient selected for care by a palliative care team is one who is a poor candidate for any further aggressive therapeutic treatments, since he or she is unlikely to benefit, and the risk of further treatment is that the patient will soon die and will only experience a longer painful dying process with such treatments.

These teams take two major forms, where a doctor who is also a palliative care medical doctor may be a part of the team or not. The first type of team, which I prefer, is a team that is led by a primary care doctor and includes nurses, religious personnel, social workers, and others who actively help the patient and family cope with end-of-life issues. That's the kind of team where I play the lead doctor role. Such a team is particularly helpful when there are deep divisions between patients and their families or within families over how to handle the end-of-life care, since the team members have the time and training to listen to and understand the views of relatives and friends when they differ from that of the patient. Then the team members can help the relatives and friends better understand why the patient wants to make certain end-of-life choices, so they can come together and support the patient, since ultimately, it is the patient's choice that determines what treatment approach to use at the very end.

Often this intervention by a palliative care team is needed when one or more family members or relatives are set in their ways about how the patient's life should end. In this case, the team members can help sway the family members and relatives to the patient's point of view. Or at least the team members can obtain their grudging acceptance, rather than letting a patient bend to the wishes of others to bring peace, when that isn't what the patient really wants.

The second type of team, which is my distant second choice, includes the same kind of practitioners as the first team, but also includes a palliative care doctor on the hospital staff who takes over the patient's end-of-life issues and can sway or control what the team does because of the authority and prestige a doctor brings to this role. Unfortunately, with this kind of team, the patient's long-term relationship with a primary care physician can be displaced or shunted aside, while this doctor-led team takes over the patient's end-of-life care.

One of the problems with the formation of this kind of team is that the doctor who leads it normally does not have any formal training in end-of-life care beyond a course taken over a short period of time, and there are few formal fellowship-training programs. But a fellowship program usually takes at least a whole year of full-time work in a chosen area of interest, usually lasting two to three years that include hands-on-training, not just a couple of weeks. Thus I do not believe that any of these palliative care doctors can do a better job at helping patients through their last days than a dedicated primary care doctor or a well-intentioned hospitalist, although the average hospitalist may argue he or she does not have the time to deal with these patients, because these last days of care are labor intensive, whereas I dedicate the time for the proper care.

Another problem with this team is that they get their information from reading the chart and looking at the notes written by doctors like me. While they do talk to the patient and the family, they usually have a short conversation that doesn't compare to the good communication with an established primary physician or a long-term patient–hospitalist relationship, like the type of care I try to provide myself, with a physician who is experienced in end-of-life care. After all, there is no true scientific answer on how to die; only more humane and compassionate ways to do so. Moreover, these new doctors may have difficulty coping themselves with the stress of knowing that someone is terminal and will die due to an intervention or lack of one, after I or another end-of-life care doctor writes the orders and executes the plan for the patient's final days. The reason for this confusion is that being terminal is not a point in time, but rather a process or development over time that usually will require several evaluation points, not just a short consultation and quick recommendations.

In short, I believe these palliative teams can work most effectively to help support patients in their last days when a palliative care doctor isn't part of the team, since I provide this direction myself. On the other hand, it can work well when a younger and less-experienced doctor has a backup team to handle the more technical details of providing day-to-day pain reduction, care, and comfort. By contrast, there can be a problem when a young hospitalist doctor who is unfamiliar with the patient alters the team's efforts to provide support to a patient in his or her last days, based on what that patient has previously agreed to in response to the input of the primary care doctor or the hospital chronic-care givers. In any case, the essential goal or primary mission of a palliative care team, however it is organized, is providing support to a patient in his or her last days, depending on what that patient has decided to do about being resuscitated or intubated or not and the current set of events.

When Doctors Disagree

At times, when two doctors are involved in end-of-life care—the patient's original primary doctor and the hospital doctor—everything can work very smoothly. Both doctors have similar conclusions about the best approach—from aggressive treatment with a hope of recovery to comfort and care in an irreversibly terminal case. As a result, the agreement of the two doctors can support the patient in making a choice in line with their recommendations.

But in some cases, the two doctors can have differing opinions about what to do, which can lead to complications in choosing what is in the best interest of the patient, while the patient can be torn in deciding what choice to make. Add in relatives with different opinions, and making decisions in this scenario can be even more difficult, especially when differing views are grounded in different religious, cultural, ethnic, and social backgrounds. With the growing number of end-of-life patients and different approaches, the potential for conflict is growing, too. Yet ultimately, the patient—or a family member acting as a proxy for a patient unable to make decisions—must decide what to do.

The other problem is communication between the primary doctor and the admitting hospitalist; a good relationship cannot be taken for granted. The other problem occurs when the specialists providing input about a given patient don't have a record of the actual recommendations of their patients' end-of-life plans, which opens the door for potential conflicting plans. It is important to know the primary doctors themselves to care for their patients as their philosophy influences their approach to their care.

The DNR/DNI Controversy

One of the big end-of-life care issues is the DNR/DNI or "do not resuscitate/do not intubate" controversy. This issue comes up because normally, in a life-threatening emergency situation, the medical professionals who deal with the patient, from paramedics to nurses and doctors, are trained to do everything they can to revive the patient. This goal of preserving life is part of the medical oath, which is taught in medical school and reinforced again and again in everything medical professionals do in dealing with patients—"do no harm and do everything you can to heal the patient."

For example, in an emergency situation, such as when a patient has been in a car accident or has nearly drowned, so their heart rhythm or breathing becomes severely irregular or stops, their blood pressure drops precipitously, or their pulse drops dramatically, the patient is normally placed in a Code 99 status. In the hospital, this situation usually leads to someone pressing a button on the wall that triggers an emergency response from all available medical personal. Within minutes, the patient's room fills up with fifteen to twenty people, and a medical team begins cardiopulmonary resuscitation to restart the patient's heart and breathing.

The basic process involves checking the patient's airway to see if it is open, determining if the patient is still breathing or trying to breathe, and examining the patient's circulation to determine if he or she still has a pulse and blood pressure. Then, since the team has only a few minutes to revive the patient's breathing and circulation, the team members quickly organize themselves based on their predetermined roles (such as to lead the team or handle a particular function, which might include monitoring the machines, providing CPR, launching compression, or providing medications by injection to an unconscious patient). To carry out these tasks, the team members may ask a series of questions, such as is the patient breathing or does the patient have a pulse. Then, to deal with the urgency of the situation, the doctor in charge of the medical team organizes who does what and the trained team self-organizes to create a very organized, coordinated effort in which everyone knows what to do to restore breathing and circulation. Each person has a clear knowledge of what actions to take to help the patient survive.

A key consideration is the way different bodily processes can affect each other. A good example is the way the lack of circulation of the blood when the heart stops can have the most deleterious effects most quickly, in that after three minutes a lack of blood to the brain can result in irreversible brain damage that shuts off other bodily functions. By contrast, a person can go without breathing for a slightly longer period of time, say up to three to four minutes, without irreversible damage. However, in practice, the two systems affect each other. For example, if a patient's circulation stops, within seconds his or her breathing will shut down, and the medical team will simultaneously attend to both systems at the same time. The process is like having to deal with a bonfire that has gone out of control, so everything is erupting in flames at once. In response, highly standardized protocols are used to deal with the evolving situation.

Certainly there are cases where a problem in breathing occurs due to congestion in an airway, such as when a person choking on food has a cardiac arrest, or when a heart attack leads a person to have difficulty breathing. In such cases, a doctor or another person has to act quickly to resolve the initial problem, such as dislodging the foreign body from the person's airway or massaging the person's heart by performing cardiopulmonary resuscitation to attempt to return the patient's circulation and blood pressure to revive the patient and return him or her to an earlier or baseline status. But generally, the heroic action of one person is the exception in most emergencies, since a full team effort is needed to revive the patient.

Whatever the situation, if a medical team is successful in this everyday emergency, the patient can be revived successfully and after a period of healing return to his or her everyday activities. Even so, the potential for saving the person can be quite low if he or she has had a true cardiac arrest, since the mortality rate is about 90 percent no matter what anyone does.

However, this recovery after an emergency is quite different from the experience of the end-of-life patient who already has all kinds of medical problems that lead to a sudden heart stoppage or the cessation of breathing. In this case, it is generally not a good idea to apply any of these emergency treatments to save the patient, because these will make his or her condition even worse than it already is, such as by breaking the ribs during a resuscitation procedure, leading to continuing pain and suffering. That's the reason for the DNR/DNI option whereby the patient can opt not to receive this emergency treatment to restart the heart or breathing, leading to more pain and suffering if the revival is successful. Then, once this option is exercised, the medical team will not do anything, so the patient can die naturally in peace within a few minutes, which is usually the result when the heart and breathing stop.

The Types of Cases That Are Most Common in End-of-Life Care

While almost anyone can end up in a life-or-death situation, such as a serious car crash, shooting, ski accident, or near drowning, in general, the practice involves treating patients with certain illnesses or conditions that have led to an irreversible terminal condition. Commonly, these conditions are associated with other problems that have not been cured, such as cirrhosis of the liver due to alcoholism or emphysema due to smoking. But whether or not they are associated with other problems, these conditions by themselves can result in the patient ending up with a terminal condition that can't be reversed, so it is only a matter of days, weeks, or months before the patient's end of life. Further complicating matters, these same conditions can often lead to a chronic state that can continue for many years, although ultimately the condition is likely to contribute to the person's death.

These three major conditions include respiratory and pulmonary diseases that interfere with breathing; cardiovascular problems that can lead to the heart stopping; and severe strokes that can sufficiently interfere with brain functioning so the patient can stop breathing or suffer cardiac arrest. I'll describe each of these in more detail.

Respiratory and Pulmonary Diseases

Commonly, respiratory problems build up over a period of days, which give us time to evaluate, reevaluate, and formulate a plan for a given patient. There are situations, however, where things happen in a rush when a patient is having trouble breathing due to a blockage, such as choking during a meal or suffering from a fluid buildup or inflammation in the lungs. The medical team usually has time to determine what is going on, such as by getting blood tests and x-rays. As a result, the team members also have time to talk to the patient and come up with a plan in which the patient can participate. Generally, patients experiencing this kind of distress will still be conscious, so the doctors and nurses caring for them will have time to talk to them or to their family making decisions for them to decide the best next course of action.

In this case, a common approach is to help the patient with breathing. One way is to start by giving the patient noninvasive support using regular oxygen off the wall via a nasal cannula, or tube, which delivers oxygen through two prongs which go into the nostrils. Or if the patient still has trouble breathing, a CPAP or BiPAP machine can be used. In this case, a tight mask delivering oxygen is placed over the nose and mouth area and is connected to a large metal box about the size of a desk computer, which regulates the airflow. The CPAP is set to a selected pressure, while the BiPAP's pressure can be adjusted for both the patient's inspiration and expiration to match what the patient needs, resulting in a less-labored breathing effort. The other more advanced approach is to place the patient on invasive support, using a mechanical ventilator or artificial breathing machine, in which a tube is placed into the patient's airway and the air is sent to the lungs through that. This breathing enables the patient to avoid what would happen if the air flow actually stops for more than three minutes. Then the patient goes into cardiac arrest where the heart stops, and death occurs if the breathing and circulation are not started again within a few minutes.

Assuming the medical team can get the breathing going in time, the patient will usually be fine and can decide whether to undergo this procedure in the future or not. At this point, many patients opt to not go through an attempt to revive them in the future, especially if a doctor advises them their condition is final. The patient can select a DNR/DNI status and no treatment will be done, and the patient is allowed to simply die with dignity by the medical team providing as much comfort as possible. In some cases, patients will want to be intubated in the future to get through an emergency situation; in other cases, they may decide they don't want this medical intervention to go on. But to be certain what the patient really wants, in either case, a doctor, nurse, or other medical-team member will repeatedly question the patient about his or her options, and the patient can always change his or her mind. To prevent this repeated questioning—which can be quite upsetting, the state of Massachusetts has created the MOLST form that once signed provides that decisions based on it can be carried out without having to question the patient again every time. The patient does, however, have the power to change opinions at any time.

Generally, patients do want to be revived when these incidents first happen and they need some respiratory help to get through the current crisis. But after a while, as the problem continues, particularly if the patient is suffering from other illnesses, the patient will decide not to be intubated in the future.

One of the most common conditions requiring respiratory support is COPD. Most patients with this condition have had a long history of tobacco abuse, and some are already using an oxygen tank to help them breathe. In fact, this type of patient is usually under the care of a pulmonary doctor who specializes in diseases of the lungs. Commonly, these patients go through a series of increasingly serious episodes where they have more and more difficulty breathing, leading them to initially require mechanical ventilation and then spend time in the ICU. For a time, they may briefly recover from an acute episode requiring this mechanical ventilation or ICU treatment. But then they may experience other, usually more intense, episodes, which occur more often, until it becomes clear they are suffering from an irreversible, terminal condition.

Thus, as the patient's condition worsens, the trend is for pulmonary doctors to discuss end-of-life options with them. Or if the patients are in the hospital, a doctor, nurse, or medical-team member will discuss their situation with them, so they can have an agreement for continuing or stopping their care, once their condition is clearly terminal and cannot be reversed.

Cardiovascular Conditions

A cardiovascular condition is another likely source of irreversible terminal cases. One of the usual causes of this condition is congestive heart failure, usually due to a malfunction of the heart muscle, resulting in shortness of breath, a swelling of the whole body, and pulmonary hypertension, in which the heart pumps blood into the lungs to provide them with oxygen, but encounters a great deal of resistance. Another cause is coronary artery disease, which results in a true heart attack due to poor circulation of the arteries that feed the heart muscle. Still another cause may be advanced damage to the valves of the heart, which are like doors that open to allow the blood to circulate forward through the heart. If these valves are damaged, they can prevent or block this flow of blood, and they may push the flow backward, too. In either case, this damage to the valves impedes normal circulation. Additionally, an extremely thick or thinned-out heart muscle can impair the pumping of the heart, and either case can result in sudden death. Finally, a cardiac arrest can occur due to an arrhythmogenic condition, in which the electrical system of the heart suddenly fires inappropriately for no apparent reason, much like the electrical system in a house can suddenly misfire, sometimes due to an unexpected surge of electricity during an electrical storm when the sky is filled with lightning and thunder.

For whatever reason, once a cardiac arrest occurs, a medical team has about three minutes in which to get the heart to beat again through manual stimulation, chest compressions, electrical shocks, or other methods to stimulate the heart to beat or pump. If the person is revived, though this is unlikely, the cure often leaves the person in a worse condition than before due to significant neurologic damage from the lack of oxygen, and often he or she will experience great agony. The particular neurologic impairment will depend on which centers of the brain suffer the most because of the lack of oxygen during the cardiac arrest. Thus, after being revived, a person will most likely find that he or she has reduced brain functioning, in addition to still suffering from any of the other conditions that led to this state, which is why many patients choose not to be revived in the event of a cardiac arrest. They would rather opt to have a DNR, meaning they will have no further cardiac resuscitation if their heart stops and they would prefer to die a natural death, which is the likely outcome of this situation.

However, before a cardiac arrest occurs, except in the case of an emergency, such as a serious accident, there are usually a number of precursors. Some of the precursors that commonly lead to the heart suddenly stopping include previous heart attacks, a history of tobacco abuse, morbid obesity, high blood pressure, abnormally high cholesterol levels, a continuing stressful experience, or a sudden, very high-stress incident, such as an extremely upsetting event.

Whatever the source of this extra pressure on the heart, a comparison might be to the rudder on a boat. Should the boat encounter very strong winds, the rudder might suddenly start to shake back and forth, and as the winds continue or get stronger, the rudder might suddenly snap. Likewise, if pressed beyond its limits, the heart can break, too.

In any event, while a number of factors may lead to a cardiac arrest, once it occurs, the effects on the body are devastating if the patient survives being resuscitated, and most often this arrest leads to the death of the patient in about 90 to 95 percent of cases.

Strokes

The third major condition that can lead to an irreversible terminal condition is a serious stroke. While strokes occur to thousands of patients every year, many strokes occur without any major consequences, although they can serve as a warning to a more devastating shock ahead. As such they are a little like the minor earthquakes that occur in certain regions of the country, such as California. They shake up the countryside and the psyches of the people who experience them a little. But they cause no major damage, and they just serve as a reminder that this is earthquake country, while warning of the big one that lies ahead and could happen anytime, though it is statistical unlikely to happen in the near future.

Essentially, a stroke occurs when the blood supply to part of the brain is interrupted or severely reduced, so the brain doesn't receive enough oxygen and nutrients. Since the brain is the most sensitive of all organs, it is the first to suffer from the absence of oxygen, which can result in irreparable damage to the brain if the lack of oxygen lasts long enough. What happens when the brain is starved of oxygen is that, within minutes, some brain cells begin to die because they aren't getting enough blood with oxygen.

Generally, this lack of blood to the brain is caused by some blockage to the blood flow—exactly the same process as it happens in the heart itself where it causes a heart attack. Here it causes a stroke. Other causes include an embolism or an artery rupturing in the brain. Or sometimes this blockage is due to a brain aneurysm, which occurs when a blood vessel there suddenly bulges or balloons out like a berry on a stem. Then this aneurysm can leak or rupture, like a piece of rubber or plastic stretched too much, causing bleeding into the brain. In any of these circumstances, once the stroke occurs, some common symptoms are a sudden loss of speech or a weakness or paralysis on one side of the body. An affected individual can have trouble thinking logically, too.

While some of these experiences of a stroke can turn into short-term inconveniences as the blood starts flowing again and the brain repairs itself, in other cases, a stroke can be devastating when major hemorrhages occur or when the blockages continue, so that a very large number of brain cells die, incapacitating the patient. In cases where the heart pumps blood into the brain, with blood bursting out of the brain vessels into the space normally occupied by the brain, this excess blood will compress the brain tissue within the skull so much that it can no longer send the necessary signals to a part of the body which it controls, such as breathing. Then that part of the body will break down and the person will stop breathing. In other cases, when there is too much pressure to the cortex, which performs all of the higher functions of the brain such as rational thinking, the resulting compression can cause the person to go into a coma, which can lead to death.

At one time it was very difficult to explain this process to family members after a loved one experienced a devastating stroke. All they could see were the outward manifestations, such as a patient who suddenly couldn't speak, had difficulty breathing, staggered while walking, fell down, or collapsed into a coma. But now with computers and monitors, a medical professional can show family members and others how the stroke caused extensive damage to the patient's brain tissue, so they can understand why these patients are facing certain death. Then these family members can better make a good decision about a stroke victim, such deciding to let the patient die a natural death without further treatment, rather than insisting that the medical team engage in all sorts of futile efforts to resuscitate and intubate a patient, when there is no hope of recovery from a permanent coma.

I had this experience with one of my dialysis patients who had been admitted to the hospital again and again for different reasons, among them a few cases of pneumonia, a few heart attacks, and a few infections. Each time, she was able to go home after a few days in the hospital to continue her recovery at home. For a while, she was even able to improve enough to walk around the neighborhood, go shopping, and carry out everyday errands. But within a few weeks she experienced another ill-ness, followed by another trip to the hospital. Soon after that, one day she passed out at home. Her daughter called 911, and an ambulance rushed her to the emergency room; she was barely breathing. I got the call to see her immediately, and as I rushed in, a nurse was just connecting her to a ventilator. However, a computer showed that she had suffered irreversible brain damage due to a massive stroke, and this time there would be no bouncing back so she could return home. Instead, as I explained to her daughter and son: "As you can see on the computer, this whole area of her brain has been blacked out by the stroke. It's like a blood vessel has burst, flooding her brain, much like what happens when a dam breaks. Due to this flooding, the key parts of her brain can no longer function to control her breathing or other bodily functions. All her neurological func-tions are essentially gone."

Thus, with the help of this computer imagery, I was able to explain how irreversible her situation was, so there was no hope for the future. As a result, the family members were readily willing to opt for a DNR/DNI status in case her heart stopped. And a few days later, her heart did exactly that.

Besides illustrating the way a stroke can be one of the major factors leading to the end of life, this case also illustrates the important role of computers and imaging programs in explaining what is going on to pa-tients and family members. Such an explanation illustrated with graphics and animations makes it easier for both patients and family members to see the damage the patient has or might experience, so they can better choose the most appropriate treatment options for the end-of-life care. As previously noted, the choice is whether they want to opt for DNR/DNI status and eventually ensuing noninterventional approach—which means no further treatment, just *care and comfort*, after a person has passed the point of no return from a therapeutic viewpoint—or whether they want a medical team to do everything they can to revive themselves or their loved one, even in the face of continued pain and suffering until the patient inevitably dies of an irreversible terminal condition.

Cancer

The fourth major condition that can lead to an irreversible terminal condi-tion is cancer, or the big " C." It has, in fact, become the predominant form of dying, since tumors can kill by invading and penetrating vital organs, thereby disabling them. For example, when a tumor invades the intestines, it actually penetrates the intestinal walls, making them part of the tumor itself, much like the infamous blob in the movie of the same name would engulf everything in its path and thereby enlarge itself. The other way that a tumor can kill is that it becomes large enough so it pushes into an essential organ or constricts it from functioning normally, such as when it pushes into the main airway or windpipe and constricts it, making it very difficult or impossible to breathe, as happened to one of my patients. The result is the tumor reduces the airflow, a little more and more over a period of time, until the patient feels like he or she is being choked—it is little like what happens when someone is strangled and their airflow is constricted until they can't breathe and choke to death.

Still another way a tumor can cause death is when it reaches the brain, which is already a fully occupied space in the body. But as the tumor grows, it pushes the brain around in the skull and can even push it out of the skull, resulting in seizures, strokes, a reduced inability to function, and eventually death. In effect, the growing tumor causes the individual to lose the abilities to think and control the various functions of the body as more and more parts of the brain are damaged, as the tumor wreaks more and more havoc in the various structures and nerve connections in the brain.

Other Facilities and Housing for End-of-Life Care

Although I see most of my end-of-life cases in the hospital and most dying patients end up there, either in the ICU or in private or semiprivate rooms before their death, a number of other facilities provide end-of-life care. As a result, while some patients end up in the hospital in their last days, many go to these other places to die—or they might end up going back and forth between these places and the hospital, sometimes at their request, or sometimes at the request of a relative or other person acting on their behalf. Among these other places where patients spend their last days are their own homes, hospices, assisted-living care facilities, and nursing homes. In addition, a palliative and hospice care team can provide end-of-life assistance and advice to an individual who is dying, wherever he or she is being cared for.

Dying at Home

Though rarer, some patients do go back to their own homes to die, because they don't want to spend their last days hooked up to a ventilator and don't want to be resuscitated should their heart stop. Returning home is also a way that some patient can spend time with their loved ones before the end. A good example of this approach is reflected in the 2014 film *You're Not You*, starring Hilary Swank, Emmy Rossum, and Josh Duhamel. It's the story of a wealthy woman who was once a pianist who comes down with ALS. She shows the first symptoms while playing for her guests, and then one and a half years later, now in a wheelchair, has a caretaker to assist with her personal needs, including getting her out of bed and taking her to the bathroom. After a failed suicide attempt where she falls out of her wheelchair before it hurtles down the stairs, her caretaker, a hippy-type free spirit, takes her home with her so the woman can spend her last weeks free of her overprotective lawyer-husband who makes her feel like a sick, caged bird. Then after a few weeks of experiencing the joy of living freely, while she increasingly loses her powers of movement and speech, she ends up after a breathing attack on a hospital ventilator. However, while her domineering, previously estranged mother wants her kept alive as long as possible on a ventilator, the caretaker who has been given the proxy in the woman's new will takes her home to die there without any ventilator to help her breathing, and her family members visit her there. So in the end, the woman dies peacefully after one last breathing attack.

Hospice

Commonly, hospice care occurs at a hospice center, where a team of healthcare professionals and volunteers provide medical, psychological, and spiritual support to help people who are dying have peace, comfort, and dignity. In the hospice system, which includes in-home and hospital outreach, patients must have a life expectancy of six months or less, while the hospice houses take only patients who are expected to pass on within two or three weeks.

Once a patient is accepted into the hospice system, the caregivers try to control pain and other symptoms, so a person can remain as alert and comfortable as possible, while the hospice generally has support services to help a patient's family and close friends deal with the dying patient.

Although some patients go to the hospice center, where they have a private or semiprivate room, the hospice team can also assist the patient and family members at the patient's home, in a skilled nursing facility that provides end-of-life care, and in the hospital, where palliative care teams may also be involved in providing the same kind of care.

The focus in the hospice system is on keeping patients comfortable and improving their quality of life in their last days, rather than on providing treatment to prolong a patient's life. As described in an introduction to hospice care by WebMD (http://www.webmd.com/balance/tc/hospice-care-topic-overview), a typical hospice-care program includes the following elements:

- Basic medical care with a focus on pain and symptom control.
- Access to a member of a hospice team twenty-four hours a day, seven days a week.
- Medical supplies and equipment as needed.
- Counseling and social support to help the patient and family with psychological, emotional, and spiritual issues.
- Guidance in completing and obtaining closure with the difficult, but normal, issues of life, such as closing bank accounts, rental agreements, and subscriptions to publications.
- Respite care for caregivers, family, and others who regularly care for the patient, so they can take a break from what they are doing to help the patient.
- Volunteer support, such as preparing meals and running errands.
- Counseling and support for the patient's loved ones after his or her death.

This hospice approach was used with one of my patients, Ellie, who was mentally retarded and aided in a group home by a hospice care team. Ellie, now in her fifties, had been in the group home for about two years, after having previously been cared for by her parents and relatives due to her low IQ—about the level of a five-year-old child, so she had difficulty speaking in more than a few short sentences or walking about on her own without getting lost. At one time, she lived at home with her parents until their deaths. About five years ago, a couple of close relatives passed away on their own birthdays, and soon afterward, her mother passed away on Ellie's birthday. Suddenly her brother worried that he would be next, since his own birthday was in two months, and that's when Ellie began her life in the group home.

Once she was there, the group-home team provided her with the kind of support she needed to get through each day—such as providing her with regular meals and with activities she could enjoy with other residents who were similarly challenged mentally, such as exercise and fitness classes, game nights, and family movie nights. But then, triggered by an infection during flu season she had trouble getting over, Ellie suddenly experienced multisystem organ failure, where different systems shut down, perhaps triggered by her coughing and wheezing due to the flu that wouldn't go away. All of a sudden, she was dealing with lung, liver, and kidney shut down.

An ambulance brought Ellie to the hospital, after a group-home receptionist called the emergency room, and soon a multidisciplinary team involving the cardiology, critical care, and primary team doctors and nurses were on her case. Almost immediately, the team arranged for her to be put in the ICU while assessing her case. Things did not look good since her blood pressure was only 70 and should normally be at least 100. Additionally, Ellie hadn't produced any urine for several days due to kidney failure, and she had congestive heart failure, so her heart's pumping power was weaker than normal and therefore her blood moved through her heart and body at a slower rate. The result was that her heart couldn't pump enough oxygen to meet the body's needs, which led her kidneys to respond by causing her body to retain fluid and salt, leading to a buildup of blood in her arms, legs, ankles, feet, lungs, and other organs.

"It looks like her condition has become terminal," one of the doctors on the team advised me. "What should we do?"

Because of her mental retardation, Ellie was in no position to make any decisions herself, so I spoke to her brother, who had already been notified by the group home that Ellie was being transferred to the hospital.

"What do you recommend?" he asked, and then described his own fears of dying. "It's like a tradition in our family. Ellie's mother passed away on her own birthday, and her sister and cousin passed away on their birthdays. And my birthday is in only two months."

"I'm sure it's a coincidence," I assured him. "These things happen, and then it looks like there is some connection, but there isn't."

He calmed down then and refocused on Ellie's case.

"I think providing her with care and comfort —which is a formal protocol of no intervention to us—would be the most humane thing to do now," he said. "Besides, this could help her join her mother who passed away on her birthday about five years ago. And her own birthday is in about two weeks."

So that's what we agreed to do—we started with a morphine dose of 2mg an hour, with an increase in the dose if the patient needed this to reduce her suffering, and we let her breathe on her own for now. Yet, ironically, as four or five days passed by, Ellie continued to be going strong. Though she continued to have very low blood pressure and passed no urine that week, she continued breathing but was not able to talk—she just made random sounds due to her mental retardation and lack of appropriate brain perfusion.

"What should we do now?" the medical team asked me.

I called Ellie's brother.

"Let's take her back to the group home where she was," he said. "That way she can finally pass peacefully in her own room."

"That makes sense," I agreed.

So the nurse and medical team made the arrangements with Ellie's brother to have her picked up by ambulance, along with a small overnight bag of clothes and toiletries that she brought with her to the hospital. They further arranged for the hospice team to continue the same type of palliative care once Ellie was back in the group home.

After five days, when I called the group home to find out how Ellie was doing, the nurse who responded told me: "She's still breathing, on the morphine drip, and drifting in and out of consciousness. She and her brother mentioned something about her mother dying on her own birthday, so that's what we expect. We expect her to pass on this coming Saturday, which is her birthday."

"I'll contact you then," I told her, thinking this was an odd coincidence, though there was no connection, since Ellie could die at any time, and if she was barely conscious, how could she know what day it was now or when her birthday occurred?

But when I called that morning, the nurse who responded told me: "Ellie just passed away. And I think she said something about 'Joining mama.'"

I hung up wondering if there was some connection after all and glad that Ellie had finally passed on in a state of peace.

Assisted-Living Facility

While many assisted-living facilities are designed for seniors over the age of sixty-five who need some degree of care and arrange to live in an apartment, small house, or condo at the facility rather than hire a home-care worker while they live at home, some facilities provide a place for the patients in the last months or weeks of their life. Sometimes long-term residents remain in these facilities for several years and are thought of more as tenants and renters than patients, since apart from care for their special needs, such as helping them go to and from the bathroom, they may participate in a range of activities at the facility, such as game and film nights.

Sometimes end-of-life patients continue to join in these activities as they are able, though commonly assisted-living facilities have a special wing for end-of-life patients, along with a twenty-four-hour on-call staff to handle their requests. In addition, the facility will have some equipment for a patient with breathing issues, as well as a trained staff to provide other needed support services, such as those provided by a hospice care team.

Nursing Home

While nursing homes are generally designed for patients with chronic illnesses who needed ongoing medical treatment for a particular condition, after which patients are discharged and return home, some nursing homes, like assisted-care facilities, have end-of-life treatment facilities. These facilities are much like the assisted-living and hospice centers by providing the requested treatment and support in the last days of life. While some patients might come from the hospital to these facilities, other patients might be transitioned from regular nursing to end-of-life care if they have a major turn for the worse like a sudden heart attack or breathing difficulties in addition to their chronic illness. Usually this transition to end-of-life care is by previous arrangements, aftera DNR/DNI in place as well as a care-and-comfort plan.

Who Decides

Generally, the rule is that the patient decides on the course of treatment and when that treatment should be stopped if the patient experiences an irreversible terminal condition. The patient generally makes the major medical decisions about his or her resuscitation/intubation or nonresuscitation/intubation status, either at the time of a medical crisis requiring a decision or early on, so the orders are already in place when the crisis occurs and the patient can no longer make a decision.

However, this decision-making process can be complicated because as a patient is cared for, undergoes different medical procedures, or recovers from a serious illness or injury, these decisions can be revisited if the patient wishes. As in some cases, the patient may be pressured by his or her family to decide a certain way. Sometimes a patient may no longer be able to make these choices, such as in the case of a stroke or a toxic metabolic state of confusion. But the possibility that a patient can no longer decide for himself or herself can lead to a conflict among a patient's family members over who decides or about what happens if there is an internal split over whether to provide further treatment to try to cure the patient or whether to accept the determination that the patient is dying, and therefore only provide care or comfort, so he or she can go peacefully and naturally without further intervention.

A good example of this complicated decision-making process is what happened with Jose, an elderly male with a very large family due to three marriages, seventeen daughters, and several brothers and sisters. At one time, he had been a successful contractor with a thriving business. He had built houses in several countries and had a dozen men working for him. But then Jose fell ill with a serious case of pneumonia. During that time, his code status was discussed, and he opted to be revived if either his heart or breathing stopped, which made sense to him at the time, since he was still a fairly strong and healthy man. He even participated in boxing fights with opponents in bars in weekends and usually won. But another serious bout of pneumonia was followed by a serious back injury when a tree fell on him at a construction site took a toll on him. Then he had a stroke while exercising on a treadmill.

When Jose awoke, he was back in the hospital and could see the face of the nurse peering down at him, but he couldn't figure out what was happening or had happened earlier that day to get him here.

"Where am I?" he kept repeating again and again. When the nurse explained he was in the hospital, he kept saying: "Where am I? Who are you? Why am I here?"

As a result, as usually occurs in cases where patients can no longer understand their options to make their own decisions, I called his relatives and children. I even called relatives he hadn't seen in some years, since even relatives and children that may have been estranged for awhile might step forward to play a more active role in the decision-making process. Plus sometimes patients may specify in their will who should take over financial or other affairs for them. In Jose's case, this determination could be fairly complicated, because of his different wives, his many children, and because some of those he was closest to lived in other states or couldn't be reached since they were out of town or on vacation. So I figured the best thing to do was to let as many relatives as I could know about Jose's condition and those who could—or who wanted to be involved—could come to the hospital.

Eventually, a dozen relatives showed up. Then, while Jose remained in bed in a semicomatose state, his now-assembled relatives had a conflict in the conference room over what to do. So I went in to try to explain the situation and urge them to decide on what to do, since Jose had never gotten around to making a decision himself, much less putting anything about his preferences in writing.

I concluded by advising the relatives about "the most humane alternative" of just providing care and comfort while ending the treatment until Jose passed away.

But as sometimes happens in these situations, these differences in opinion cannot quickly be overcome, and the family members split into two groups in which some relatives thought the patient should be given every chance to recover while others opted for a more quick and humane passing.

So for a time, we were at an impasse, like two trains at the entrance of a tunnel, and one has to pull back for the other to get through. Meanwhile, in the face of no decision, the medical team was preparing to do what was necessary to revive Jose no matter what when the time came, because if a patient or relative doesn't make a choice, the hospital or center caring for him has to do whatever is necessary to keep that person alive, even if the procedures prove painful and only prolong the dying process by a few hours or days, which is what I felt would happen here.

Thus, I presented my case again, concluding: "So please. Your loved one will only suffer more pain, and he is likely to remain in a semiconscious state like this before he dies, because of the extent of his brain injury due to the stroke."

Finally, there was some movement. One daughter volunteered: "I'd like to join the team voting not to revive him." Then another came to the same conclusion. "I think my father led a good life, even though I lost touch with him in these last few years. So now I'd like to do what I think he would want."

Thus, we had a quorum, and the spokesperson for this group now announced: "Okay, make it DNR/DNI," while those in the other group remained silent. They realized they had lost, and I was relieved that I was able to persuade still another family to go the DNR/DNI route as the most humane approach, since today this is the preferred medical option to prevent further pain and suffering. I wish all patients would consider putting this kind of decision in place as soon as possible. Or if they can't do it, a relative with a proxy to take over the decision making should make this decision for them, as finally Jose's family did.

It is a decision-making process that is required again and again in any end-of-life case, like making provisions for any worst-case scenario. Thus one of my roles in dealing with dying patients and their relatives is to help them make that decision if they haven't already made it, though the circumstances and procedures for getting to that decision vary greatly from case to case, as illustrated in the many different cases in this book.

2

CORRECTING COMMON
MISCONCEPTIONS

When people think about doctors dealing with patients at the end of life, they often are influenced by popular TV shows, like *ER* and *Grey's Anatomy*, to imagine that doctors are miracle workers who can do almost anything with the aid of modern technology. Thus, they often have extra-high expectations about survival and recovery rates from serious illnesses and life-threatening injuries that aren't true. They believe if only they can get the patient to the hospital in time that a team of doctors and other medical professionals will enable them to make it.

But that isn't true, especially when these illnesses or injuries lead a patient to suffer a cardiac arrest, where the survival/recovery rate is very low—commonly around 6 to 13 percent. When a cardiac arrest occurs, this means that the heart stops beating, and thereby stops pumping oxygen to the brain, so even if the heartbeat is restored, after a very few minutes, neurological damage can result from the brain being deprived of oxygen. Once this damage occurs, it is irreversible, though with healing and training, some parts of the brain can take over the activities of other parts of the brain. But if the damage is too extensive, this repair-and-replacement function cannot happen, and the person suffers permanent brain damage, which is reflected in some of the cases in the news where a patient has recovered some bodily functions but remains hooked-up to machines that keep the body functioning, though the patient is now in a coma or persistent vegetative state. One of these stories is that of Jahi McMath, who has been in a coma since her parents took her off a ventilator and placed her in a nearby hospital for continued care; they are claiming she is still alive and are seeking to get her death certificate revoked. [1]

Another case is that of Bobbi Kristina Brown, who was similarly in an unconscious state after being found submerged in a bathtub. While she, too, was able to breathe on her own, there was little hope for recovery, and as much as the family hoped and prayed for her recovery, after many weeks, she finally died. [2]

A key reason that family members have continued to maintain these individuals who have been declared brain dead is because they still hold out the hope that these individuals will recover, and this hope is nurtured by the few unusual cases where someone has suddenly woken up from a coma after months or years, though doctors have deemed them dead. So the flame of hope continues to flicker, although with each month or year that passes, the hope of recovery grows dimmer and dimmer. Under normal hospital procedures, with a DNR/DNI order in place, such a patient would have been allowed to die a natural death, rather than being kept alive by herculean efforts. If these patients were conscious, they would generally be experiencing great pain and suffering, and they normally would not want the effort to prolong their life by any means possible, resulting not only in exorbitant costs for the surviving family members but in extended pain and suffering, along with no meaningful life for the patient.

Thus, I want to provide a reality check on what people can expect of a doctor and medical team treating the patient, so they have a better understanding of what the doctor and medical team really do—and what they can hope to achieve in treating a patient with a terminal prognosis. This way readers can better understand the limitations and pressures under which the doctor and medical teams work, so readers can more realistically understand what happens when a very serious illness or injury means that the patient is likely to face an end-of-life assessment and the treatment to experience less pain and suffering in these final days.

This background will help to clear away the many misconceptions which patients, their family, and friends often have about the different conditions patients have that are terminal rather than conditions that might be cured. I also want to discuss the different types of treatment that doctors can provide at the end. As illustrated in this overview, doctors and their medical teams are not miracle workers; they are subjected to many limitations in what they can do to help the patient recover, including the patient's presenting symptoms and medical history. In addition, and most importantly, they are faced with the reality of time—the time between the onset of the patient's condition and whether or how long the patient has suffered from a cardiac arrest—a stoppage of the heart and the end of blood flow. If the stoppage is too long, all the other factors don't matter, because once the heart stops, the blood with oxygen can no longer travel to the brain, so within minutes the body starts to shut down, and after twelve minutes, that is normally the end. After that, any possible revival will usually be accompanied by some brain damage, with the amount determined by other factors, such as the patient's age, sex, and general level of health.

HOW THE MEDICAL STAFF RESPONDS TO PROVIDE END-OF-LIFE CARE

A terminal diagnosis can occur for a number of reasons. One major category is chronic conditions and illnesses, such as cancer, emphysema, Alzheimer's, and ALS, which grow increasingly worse over months or years as the patient loses more and more bodily and mental functions. Finally, it becomes clear that the illness has progressed to a terminal phase, at which point patients not only finalize their arrangements to leave their legacy to others, but they make arrangements for their medical care. Commonly, this involves agreeing to a DNR/DNI status, which means that the medical staff will not engage in any aggressive measures to keep reviving the person, since doing so would result in unnecessary pain and suffering before the inevitable end. Thus, a usual recommendation is for the patient to agree to this status while still competent to do so, although, as this book describes, in some cases patients aren't sure what to do, or there may be disagreements with relatives or battles with family members over whether the patient is competent to make his or her own end-of-life determinations.

Another reason for an end-of-life prognosis is that the patient has experienced a life-threatening event, such as a serious accident, fast-acting illness, or being the victim of a violent crime. In many cases after such incidents, the patient is brought to the hospital almost dead, so he or she isn't able to make any determinations about future arrangements and the issue is who should take charge of what should be done to at least reduce the patient's pain and suffering before the end, which is expected to come relatively quickly. As the book describes, I have been in many of these situations, where my role has been primarily to inform the family and relatives that the medical staff did the best they could, but the patient's condition was too poor for anything to be done.

HOW DOCTORS AND MEDICAL TEAM MEMBERS HELP PATIENTS AND FAMILIES

Whatever the patient's reasons for having a terminal prognosis, the hospital staff quickly mobilizes to give the patient the best care possible, and I and other doctors who specialize in end-of-life care act as a liaison between the medical staff and the patient's family and friends who come to the hospital. Often we are involved in the treatment, too, such as engaging in surgery or advising the nursing staff what medications, painkillers, or other treatments to use with a patient in this situation.

We may also spend time talking to the patients to give them information on their prognosis and treatment plan, as well as obtain an agreement from them to approve being considered DNR/DNI status, which means there will be no last-minute heroics to try to keep the person alive after their vital signs drop down, indicating the patient's impending death.

The average person is unfamiliar with the option given to patients or their families to choose a DNR/DNI status and the recommendation by end-of-life medical personnel that they choose this. Perhaps this lack of awareness is due to a reluctance in society to think about the subjects of death or dying. The focus in our ever-present media is on life-affirming activities and events; on humorous exchanges; and on lovable animals, especially kittens and puppies. When death comes up it usually is in the context of a tragic accident, violent crime, or savage beating, with the social media drums urging that anyone who is a perpetrator or a stupid victim receive a punishment in kind. Or death is presented as something which is grim and gory, so the tendency is to want to hide it away, not acknowledge it; so many people are uncomfortable with the whole idea of terminal care. But the DNR/DNI option is an important part of this end-of-life compassionate care, so it is important to understand to provide a context for reading my accounts of my interactions with patients, family members, and relatives.

The reason for recommending DNR/DNI status is it avoids prolonging the dying process, which can mean days or weeks of agony at the end, as the medical staff repeatedly resuscitates the patient, thereby keeping the inevitable from occurring quickly, when there is no hope of the patient resuming a meaningful, productive life. Rather, the goal of a DNR/DNI status is to let nature take its course, so the patient dies a more natural death, with a minimum of pain and suffering.

Explaining Key End-of-Life Issues

Besides helping patients, family members, and friends understand the DNR/DNI option, there are many other issues that come up that need an explanation, since besides having misinformation, patients, family members, and friends are often confused. This explanation is very much needed, because the end of life is a scary time for patients and their families and friends who come to visit them or who stay in close touch by phone when they aren't able to come to the hospital.

Thus, in this book, I will be incorporating these explanations into my discussions of how I worked with different patients, family members and friends, though here I want to briefly introduce some of the key issues and experiences, such as what happens to those who suffer in a cardiac arrest, since there is much misinformation out there, spread by popular TV shows and social media, that suggest doctors have a nearly magical ability to bring ill or injured patients back to life and health after a heart attack.

Another popular misconception is distinguishing a cardiac arrest from a heart attack in order to know the best way to respond when a person goes into a cardiac arrest, which is completely different from the way to respond to a heart attack or myocardial infarction. Accordingly, before describing my experiences in dealing with end-of-life patients and their families, I wanted to discuss what happens in a cardiac arrest and what medical practitioners can do or not do in responding to this situation.

What Happens in a Cardiac Arrest

One of the most popular images in films or TV programs is a medical team rushing a patient on a gurney down the hall in a hospital. People are yelling, sirens are blowing, and medical team members are urging others in the hospital to move away quickly and let them through, because it is *literally* a matter of life or death. Often, regardless of whatever led up to the cardiac arrest, from a serious illness, accident, or a gunshot wound to a vital organ, a key reason for the rush for treatment is that the patient has suffered a cardiac arrest, which occurs when the heart suddenly stops.

Commonly, people confuse what has happened in this emergency scenario with a heart attack, which occurs when something causes a blockage in the blood flow in the arteries to the heart muscle, also known as a myocardial infarction. Sometimes this arterial blockage may result in momentary heart-rhythm irregularities like pauses and last a few seconds, or it may lead to a much more prolonged situation called a cardiac arrest, which is a full-stoppage of the heart that may occur when any of the arteries leading to the heart muscle walls become blocked.

This difference between a heart attack and cardiac arrest is why many people who have heart attacks can often "survive," since they were not dead in the first place. In a true cardiac arrest, a patient can potentially be revived if a rescue team—or even a friend who knows CPR—acts quickly enough to stimulate the heart to get it beating again. But generally, once the heart experiences a true cardiac arrest and the patient is technically dead—at least temporarily since there is no ongoing circulation—advanced emergency medical care is needed to get the heart to work again. In all these cases, the survival rate is very low because a cardiac arrest is a much more serious condition than just a heart attack. The usual survival in a heart attack is about 79-89 percent, depending upon their time of arrival at a hospital.[3] In a cardiac arrest, the survival rate is about 10 percent, according to worldwide statistics.[4] The usual symptoms of a heart attack involve chest pain, mostly with an otherwise well-functioning heart muscle and pump function. In a cardiac arrest, the patient becomes unconscious and is soon dead.

While sometimes a cardiac arrest can occur in a patient who is already receiving treatment for an end-of-life-related condition—which is what I normally provide—in other cases, it is due to a sudden emergency such as a patient who has been deprived of oxygen from drowning, a serious accident, or a gunshot wound. My own cases involve mostly the former, since these patients are normally in the hospital environment for at least several days or weeks while being treated for their condition. But in the latter case, everything happens so quickly that I don't get involved, unless a patient who is brought back from the brink manages to survive and needs further care.

What Causes a Cardiac Arrest

Given the confusion about what causes a cardiac arrest and the difference between a cardiac arrest and heart attack, I wanted to explain a little more about it.

In a heart attack, the blockages that lead to it usually develop over many years, and these can be due to either a critical or complete acute arterial blockage or due to the slowly closing vessel resulting from a chronically enlarging plaque, which can occur in various ways. The most common cause is the rupture of an aging plaque, which is a deposit of pulpy materials on the inner aspect of walls of the cardiac or coronary arteries. The problem in the heart develops when this aging plaque ruptures, so that the plaque that is normally present on the arterial walls breaks off and these pieces of plaque can get stuck further down in the coronary arteries, thereby blocking the flow of blood and the oxygen it is carrying to the heart beyond the blocked point. Furthermore, this growing blockage from the plaque rupture can become even worse, resulting in even less or no blood flowing into the heart muscular walls. This is the heart attack part. More rarely, a clog can develop somewhere else in the arteries, and eventually this clog can migrate to the heart muscle, resulting in a heart attack by mechanically blocking the blood circulation.

Or sometimes a heart attack or a cardiac arrest can be triggered by a more sudden development, such as an embolism, which can occur when a bubble in the bloodstream enters the heart and lungs; more commonly, an actual blood clot enters the pulmonary circulation. These clots normally form in the legs, such as when someone sits too long in one place, often in a confined space like on a plane. This extended immobility might cause the circulation in the veins to become stagnant, and the resulting clot flows up to the heart, causing a blockage in the pulmonary arteries that creates a reflex that paralyzes the heart.

While a cardiac arrest may occur for numerous reasons, it commonly occurs when a heart attack isn't quickly treated to get the heart circulation restored promptly again. In this case, this blockage in the circulation not only keeps the oxygen in the blood from reaching the heart walls, it can lead to a disruption in the heart's electrical system, which is like an engine, and this can cause the heart to stop pumping. Then, this stoppage quickly leads to a loss of blood pressure and patient collapse, and very soon after that, death, if nothing is done within a couple of minutes to restart the heart again.

The initial heart attack, which could lead to a cardiac arrest, may occur for many reasons, including in healthy individuals—or at least in individuals who seem outwardly healthy. But suddenly, they start exhibiting the classic signs of having a heart attack—lifting their hands to their chest in response to the pain they feel there. At this stage, this is not yet a cardiac arrest, since the heart is still pumping. But if something isn't done quickly to get the heart stabilized, like restoring the coronary blood flow, this attack can lead to a cardiac arrest. If the individual is still conscious, this process will last just a few seconds, or the individual may have already passed out from pain or low blood pressure.

There are a number of reasons why a heart attack might occur. A common reason is when an individual, even one who is normally healthy, engages in too-strenuous activity causing undue pressure on the heart, leading it to beat abnormally. Another reason is when someone experiences too much stress in their life, causing emotional tension that may also lead to excess pressure on the heart, usually called the broken heart syndrome. In such cases, like alcoholism, this pressure can impair the pumping ability of the heart. The big villain here is increased cholesterol in the blood and high blood pressure, both of which can not only trigger a heart attack but can lead to a stroke. What happens is that as the amount of cholesterol in the blood increases, it hardens into cholesterol plaques on the walls of the arteries, making the openings smaller. Then these smaller openings restrict the flow of blood and make it harder for the blood to push through these narrower walls. So it is harder for the blood to get through the heart—and any exertion makes this effort to get through harder than ever.[5]

A heart attack might also occur in patients who already have a cardiac history, since they are usually more prone to another attack because they have the same disease that caused the first heart attack. When they do have such an attack, given their history, they have a reduced resiliency and ability to survive, much like when the walls of a castle moat are continually eroded away from repeated attacks, so a subsequent attack breaks through the wall and proves fatal to those inside.

In any event, for whatever reasons it occurs, a heart attack is reflected in a series of symptoms. Besides a crushing chest pain, an individual can experience difficulty breathing, sweating, and nausea or vomiting. The individual may also experience a sudden pallor or pale skin, and will commonly feel very anxious, knowing something is terribly wrong.

Whenever a person experiences any of these symptoms, it is important to quickly get that person treatment, or he or she can soon go into cardiac arrest or sudden cardiac death, when the heart stops for good and blood pressure collapses.

As part of my role in dealing with end-of-life patients, I sometimes counsel patients and their families to be alert for these signs, such as when a patient appears to have a terminal condition but recovers enough in the hospital to go home again. An example is the cancer patient who seems at death's door, but then goes into remission, or the accident patient who recovers after a touch-and-go situation. Though someone has escaped death once, they are often at greater risk of a relapse, and so should be aware of certain signs that their system might be failing, triggering a disruption of their circulation that can lead to a heart attack or cardiac arrest. Thus, a part of my responsibilities in dealing with end-of-life patients who have this reprieve is alerting them to the possibility and signs of a relapse, so they can quickly respond to any signs by returning to the hospital to perhaps prolong their life once again.

The Low Rate of Surviving a Cardiac Arrest

While I might work with some patients who experience a cardiac arrest, either those in the hospital for end-of-life care or those who survive a cardiac arrest and remain in the hospital for further treatment or end-of-life care, the statistics for survival are quite grim once a cardiac arrest has happened, despite all the advances in treating heart disease. Often the general public has a misconception of a person's real chances of surviving a cardiac arrest because of the medical television shows and news reports showing miraculous recoveries, including near-death revivals.

But, in fact, a successful outcome after the heart stops remains poor. Some recent sad cases in the news illustrate what can happen. This is because of the extent of brain damage due to brain cellular death which follows a heart stoppage, because the brain suffers a lack of oxygen and the neurons are the most sensitive of all body tissues to this particular insult.

The examples of Jahi McMath and Bobbi Christina Brown illustrate the way the bodily functions of individuals who are brain dead after a cardiac arrest can be kept alive, but any meaningful recovery of brain functions are very unlikely if not impossible.

Some recent stats show this low level of success in a patient's recovery from a cardiac arrest worldwide. For example, in the United States as a whole, out of seventy thousand patients who experienced an out-of-hospital cardiac arrest, only 8 percent survived and were discharged from the hospital in 2012. This was a slight improvement from 6 percent in 2005, but still a very low success rate.[6] There is some variation from state to state or city to city, with the rates a little better in some areas, such as in Seattle. There, out of twelve thousand patients treated over twenty-four years, the survival and hospital discharge rate was 16 percent.[7] But even this is a low survival rate. So in general, the stats show a very bleak picture for a patient who has experienced a cardiac arrest, because of the short amount of time—about three minutes—before the lack of oxygen to the brain results in loss of brain function; within a few minutes, this loss can lead to death.

But, as I tell patients and their families, some factors contribute to both experiencing a heart attack and a cardiac arrest and to a reduced chance for surviving the heart stoppage. Even if patients might not be able to do anything to improve their chances based on these contributing factors, it may be possible for their family members and relatives to change their own behavior, where that is a contributing factor, and therefore reduce their odds of experiencing a heart attack or cardiac arrest.

For example, these contributing factors include an advanced age and poor health, such as a history of strokes, cancer, Alzheimer's, heart disease, and chronic conditions such as hypertension (high blood pressure), diabetes, end-stage kidney disease, a prior history of congestive heart failure, or a prior myocardial infarction, which results in an irreversible death of the cells or tissues of the heart muscle. Also, having sepsis or septicemia—an infection that spreads through the body after bacteria takes root—can reduce a patient's survival chances. In addition, men are more likely to experience a cardiac arrest than women, perhaps because men tend to have a higher level of stress at work, which results in higher blood pressure and puts more pressure on the heart.

A cardiac arrest can occur for a number of reasons and the survival rates can vary under different circumstances, influenced by the patient's age, level of health, and past medical history, as described above. In all of these situations, if a patient is healthier, younger, and female, he or she is more likely to survive, all other factors being equal, though the difference is minimal between the different groups. While a history of heart problems accounts for a majority of cardiac arrests following a heart attack, about a third of cardiac arrests are due to noncardiac causes. Among the most common causes are: trauma resulting from major accidents, bleeding, intoxication, near drowning, and a pulmonary embolism due to various factors, including smoking, a long period of being immobile, taking certain medications, a genetic predisposition, and cancer.

When a Cardiac Arrest Is Due to What Happens in the Hospital

While most cardiac arrests are due to the conditions the patient experiences outside of the hospital, such as having a serious illness, being in a life-threatening accident, or suffering from a violent crime, some cardiac arrests are due to what happens in the hospital, after a patient is brought there for a cardiac-related problem or some other reason. Sometimes I have to explain this to patients and their family members or relatives, too.

One common cause is the formation of a blood clot in the leg, such as one caused by sitting or lying in a single position for too long or triggered by a trauma. Once formed, this clot travels to the lungs and triggers a reflex that paralyzes the heart so it stops pumping. As a result, blood and oxygen stop circulating, and death soon follows. Another in-hospital cause of cardiac arrest is when the patient experiences a lack of oxygen to the heart. Patients who develop an altered mental status can easily choke and trigger a cardiac arrest, as well. This altered mental status can also be triggered by low blood pressure, usually resulting from infection or sometimes due to overmedication.

The Effectiveness of Resuscitation Methods

Whenever a patient experiences a cardiac arrest or other life-threatening situation, I always talk to patients and their families and relatives about the different methods for resuscitating a victim of a cardiac arrest, which can help an individual survive. In doing so, I point out the difference between resuscitating someone who can then recover and go on to live a productive, everyday life and resuscitating someone at the end of life, where survival probably means continued pain and suffering. Explaining these differences is important, because often people think that resuscitation means a person will fully recover, such as when a healthy person is lying unconscious on the beach after nearly drowning and is revived successfully. But reviving a healthy person is very different from resuscitating an already ill person who is near death in the hospital. While the resuscitation methods are the same, the outcomes are most likely very different, since the patient near death who is returned to consciousness, but otherwise has no hope of recovery, will most likely only experience a prolonged painful dying process.

As I explain to patients and their relatives, one common approach is CPR, which stands for "cardiopulmonary resuscitation," and even bystanders who know CPR techniques can help. Additionally, medical personnel or just about anybody may use a now widely distributed device called the "automated external defibrillator" or AED that greatly advances the CPR process, which involves repeatedly and intermittently applying pressure to the patient's chest to get his or her heart pumping again and provide oxygen with available means, like mouth-to-mouth breathing.

Another approach, which usually involves trained medical personnel and more sophisticated equipment in the field, includes providing oxygen, such as by using a defibrillator or an advanced airway-management system, such as endotracheal intubation. These methods are designed to give a person suffering from a cardiac arrest a therapeutic dose of oxygen and electrical energy to the heart. This energy helps to reestablish a viable heart rhythm, much like a regular heartbeat, to get the blood flowing regularly again by overcoming the electrical disruption triggered by the cardiac arrest.

However, I point out that contrary to the impression of the success of these techniques shown in the movies and on TV, such techniques are only successful to a limited degree. For example, CPR generally can increase the survival rate from 3 to 16 percent, while defibrillation can increase it from 8 to 40 percent for selected populations, based on a study of ten North American regions.[8] Even when emergency personnel come to the scene, an initial successful resuscitation outside the hospital only occurs in up to 33 percent of the patients. Even then, only about 10 percent of these patients are ultimately discharged from the hospital, and many are neurologically impaired, meaning that they have suffered irreversible brain damage as a result of their attack.[9] I feel that giving patients and their families and relatives this information is helpful in presenting the case for an DNR/DNI status, so they don't have unrealistic expectations about a miraculous recovery after a CPR or defibrillation revival. Just as patients may not want to be resuscitated to live in a state of continued pain until an inevitable death, they may not want to be revived if they will have only minimal brain function because their brain has undergone irreversible damage.

Additionally, I point out that perhaps the most critical factor to both increase the chances of a patient's survival and successful recovery is the speed of response to a cardiac arrest. Regardless of a patient's health, age, sex, or other factors that affect survival and reduce the potential for brain damage, the time taken to resuscitate a person makes a major difference in both survival and recovery rates.

Whatever the technique used—whether it's CPR or defibrillation—the time to revive the person makes a big difference to not only whether or not the person can breathe again on his or her own, but to what extent the lack of oxygen to the brain may result in brain damage, also known as "anoxic encephalopathy." As extensive research has shown, the longer a cardiac arrest lasts, the lower the likelihood of reviving the person and the lower the likelihood of the person avoiding brain damage due to neurological impairment. So even if CPR or defibrillation is eventually successful, this brain damage can occur if the resuscitation takes too long, with damage increasing by the minute, while the chances of surviving go down minute by minute, too.

To illustrate this potential for brain damage after CPR or defibrillation, I use this example of what occurs when a person suffers a cardiac arrest in a public place, such as at the mall, supermarket, and restaurant. Say a person is found on the floor after suffering from a cardiac arrest. After an initial two- to three-minute period—the critical time after which the brain begins to suffer from the lack of oxygen, the survival rate declines about 10 percent for each minute without resuscitation efforts. And after twelve minutes without resuscitation by CPR or defibrillation, the survival rate is only 2 to 5 percent. If a person is not resuscitated within twelve minutes, the chances of dying are 98 to 99 percent according to commonly cited statistics by other doctors I know. And even if the patient does survive, neurological damage becomes increasingly likely with each minute it takes to revive the person.

However, when a cardiac arrest is witnessed, a person often receives immediate support, since emergency systems are quickly activated and a rescue team, such as an ambulance or fire department medic, may come immediately. So such a patient might have a good chance for survival with minimal damage, especially when the immediate responders can activate an automated external defibrillator, which are common in many public places. In such cases, patients with a good chance for survival are otherwise healthy, but their heart attack is brought on by circumstances, such as overexertion or experiencing a high level of stress or anxiety. By contrast, when someone has an unwitnessed cardiac arrest in a public place, they are commonly found dead, because they aren't rescued in time. These cardiac arrests in the field are also different from the arrests experienced by patients in a hospital, since they usually have ongoing health problems, some of which can be quite serious, like a previous heart attack or cancer, and in this situation, resuscitation can't really help the patient since he or she is already near death.

Finally, I want patients and their families and relatives to understand the limitations hospitals have in treating patients who suffer a cardiac arrest, since many people imagine that hospitals have all kinds of modern equipment to revive patients. They may think the outcome for a patient who experiences a cardiac arrest in the hospital will have a successful outcome, because they believe the patient will have ready access to the equipment needed to quickly resuscitate him or her, along with the trained medical personnel who can quickly swing into action. However, this isn't the case, even though hospitals generally do have this equipment and the medical teams are trained how to use it. The problem is that a patient in the hospital already either has a serious end-of-life condition or an acute debilitating illness, and a cardiac arrest is like the final straw that breaks the camel's back—or in this case, ends the patient's life.

In practice, this quick and generally successful resuscitation response in the hospital only occurs in a specialized cardiology laboratory where patients, under controlled circumstances, are intentionally caused to have the erratic rhythms that are common in cardiac arrests. Then medical personnel uses a defibrillator to shock the patient out of this rhythm within seconds, so his or her heart can resume beating normally. By contrast, in the regular hospital, the response is often not quick enough to assure survival or avoid brain damage, simply because of the very short time involved to first diagnose what's wrong and then attempt to revive the patient.

For example, suppose monitoring equipment is already connected to that patient. Then, once he or she has a cardiac arrest, indicated by the monitor showing that a normal heart rhythm or breathing has stopped, it can take the medical team at least two to three minutes to respond and effectively start meaningful resuscitation. Then, even if the team rushes to the patient's room, it can still take a few precious minutes to get the equipment set up for either CPR or defibrillation. Then it can take a minute or two more once the procedure starts to get the patient breathing again, if that is even possible. And, as noted, every minute's delay reduces the chances both of having a successful resuscitation and not having any brain damage. In other words, because a quick response is so crucial, there may not be enough time to successfully revive the patient and prevent any neurological damage.

Moreover, if a patient is not in a cardiac monitored bed, the delay can be even longer, since once a nurse or other medical team member finds an unresponsive patient and asks for a medical team to respond, it can take much longer than five to ten minutes to begin resuscitation efforts after the patient's initial cardiac arrest. After all, the time needed to successfully resuscitate a patient starts from when he or she has the heart stoppage, not from when he or she was discovered.

That's why the survival rates are only about 6 to 15 percent. For example, in the largest study conducted at 435 hospitals of patients who had cardiac arrests in the hospital and were revived using standard resuscitation procedures of CPR or defibrillation, 50 percent of the patients were actually revived so they regained their pulse after their heart began pumping and circulating their blood again. However, in the end, only 15 percent survived to be discharged by the hospital.[10] While some of this poor survival rate was due to the patients' original condition leading to hospitalization, much of this low rate was due to the patients' failure to fully recover from the cardiac arrest.

3

CLOSE FAMILY, CLEAR MIND

For some patients, the end of life can be a very calm, logical process, where they organize everything as long as they can, and their family members carry out their instructions. In such cases, there is relatively little drama; everyone understands and feels comfortable with the process of letting go. They accept the inevitable, as physical and mental deterioration occurs, and there is none of the shock, denial, anger, bargaining, testing, or depression that occurs in some patients. It is as if, to take the first stages of dying initially developed by Elisabeth Kübler-Ross, the patient and his or her family have come to the hospital in the stage of acceptance without going through any of these other stages. They are prepared or ready for whatever comes next in this final stage of life.

That was my experience with Gertrude, a sweet stoic German woman, who had immigrated to the United States from Germany in her early twenties, and still had her thick accent and staccato pattern of speech. During her life, she had been a shop owner, who learned the skills of managing a small office and handling the books, so she knew how to be well organized. In her prime, she had been stocky, with the build of a heavyset German woman who enjoyed a diet of rich meat, potatoes, and pastries, although now she was skinny, because cancer had robbed her of her hearty appetite and gradually caused her to waste away. Even so, when she first came to the hospital, she was still feisty and determined.

As I sat at her bedside at our first meeting, her daughter and two sons seated nearby, Gertrude told me: "Doctor, I don't want to fool around. I lived my life, and I know it'll be over soon. But I talked to my family, and

I know exactly what to do, just like I have always known what to do in running my business to be successful. So now my family and I have worked out a very clear plan."

As I took notes, it was hard to imagine that she was gradually declining from a spreading cancer in the last few years of her life, for she still had the same feisty spirit and the same desire to stay in control as long as she could. She wanted to manage her death, much as she had managed her life. She continued explaining the plan.

"I have decided that when it is no longer worth living, I will just go away in a peaceful manner. My family understands this very, very clearly. They know I don't want to be resuscitated when the time comes. I just want you to take away any supporting tubes and wires keeping me alive and let me go."

For now, since she was still able to be active, though often in pain due to the cancer, I prescribed some painkillers to ease her pain.

I told her children who were caring for her: "Your mother can go home with you for now."

Then I told Gertrude: "If you have difficulty moving or experience increased pain, come back to the hospital, and we'll care for you here."

She and her family members nodded their agreement. But a few weeks later, Gertrude was readmitted again. As she, her daughter, and two sons sat across from me in my office, her daughter reported that her mother had experienced a few small strokes, so she now had difficulty raising her arm and her speech was slurred. Gertrude also seemed slower in responding to the questions I asked her about the common knowledge most everyone has to know if they are oriented to the present, such as "What date is it today?" and "Who is the President?" Though Gertrude answered correctly, her answers came after a long period—nearly fifteen seconds—of thought. So I told Gertrude and her daughters and son:

"I would recommend that you undergo carotid surgery to prevent strokes in the future. This is done when a stroke might be likely to occur and a large clot could be dislodged in the bloodstream and cause massive brain damage. Without surgery, the risk is too high, but if you get the surgery, you could live for several years."

"Yes . . . yes," Gertrude and her children agreed.

"And you understand the risks," I reiterated, since I wanted to be sure they knew this procedure might not be successful, especially in a woman of Gertrude's age and condition, since she was already in a very fragile state. "But the alternative is continued strokes and more serious ones," I explained.

With that understanding, the next day the vascular surgeon wheeled Gertrude into the operating theater, accompanied by another doctor and two nurses to assist. As usual, the anesthesiologist administered the general anesthesia, putting Gertrude in a relaxed and unconscious state, so she was not aware of the operation, rather than using a more localized anesthesia where the patient remains awake. For this delicate procedure, this state of total unawareness is best.

At first, during the surgery, all seemed to go well. The surgeon suctioned out the blockages, where there had been a buildup of coagulated blood, so now the blood flowed more strongly. But suddenly, like a car's engine that gets flooded with gas and shuts down, Gertrude had a major stroke during the surgery. I realized she had the stroke when she woke up, due to her sudden muscular weakness, and when she became more alert, she had an even more marked deficit in her ability to understand language or recognize what was happening around her due to the stroke.

Unfortunately, a stroke was a possible occurrence, which happens in a very small percentage of cases, but there is no way to know in advance which patients will be affected. For the vast majority of patients, the surgery we performed is a safe and recommended procedure to prevent future strokes. Nevertheless, there is a slight risk for a small minority. Regrettably, Gertrude provided to be that one or two in a hundred patients who experienced a major stroke.

Since Gertrude could no longer understand what was happening due to the stroke, I spoke to her daughter and sons about what had happened and what we should do next. As I told them:

"Unfortunately, Gertrude experienced a serious stroke during the procedure, which has left her unable to understand and communicate as she did before. However, her condition was already deteriorating before the operation, so it was just a matter of time before she had further strokes."

"We understand," her daughter said. "At least you gave us some hope with the operation. But we realize there is nothing more anyone can do now except make her last days more comfortable and end her life like she wanted."

I felt relieved that the family members understood what had happened and did not blame the surgeon and operating team, which sometimes happens when an operation doesn't go well. But as long as a doctor provides the best care possible based on the current standard of care, that's the best we can do. We are still at the mercy of the patient's condition, genetics, and will to survive, as well as the ravages of his or her disease.

For a time, right after the operation, we put Gertrude in the ICU to heal physically from the surgery incisions. When the family came in to see her, she still was connected to tubes, as she pulled herself up to greet me and her daughter and sons. They spent a few minutes with her, asking questions like "How are you, Mom?" and telling her: "We're glad you're okay." In response, she just smiled wanly, letting everyone know she could still hear and recognize the family members, though she couldn't speak.

Later, her daughter and sons came to visit her briefly each day, and the exchanges went much like that—the family showing their care and concern and Gertrude smiling to acknowledge their presence. At least I could tell by Gertrude's wan smile that she was gratified by these visits. They helped her feel connected to her family, whom she still loved, even though she couldn't speak about her feelings, which is characteristic of many patients in these last stages of life.

After a few days, Gertrude's physical wounds from the surgery healed and the tubes came out, so we were able to transfer her from the intensive care unit to the floor. There she shared a curtained room with another patient, and the nurses placed her in a dayroom during the day with other patients in a similar condition. During this time, I checked in twice a day for a few minutes to examine how she was doing. I checked her reflexes, listened to her heartbeat, and prescribed painkillers to ease any pain. But for the most part, the nurses now took care of her, which, among other things, including getting her ready to sit on a couch or chair in the dayroom, helping her to the bathroom, and bringing her meals on a tray.

Unfortunately, Gertrude's overall situation remained poor and there were no major signs of improvement. Mostly, she lay or sat up in bed or perched in a chair in the dayroom, staring out into space and not speaking to anyone, unless I, her family members, or the nurses came over to speak to her. At least, Gertrude seemed by her faint smile and nods to understand their comments on an emotional level, as if she understood they were there to show their continued support and that seemed to make her happy for the short time they were there. Otherwise, her appearance was one of chronic sadness, as if she now realized that she had no hope of a meaningful recovery.

After one of their last visits, as we stood in the hallway outside of the dayroom, I asked the family members what they wanted to do. They walked down the hall to confer, and a few minutes later they returned. As before, the daughter spoke on behalf of the whole family.

"We discussed this, and the family wants to honor Gertrude's wishes of taking a generally conservative approach to her passing given the circumstances. So we don't want to take any active or heroic efforts to keep her alive."

I immediately agreed this was the best course. Clearly, we all hoped for a quick outcome, and from their conversations with Gertrude in the months before her final days, the family members felt she would want this, too. Then nature could take its course and Gertrude would naturally pass away. The family members hoped for this, since they were rather hesitant but were seriously considering asking me to take some action to bring this kind of limbo to a conclusion, such as giving her a lethal dose of painkillers or sleeping pills.

In that case, pushing her into a peaceful demise would seem like an assisted suicide, even if somebody left the pills on her bedside table and advised her to take them herself if she wished. Technically and legally, leaving the pills within reach might or might not be considered an assisted suicide, since no one actively gave her the pills. Yet defining "assisted suicide" was still a legal gray area. One of the complicating factors here is that Gertrude might no longer have the ability to knowingly make a choice—she might be just responding automatically to my or a family member's directive to take the pills.

Another worrying, though less likely concern, was the possibility that Gertrude might get better to become more cognitively aware and function on that level for a while with no immediate risk of dying. If so, she would be in a state of chronic suffering, because of her limited functioning, even if she wasn't in physical pain. But she still could experience the emotional and mental pain of feeling trapped in her body with limited movement and limited ability to communicate with others.

Meanwhile, as we waited, still unsure of what to do, a team of continuity of care nurses who specialize in planning where patients are going after they leave the hospital based on their limitations, contributed its expertise. The nurses helped the family to arrange for an in-home team of nurses to care for Gertrude with a series of eight-hour shifts throughout the day, much as the nurses did in the hospital by helping her sit up in bed or in the dayroom. But now she would be at home, which would be an advantage for her in being in familiar surroundings, and for the family in reducing the costs of hospital care. At the same time, the family and I met with the primary care nurses who would provide this care once she was home.

It was my job to coordinate what the teams of nurses would do to make sure that they provided the kind of care the family members wanted and that they would be as upbeat and humane as possible in caring for Gertrude. As I explained to the family members:

"In keeping with Gertrude's wishes, these nurses will come to her home to make her last days as peaceful and comfortable as possible. But they won't do anything to prolong her life or hasten her death."

The family members agreed that this home care was the best approach, since it prevented us from making a decision to actively bring on her death, since any such death could be considered not due to a natural outcome and therefore might be regarded as an "assisted suicide." At the same time, a home care arrangement would provide the family with the peace of mind of knowing that Gertrude's wishes had been honored, since she would be passing away peacefully without any further interventions. She had clearly stated that she did not want any artificial nutrition or support, and that's what we agreed to do.

After that, Gertrude lingered in this state of barely living but not dying for several more weeks, but the family members and I felt satisfied that she was comfortable and in no pain. She continued to sleep much of the day, and when she was awake, she mostly stared straight ahead, whether sitting up in bed or on the living room couch, and she no longer spoke much more than to softly grunt her approval when a nurse came to give her some water or juice or to change the large white adult diapers she now wore. At least Gertrude continued to smile happily, as if to let us know she felt at peace and was thankful for the ongoing support of her daughter and sons, who came from time to time to hold her hand or kiss her forehead to show they were still there with her.

Finally, after a couple more weeks, Gertrude slipped into a coma-like state and clinically her condition quickly deteriorated, as one by one her organs began to shut down, although in this coma-like state, she had little awareness of what was happening. Meanwhile, to be sure she felt no pain though such a feeling was unlikely in this state, I started her on a low-dose morphine drip, whereby the nurses set up a bag and tube that injected her with morphine, which cut off any signals of pain to her brain. Then, since there was no medical hope of recovery, I spoke to the family, and with their agreement, I facilitated her passing using medications to provide what we call "the care and comfort protocol."

As I explained to her daughter and sons as we sat by Gertrude's bedside while the nurses set up the morphine drip:

"This morphine drip is here to give Gertrude a sense of comfort and pain relief. Even though she is in a semicoma, we do this to make sure that no pain signals come through and cause her any discomfort or distress."

As the nurses finished setting up the drip and moved away from Gertrude, who appeared to be in a quiet sleep, I continued my explanation.

"This drip also gives the patient a very calm, peaceful appearance, which as you can see shows that Gertrude is in no apparent distress. Should the nurses later notice any tightening of the muscles or cries from her that might suggest she is experiencing some tension or discomfort, they will increase the dose and as needed give her a strong sedative, such as Ativan, either by injecting it or placing it under her tongue. Should her breathing become noisy or should any saliva accumulate in her mouth, the nurses have another medication called Levsin that dries up the secretions in the mouth, allowing for a more peaceful, comfortable end of life. This process is less stressful for the family members who are with the patient, too."

After this explanation, Gertrude's daughter and sons looked very peaceful, almost serene, as they waited for the end, which was very near. Thus, this is an approach I commonly use with many patients at the end, when they want a calm and peaceful death, letting nature take its course, as Gertrude wanted in this case. It's an approach which makes the whole process of dying and death much more humane for both the patient and his or her family members, especially when the patient has given a "do not resuscitate" order and wants no active intervention to prolong life in these last difficult days.

4

ALONE AND IN DENIAL

For some patients, the dying process can bring together members of the family and friends through shared grief over the passing of the patient. They join together to show the dying person that he or she is loved, and in so doing, they make it easier for that person to accept the ending of life.

For others, this last phase of a person's life can be a very lonely one indeed. In fact, this loneliness and fear of being alone can contribute to dying people not wanting to acknowledge that the end is near. So they deny what is happening to them, and that denial can contribute to their further separation from others.

That was the case for Victor, a Hispanic man in his late twenties, an immigrant from Puerto Rico who spoke a mix of English and Spanish, sometimes called Spanglish. His lifestyle contributed to his isolation at the end of his life. He lived in a housing development where he shared the space with a Cambodian family to whom he had no ties, and he was estranged from both a significant other, who worked as a prostitute, and their daughter. He hadn't seen either of them in years, and after the relationship with his partner broke up, he led a vibrant, happy-go-lucky life as a member of the gay community, but his lifestyle contributed to his isolation from others. Rather than develop relationships, he was happy with one-night stands, and he participated with others he met through a bar-hopping community of young men who pursued this way of life. Like many of the other men, Victor enjoyed getting high on whatever was available at the parties with the rocking music which he attended—pot, ecstasy, speed, cocaine, sometimes even heroin—he tried them all. At the same time, this way of life helped to disconnect him and the other gay men at these parties from their families. In some cases, this was because their families had difficulty accepting their gay orientation and disapproved of their casual approach to sex. In other cases, the men were married, though in name only to keep up appearances, whether their spouses or partners knew or didn't, as in Victor's case.

At the same time, Victor's work provided only limited personal relationships with others, since he worked as a low-level employee in a stock brokerage firm in training to become a broker. In the business, relationships were based on one's success in the market, and as individuals moved up the ladder financially, they were only too ready to push their past associates aside to connect with others on the way up or already there.

Thus, both at work and in his personal life, Victor had limited connections with others, and he experienced further isolation when he discovered he had AIDS. Further complicating matters, he also contracted hepatitis, which frequently is transmitted by sexual contact or by the dirty needles often used by drug abusers. He discovered the problem when he went to a local clinic, because he was puzzled by some of the odd blue bruises that appeared on his arms and legs—a symptom of Kaposi's sarcoma, which is a tumor caused by human herpesvirus 8.

He actually had had the HIV virus for a while without knowing it, but these blue bruises were the first signs he was infected, since his weakened immune system due to HIV had provided a fertile breeding ground for Kaposi's sarcoma.

At first Victor tried to deny the disease by taking some pills for the headaches and upset stomach that accompanied it, though he went to parties and had sexual encounters as usual. But gradually he became weaker and weaker, which led him to come to the hospital, where I first saw him. After the nurse at the reception desk admitted him and another nurse gave him a workup to check his weight and blood, I came into the examination room, where he was lying down. I could see by his record that he had been losing weight over the last few weeks, so he was noticeably thin now, and I saw the tell-tale bluish splotches on his arms and legs, which he had tried to cover up with a beige make-up powder.

When I asked him about his health and nutrition over the last few weeks, he told me:

"I've been getting weaker, doctor. I don't feel very hungry anymore, and I've been having trouble keeping things down when I try to eat something."

I realized that he had been getting worse, both because of his poor nutrition and because the viral disease HIV had taken over, and I knew that he would soon have a full-fledged case of AIDS. This would happen once his T-cell count, one of the subsets of white blood cells in his immune system, dropped below two hundred, though it is normally is about a thousand. I was also concerned that once the HIV turned into AIDs, he might be likely to get other conditions that often accompany the disease, including pneumonia, the HIV wasting syndrome, and respiratory tract infections.

I cautioned him about what to expect and recommended that he consider getting his affairs in order and arrange to go into a treatment program to prevent him from needing hospice care, since he was diagnosed with end-stage liver disease due to his hepatitis and alcohol abuse. However, he didn't want to hear about any of this. Instead, he thought if he took the few medicines I prescribed for him to improve his appetite and ease his pain, he would be fine. Then he left, presumably to continue his past lifestyle as best he could by going to work for the stock brokerage firm and going to bars and parties at night.

But a couple of weeks later, he could no longer do either because he had become even weaker, so he stopped going to work, left a couple of parties early, and finally collapsed at one of them, after which one of the attendees dropped him off at the hospital. That's when I saw him again, soon after he woke up in his hospital bed.

At this point, he looked extremely poor. He had more Kaposi's sarcoma lesions, with a few blotches now on his neck. He looked even thinner. His face was now gaunt and his eyes were watery. He had a nasal drip and coughed from a respiratory infection. I also noticed that despite his thinness, his waistline had increased and his stomach protruded out and down, which is a sign of the late stage of liver cirrhosis, commonly due to excess alcohol consumption and/or hepatitis.

"How much do you usually drink?" I asked him.

"Maybe a few drinks at parties, and a few more drinks when I get home," he said.

Ultimately, I determined he was drinking about a bottle a day.

"It makes me feel better. It eases the pain," he said.

"But it's even worse for your general health," I explained.

I asked him if he could get out of bed. "I'd like to see how you are walking," I said.

But when Victor put his feet on the floor, he immediately became dizzy and his legs buckled under him, so he grabbed onto the bed and pulled himself back into a sitting position.

"I guess I can't walk right now," he said.

I then had to figure out how to tell him that his disease was terminal, since all the signs pointed to him only having a few months to live, given the Kaposi's sarcoma, his liver disease and distended stomach, his general weakness, his inability to walk, and the certainty that he now had full-blown AIDS. Giving someone this pronouncement is always difficult; but now it was even more so, because I knew Victor had a pattern of denying the seriousness of his condition, so he might be likely to deny this diagnosis as well.

"I'm sorry to have to tell you this, but your condition is not going to get any better."

Victor at first glared at me angrily, as if he was ready to fight back against the truth. But ultimately he lay back on his pillow, as if he was too tired to fight against what was increasingly obvious and hard to deny. So his pattern of continued denial was over.

The next question was what to do about his continued care, since no one came to visit him at the hospital; he no longer lived with his partner; and he had no close friends or family who seemed to care.

"Is there anyone we contact about your condition?" I asked. "Is there anyone who can help you wrap up your affairs?"

Victor looked at me even more weakly and uncertainly.

"I guess you could contact my mother," he finally said reluctantly, since she was the only one left to contact.

A few days later, after I called his mother to explain the situation, she arrived. As she sat with me by Victor's bedside, he was barely lucid, slipping in and out of consciousness.

"We don't have a particularly good connection," his mother explained. "His father, when he was alive, and I never really approved of Victor's lifestyle, but we couldn't change him. So eventually we accepted who he was, but after he moved to a big city, we didn't speak very much anymore. But now I'm here."

"Thank you for coming," I said.

As Victor sat up again, we discussed what to do about Victor's DNR/ DNI status.

"It means you don't want us to resuscitate you, when you can no longer breathe on your own."

But Victor refused to consider that option.

"I want to be resuscitated at any price," he said. "Whatever it costs, however painful it is, I want to keep on going."

"But why?" his mother asked.

"Because as long as I'm alive, there's always hope," he said.

Victor seemed to think there might be some miracle cure that would suddenly be discovered, though in the next few weeks when he was likely to die such a cure was unlikely until there was some future medical breakthrough. So even with resuscitation, Victor's best hope was to live several more weeks, but he would experience even more weakness, confusion, and eventually fall into a coma, which is what a liver disease causes, requiring even more medications to help him feel better, though that would mean he would spend more time in a barely conscious weakened state. Though his determination to be resuscitated no matter what was not a decision I would recommend, in the end, Victor was the patient. So the final decision about how to die was up to him.

Finally, the decision made, I spoke to the nursing team that would handle the end-of-life care for Victor. There were three nurses on the team—one for each eight-hour shift, and we discussed how aggressive to be in treating Victor, since the nurses knew they had to resuscitate him should he have any breathing problems. Eventually, we decided we needed more help in deciding on how to respond and asked the palliative-care nurse to assist us. Such a nurse is part of these new teams that deal with end of-life-care, and seek to reduce the patient's pain and suffering at the end, whether that pain is physical, emotional, or mental. The palliative nurse explained what she could do.

"With a patient like Victor, who is trying to delay the end of life as long as possible despite his deteriorated and painful condition, the basic goal is to have a straightforward professional discussion with him, so he fully understands what he will experience if he keeps getting resuscitated. When told this again by another party, the patient is more likely to finally get the message about what the end of life really means and how he would like the medical staff to proceed when it comes to that."

Thus, later that day, the palliative care nurse spoke to Victor, holding his hand by his bedside as she spoke to show her continuing care and support.

As a result, Victor did finally get the message and changed his instructions to a DNR/DNI status. He died peacefully two days later. His mother came shortly after I called to tell her what happened, and thereafter she took full charge of signing the release papers to send his body to the local crematorium, as he wished, so his ashes could later be released in the wind from a boat at sea.

The experience also provided a good lesson for future dealings with patients who have a very serious disease where no cure is possible to gently help them understand this situation. This way they can better be ready to face their death without resisting and prolonging the process, which results in them living their last days in a state of shifting between unconsciousness and pain. While doctors, nurses, and other medical practitioners may not be able to hasten the dying process, as the law now stands in most states, we don't have to prolong this process. Rather, we can advise the patient how to avoid this by agreeing to a nonresuscitation status. In many cases, a palliative care nurse who is trained in this process can help get the patient's agreement.

Unfortunately, as Victor's case indicates, while many doctors and nurses may join together to let a patient know how bad things are, some patients tend not to want to hear this information. They may think the doctors or nurses are wrong or that an end-of-life diagnosis doesn't apply to them, because they expect to somehow pull through. In many cases, the patients may wrongly believe they may not die this time, because they have recovered from previous episodes where they were near death. Or even if they haven't had such an experience, they still may want to deny that they are facing the end of life.

Thus, as in Victor's case, it can be very difficult to communicate to somebody that the end is very near and inevitable, based on our best scientific knowledge and past experiences. Some patients may express doubts about this assessment, since we don't have hard numbers to support this determination, which some patients expect, especially when they come from a financial, scientific, or engineering background. But medicine can never be exactly precise; it always depends on our best assessment based on the patient's perceived condition as determined by our current diagnostic tools and on the medical treatments available at the time.

In turn, communicating this kind of information to help patients decide what to do at the end requires a special individual, such as a palliative nurse, to provide this input, since these nurses are well trained in what to say and do. So they are at times better able to connect with the patient than doctors and nurses, whose training focuses on what medical procedures to provide. While some doctors and nurses may be better at providing more scientific or data-based information, it may be more comforting for the patient to hear about how to deal with the end of life from a more religious or practical perspective.

Thus, combining all of these opinions can help in making the final assessment and getting this message to patients, so they can best understand it. Then, they can realize that they will get no benefit from prolonging their life. Rather, prolonging it will just bring about increased bodily suffering and "torture" from the procedures used to prolong life at a time when there is no hope of recovery. So all their continued pain, which is too great to be fully relieved by any pain medications, will only make them suffer for no purpose, because there is no meaningful hope for any sort of recovery.

In some cases, the patient's primary care physician, who has years of knowledge through a close relationship with the patient, may be the best one to express these views, because of having more credibility due to the long years of taking care of the patient. However, more and more primary care physicians may not offer this input, because they are increasingly distancing themselves from their patients' care in the hospital setting, especially when patients are there at the end of their life. So in that case, a doctor in the hospital or a palliative care nurse might best present this information.

5

LAUGHING 'TIL THE END

In some cases, patients approach the end of life with a positive, humorous attitude. Commonly this occurs when an individual has always been a good-natured, easy-to-get-along-with person. Sometimes these patients may even be a comedian or jokester in their everyday interactions with others both personally and at work. So that attitude carries over when they experience anything bad in life—including the knowledge of their impending demise. But in some cases, treating their coming death through jokes and humor can be a form of denial. They laugh away the inevitable, thinking of the deadly prognosis they have received from the doctor as a kind of joke—or at least they want to think that to feel better.

Such an approach was characteristic of Jack, who was a very nice, always smiling heavyset guy with a very good sense of humor, who everyone, including me, liked to be around. He made everything in life fun, and his thirtysomething normal-weight male roommate, who shared a small two-bedroom apartment with him in a busy downtown neighborhood, seemed to enjoy his company, too. Sometimes Jack's roommate even watched TV with him, though Jack had a fairly active social life in the local singles community, so he wasn't often home.

Besides his humorous approach to everything in life, Jack had a ferocious appetite for any type of food. At one time, his love of food and large girth was a perfect fit for his job as a salesman, since it gave him a roly-poly look like a friendly bear, and combined with his witty repartee, his sales approach and appearance helped him sell anything because he seemed so lovable and trustworthy. Thus, whether he was selling furniture, office supplies, or décor for a house, Jack was very successful. However, over the years, as Jack put on more and more weight and ultimately became morbidly obese at four hundred pounds, his heavy weight made it impossible to do the job since it was hard to go to personal meetings. Though he had a gastric bypass done years before to get down to an acceptable weight, that goal didn't last very long, and he was quickly up to four hundred pounds again. He adapted to his high weight by becoming adept at telephone sales, and he gave up any hope of having another gastric bypass, because that would be too dangerous due to possible complications given his previous surgery. Moreover, his lack of discipline meant that he might quickly go back to his heavy weight again.

I met Jack when he was back in the hospital because of the classic complications of obesity. One of these problems that I noticed immediately is that he had cellulitis, which occurs when the skin is stretched, especially on the legs, so that small holes in the skin called "micropores" develop. These break the integrity of the skin, and bacteria can freely cross through the natural skin barrier and lead to infection. As I examined him, I saw the tell-tale signs of this—a large red puffiness around many micropores that were signs of bacterial infection.

"I've noticed these sores for a while," Jack explained.

When I told him what these large red sores were and why they occurred, he showed his natural tendency for joking by making fun of his condition.

"You mean I'm holy," he kidded.

"You might say that," I said. "But you have to understand these micropores are a very serious complication. We can get the infection under control for now with some antibiotics to kill the bacteria. But when you have a break in the skin permitting bacteria to enter and infections to develop, you could easily get in some bacteria that are much more deadly, so this complication could be fatal."

At least Jack quieted down and relaxed as I continued the examination and looked for other complications of the morbid obesity syndrome. One common complication is breathing problems, which may occur because of excessive water accumulation, which occurs as fat accumulates. Another related condition is having pulmonary problems due to fat pushing the tissue into the chest cavity, causing the person to hyperventilate because he or she has less room in the chest to breathe normally, so less air is moved in and out. As a result, after such patients breathe in oxygen, instead of exhaling all the carbon dioxide, or CO^2, as they should since this is a waste gas, they retain it, so CO^2 builds up in their lungs. It is like driving around with a clog in your car exhaust system.

I noticed this symptom through Jack's slow and labored breathing, reflected in his long deep breaths, like he was gasping for air, and I asked him about this.

" Have you had trouble with your breathing?"

"Yes," Jack agreed. "I sometimes feel I need more air, especially when I try to stand or move around."

"That's exactly it," I replied. "It's your heavy weight that has been causing your breathing problem, because your excess weight puts pressure on your chest cavity, so you have less room for your lungs to go in and out. So you have to breathe even harder for them to push back against this pressure."

"I know. It's like lifting weights," he said, trying to be cheery. "When I was younger, I tried to lift heavier and heavier weights, and I had to breathe harder from the extra exertion. But after I lifted them and put the weights back down, I could relax and I breathed easier again."

Then, as I continued my examination, I checked his heart rate and pulse. I looked for any signs of high blood pressure, heart flutters, or arrhythmic beats, because these cardiac complications commonly occur due to obesity. Grossly overweight people often have highly elevated blood pressure or irregular heartbeat, because their heart is overworked by the extra weight, and it might readily skip a beat from doing this extra work.

"Yes, I sometimes experience these skipped beats," Jack agreed. "And it can be a little scary, because it's like my heart is standing still. It's like the car I used to have when I could drive. It might not start right away. So I would step on the gas again, and it would rev up."

"That's a good analogy," I said. "However, you can always take your car in to get it fixed, so you can repair the engine and it's good as new. But your heart doesn't work that way. If it stops because it's working too hard, you have to start it again within a few seconds or at most a minute or two. If you don't, not enough blood with oxygen reaches your brain, and your brain can be irretrievably damaged or you can be dead."

Jack nodded somberly, as if he was finally recognizing the seriousness of his situation. "You're right, doc. I didn't realize how badly I was doing with all this extra weight."

Then my examination continued, as I checked the level of water accumulation in Jack's body by looking for swollen legs or edema, which is a swelling caused by excess fluid trapped in the body's tissue. A high level of fluids often occurs with obesity, and this can trigger respiratory failure and further water accumulation, which shows up on the legs as gravity pulls the water down during the day. However, this water is also diffusely distributed throughout the body and tends to accumulate in the lungs, so a patient can feel like he is drowning from inside.

This buildup occurs because eating a very high-calorie diet puts extra pressure on the whole body including the kidneys, and an overweight person has difficulty processing all the additional foods. It's like putting too many items on a factory assembly line or too many messages on an Internet server, which overloads the system. As a result, the operations of the kidneys or other organs can slow down or stop. So water and other toxins begin to accumulate throughout the body, putting further pressure on the kidneys, so they are prone to malfunction even more, reflected in some degree of renal failure. Furthermore, besides being prone to slowing down or stopping, the kidneys can get inflamed, leading to further slow-downs and stoppages. Likewise, this pressure can impact other organs, including the lungs and the heart, and the stress on these systems tends to make matters even worse, as even more fluids accumulate in the body.

However, it was difficult to know what the problem was for Jack, since when people are so big, it is not possible to obtain a biopsy to explain what is going on with their kidneys. Moreover, due to all the excess weight, it becomes more difficult to reach the kidneys by the usual methods, because they are further away from the exterior of the body. Thus, I simply told Jack:

"There appears to be a problem with your kidneys, too, and you have an accumulation of extra water in your body, which is reflected in further bloating. But we can't tell exactly what's going on, because we can't do a biopsy since there is a very thick layer of fat under your skin, which is too thick for us to cut through to extract some cells to test."

Then I had one more bit of dire news, since I discovered Jack had diabetes after I had drawn some blood for a lab test and got back the results.

"Unfortunately, you have a very high level of sugar in your blood due to diabetes, so to get that level down, you need to start taking insulin. You can start with some medications to do this, though if the problem becomes more severe and your blood sugar level doesn't come down enough, you will need to get shots. Either a nurse can do these injections, or I can show you how to do them yourself. Otherwise, a high level of blood sugar, along with high blood pressure, can cause a stroke."

Jack looked surprised. "Oh, that might have been what happened to me last week. Suddenly, while I was sitting on the couch watching TV, I saw the room go dark, and I couldn't raise my arm or move my feet. It was like I was frozen into place or stuck in concrete. Then the feeling of being frozen or stuck lifted, and I could move and see again."

"It sounds like you had a stroke," I agreed.

To check if a stroke had caused Jack's experience, I arranged for him to have a CT scan—a computerized tomography scan, which combines a series of X-ray images taken from different angles. Then it uses computer processing to create cross-sectional images or slices of the bones, blood vessels, and soft tissues inside the body, which provides more detailed information than a plain X-ray. This kind of scan is especially good to quickly examine people with any kind of internal injuries, and it can be used to diagnose disease or injury as well as to plan medical, surgical, or radiation treatment.

To perform the scan, two nurses came into Jack's room and wheeled him into the room with the CT scan equipment. As Jack lay down, the X-ray screens were placed around his body to take a series of X-ray images. A few minutes later, the images were recorded so I could look at them. The process is much like having X-rays in your dentist's office. However, since Jack's stroke had come and gone without causing any lasting damage, the photo images did not reveal whether he had a stroke or not. An MRI (which stands for magnetic resonance imaging) would have been a better test, since this is a radiology technique that uses magnetism, radio waves, and a computer to produce images of the person's brain. But Jack could not fit in an MRI machine because of his excessive size.

Finally, after telling Jack about all the problems he was presenting, I sent him home, explaining, "There's nothing more we can do for you now."

I urged him to take care of himself and try to reduce the number of calories he was getting each day. "If you can bring down your weight that may help to reduce your blood pressure, your excess fluids, and the pressure on your systems. If you eat less sugar, that can help with your diabetes. Then come see me in two weeks to see how you are doing."

But two weeks later, Jack was not doing very well. Once I met with him in my office for a follow-up session, it was clear that he was not about to change anything. Instead, Jack simply joked about his situation, another sign of denial of how serious his condition really was. For example, when I asked about his diet and if he had made any changes in what he was eating, he smiled and told me how he persuaded the girls in the apartment next door to bring him pizza and bagels from the cafeteria.

Though I told him that these behaviors would lead to his early demise, he seemed uninterested in even entertaining the possibility. Instead he was full of jokes again.

"Everyone dies. If you gotta go, you gotta go, but I'm not going yet."

He didn't understand with his history of strokes, high blood pressure, diabetes, and everything else that I found wrong with him, he could go at any time. So there was no way I could bring up the end-of-life decisions he would have to confront very soon, probably on his next visit to the hospital, such as his choice of resuscitation status—to resuscitate or not. He did not want to hear about these choices. Instead, he found a way to twist everything I said in a different direction and with some humor to get a laugh almost every time, if not from me from my office assistant, who did the typing and filing and transcribed my notes with patients.

For example, when I said I hoped we could talk about his choice of resuscitation status, he just laughed and began a series of plays on words, telling me:

"Oh, yes. Recitation. I've always liked doing that. So you can always call on me to recite something."

Thus, it was clearly impossible for me to talk about the subject of resuscitation seriously, because Jack wanted to maintain a positive, humorous attitude anytime I tried to bring up his likely death in the near future, since he had stopped trying to take care of himself.

But at our next meeting at my office, he brought along his sister, a woman in her forties, who worked as a lawyer and was the family legal adviser, perhaps because she saw his deteriorating condition and felt it was time to take what was happening to him seriously. As a result, I was able to discuss planning for his future hospitalization and possible death, and his sister agreed he should do this, telling him:

"You have to take what the doctor is saying seriously. We need to plan what will happen, not just for you but for the whole family."

Reluctantly, Jack agreed.

So he was truly a very frustrating person to deal with, although in our next follow-up meeting he told me that he finally got the message. Even so, he tried to treat the subject lightly, with even more jokes. For example, when I told Jack: "If you have a resuscitate order in place, you'll receive the maximal medical therapy available within your means," he joked back:

"Okay. So that means if you've got the means and I've got the means, you'll do everything within your means to keep me going."

Again, I agreed we would do that. Though I felt I needed to explain what could potentially happen, if we tried to maintain life in the face of indicators suggesting it would be better not to resuscitate. As I explained:

"You have to understand that if you experience a cardiac arrest, which could occur at any time because of your heavy weight, you might not want us to attempt to resuscitate you because of the terrible results. Any CPR will be difficult, since it will require so much extra pressure on your chest due to your weight. And since the CPR will be hard to do, this will cause a lack of sufficient oxygen to your brain. The experience will be like drowning and staying under water for too long."

Jack seemed to finally understand what he faced because of his weight—that he would be more likely to suffer such a heart stoppage in the first place. Also, he seemed to recognize that if he suffered a cardiac arrest, it would not be the same thing as a cardiac arrest in somebody younger and healthier, where CPR might be able to quickly get the person's heart pumping again. So there were no more jokes this time. Instead Jack remained silent and thoughtful, and I went on with my explanation.

"You also have to understand that a cardiac arrest is a terminal event for about 95 percent of the people who have that experience, and it will be close to 100 percent for someone with other complicating factors, such as diabetes and kidney problems, in addition to being obese. Moreover, most patients who escape death from a heart stoppage requiring CPR are likely to end up being subject to horrible intensive care, including being hooked up to a mechanical ventilator and nutritional support through tubes for the rest of their life. And most will probably have only limited or no mental functioning, so they are in a vegetative state."

Jack looked truly shocked to finally face what could happen. His face blanched so he looked white as a ghost, and for the first time, he was almost speechless.

"I don't know what to say," he said.

Yet, Jack still wasn't quite ready to make any final arrangements for his death, as if just realizing what could happen was too much to cope with for now.

However, as it turned out, Jack never needed to discuss his dying arrangements or end-of-life status, because a few days later, he went to bed and never woke up. A neighbor discovered this when he heard Jack's phone ringing repeatedly during the day and knew Jack was home, since Jack almost never went anywhere. After the neighbor contacted the apartment manager who let him into the apartment, he found Jack dead in his bed.

I found out what happened after I got a 3 a.m. phone call from the coroner, who had several questions for me, since I was listed in Jack's phone book as his physician.

"Did you know about Jack's health status before he died?" the coroner asked me. "Did you think there was any reason to believe his death was unnatural?"

At once I told the coroner "My answer is absolutely no. Jack was obese and had many medical problems, so he was likely to die of any one of these problems at any time."

As I once told Jack, as we grow older, we accumulate points against us, which reflect our different health, medical, and personal factors. Among them are aging, being a male, being obese, having diabetes, experiencing high blood pressure, and smoking. Unfortunately, Jack had almost all of these factors, causing him to score more points. So there was no surprise that he would die young, in his early forties, soon after I first saw him in the hospital. Though Jack joked about it and tried to deny that the odds were stacked against him, ultimately, he did nothing to change those odds by trying to lose weight or live a healthier lifestyle. So his early demise was a foregone conclusion.

I truly felt really sorry for him, because he was a really nice guy who tried to maintain a positive attitude and treat the difficulties he faced in life with humor. But unfortunately his jokes and humor were of little use, because he had all the odds against him. There was no way he could last much longer.

Accordingly, as I tell my patients, to improve your odds, you can't deny and joke about the reality you face. You have to do something proactive to change those odds, such as by living a healthier lifestyle and dealing with the causes that may be undermining your health and contributing to an earlier death.

6

COMPLICATIONS

Unfortunately, a history of heavy smoking can bring about an untimely end, as was the case for Mrs. Jan Collins, a white female in her early sixties. Today, a great majority of women in their sixties live active, socially engaged lives, much like women in their forties a few decades before. But Mrs. Collins came to the hospital with numerous complications due to several decades of smoking. Her treatment was further complicated because she had relatives who hoped to extend her life as long as possible, whereas Mrs. Collins wanted to end her suffering with a DNR order at the end, once she realized she would be dying early due to her smoking. I knew her wishes and obtained the DNR for her because I knew her from a prior admission.

Initially, Mrs. Collins was under the care of another physician in town, who sent other patients to the hospital. But even though I had a working relationship with him, he wasn't able to give me her medical records due to the regulations of HIPAA—the agency created under the federal Health Insurance Portability and Accountability Act of 1996—which protect the confidentiality and security of healthcare information, along with other healthcare insurance and administration regulations. Mrs. Collins couldn't consent to the release of the records herself, since the records would come from various sources and it would therefore be overly time-consuming to gather them.

When she arrived at the hospital, she already had a machine to help her breathe because she was suffering from chronic respiratory failure.

Without the machine, she wouldn't get enough oxygen and would gradually become increasingly tired and finally pass out from fatigue.

She was still in the emergency department by the reception desk being processed by the receptionist when I came down to greet her. Several of her close relatives were with her—a sister and two daughters.

"I'm Dr. Sepulveda," I explained, "and I'll be your doctor here."

"Then you are just the person to talk to," said her sister Frances, speaking on behalf of Mrs. Collins, though I generally prefer to speak with the patient directly if he or she is able to speak. "We'd like to get her off the machine she is hooked up to in order to help her breathe as soon as possible."

"Of course," I said. "We can do what we can to wean her off the machine entirely once she gets settled in her private room in the ICU, which has private rooms for all patients. She'll be cared for by the pulmonary-critical care team there, because of the damage to her lungs."

"So what do you suggest when it comes time for us to decide on the best treatment for her?" Frances asked.

I could sense there might be a looming conflict, since Frances seemed to want to take over Mrs. Collins' treatment, although relatives have no legal right to make any decisions for the patient. Another problem was that one of the daughters indicated that she was firmly opposed to the DNR order, since she considered it an order to kill the patient. But whatever her opinion, I can only talk to any family members or relatives about the patient's decision if the patient authorizes me to do so.

"Mrs. Collins has to make all of these decisions," I explained. "I can convey your views to her, but then it's her decision."

Frances frowned, showing her displeasure at not being able to take the lead, but remained silent.

Several minutes later, Mrs. Collins was in her private room in the ICU, and as is usual procedure, the ICU nurses and doctors took over her care while I came by from time to time to see how she was doing and make recommendations.

Initially, she lay in bed, a once-vibrant woman who loved to hike, now barely able to move. A long tube connected to a face mask, which was in turn connected to a large BiPAP machine that dispenses oxygenated air under pressure while the patient releases carbon dioxide into the air.

Then, as another nurse stood nearby, a respiratory therapist removed the face mask and asked Mrs. Collins to try breathing on her own. The nurses played a supportive role in this situation, since the respiratory therapists handle all the respiratory equipment because of their speciality training, based on the treatments prescribed by the doctors handling these cases.

Mrs. Collins tried breathing on her own for a few minutes, but soon her breath became more and more labored, and she gasped for air. The respiratory therapist quickly put the face mask back on. Mrs. Collins lay back in bed, tired from trying to breathe without the respirator or BiPAP machine.

"We'll come back and try later after you are rested," the nurse told her.

A few hours later, the nurses tried again, but as before, within minutes, Mrs. Collins was gasping for breath, and the respiratory therapist put on her face mask and rehooked her to the machine.

Finally, after three failed attempts, the nurses and respiratory therapists reported what happened to the ICU team leader, a doctor specializing in lung diseases and intensive care medicine. He then reviewed her case. A big question was why Mrs. Collins got tired when she tried to breathe on her own. Normally, once she was back on the respirator after a few minutes off it, she shouldn't feel any major fatigue; rather she should feel more relaxed since the respirator supported her breathing. Thus, the doctor leading the medical team thought that Mrs. Collins might have another factor causing her condition beside the chronic pulmonary disease. Fortunately, Mrs. Collins continued to improve, so she was able to leave the ICU for a private room on the main floor, and soon after that, since I now was in charge of her care again, the medical team asked me for another opinion. Why did I think Mrs. Collins was getting so tired after briefly breathing on her own and did I agree with their opinion? Was it due to having an additional condition besides her chronic pulmonary disease, such as congestive heart failure or even chronic poisoning or a debilitating neurologic disease?

As I flipped through the report the team sent me, which included printouts from the respirator that showed her rate of breathing, oxygen flow, blood pressure, pulse, and weight, I noticed her chest X-rays and cardiac reports did not show any functional abnormalities of the heart or any chest congestion in her heart that was causing her fatigue.

So her case seemed to truly be a medical mystery, since it was such a difficult case to diagnose. As I sat by her bed, assessing what was wrong,

Mrs. Collins sat propped up against her pillow, still hooked up to the BiPAP machine, while we talked and I took notes on a small yellow pad. I noticed she seemed extremely weak, since she had trouble lifting and moving her head as well as her legs and arms.

"I do feel very weak," Mrs. Collins agreed. "I used to be so energetic. I used to go hiking in the mountains and regularly walked or bicycled around my neighborhood. Over the past couple of years, I kept getting a shortness of breath, and I started to feel very tired, so eventually, a doctor prescribed that I go on a breathing machine like this. Then, a few days ago, I was sent to this hospital."

"Okay. Let me first order a weakness workup, so we can see what's going on. We want to look more carefully at when you feel weak and what were you doing before then. We also want to see what other symptoms you have when you feel weak, apart from your difficulty in breathing."

I then did a complete screening and diagnostic tests on almost every single body organ. I even included a test for chronic poisoning, such as from arsenic.

A few days later, the report came back, and I consulted about the results with the hospital's neurology team, which included a neurologist, who is a medical doctor trained in diagnosing, treating, and managing nervous system disorders, including diseases of the brain, spinal cord, nerves, and muscles.

When the doctor advised me that the weakness might be because her chronic pulmonary disease caused a lack of oxygen to the muscles, I realized this could be the major cause of her condition. That's because when the muscles are weakened, people lose their ability to breathe comfortably, so if they experience any stress or engage in any kind of activity, they need help in continuing to breathe. While this disease strikes many individuals, especially seniors who have less resistance to any kind of disease, I felt her heavy smoking was a major contributing factor, resulting in her COPD. The irritants from smoking could readily scar her lungs, so she had less lung capacity and therefore would be more prone to having difficulty breathing due to any disease, stress, or an increased level of activity, such as walking even a short distance.

Since Mrs. Collins wasn't allowed to smoke in the hospital, she gradually got better and her strength increasingly returned, until at last she could breathe on her own and started walking again.

She demonstrated her success one morning when I came to review her progress. I saw that her face mask was no longer in her nose, although patients with her condition normally require masks delivering oxygen to their lungs at all times. As soon as she saw me, she sat up spryly in her bed.

"You see, doctor," she said. "When the nurses removed the tubes this morning, I found I could breathe on my own. And now look."

She got out of bed and walked a few steps. "I can walk again."

Yet, since Mrs. Collins still couldn't walk very far without becoming weak, I recommended that she join a rehab program.

"You'll build up your strength again by regularly exercising," I said. "Each day you should be able to walk a little more and your breathing should become stronger."

After Mrs. Collins agreed to my recommended regimen, I recommended some additional tests, because I knew about her history of smoking and the propensity of smokers to get other diseases after a decade or more of smoking due to the buildup of chemicals in their lungs.

To illustrate how this buildup could occur, I pulled out a sheet of paper from my notepad and drew a picture of the heart in the chest cavity. Near it I draw the lungs like two sacks of wine, which came together to form a long tube up into the throat and nasal cavity. Then, I drew an arrow to show the normal flow of air.

"This is the way we breathe normally."

I paused and drew some dots to represent the blockages that might be caused by obstructions due to inflation and infection.

"You can see that any blockages not only can make it more difficult for you to breathe, but they can put pressure on your heart. This condition is much like an infection in the lungs due to pneumonia, which is a serious disease caused by bacteria. The disease is characterized by fever, a cough where you might cough up phlegm tinged with blood, and difficulty breathing. You can get the same kind of inflammation of the lungs with congestion due to chronic smoking, which sometimes results in the heart failing to maintain a good circulation."

"You think that's what's wrong with me?" Mrs. Collins asked.

"Possibly. That's why we need to do more tests to look at the underlying causes of your breathing problems."

I noticed a crumpled up cigarette package on her table, as if Mrs. Collins had gotten hold of a package of cigarettes even though smoking was forbidden in the hospital and would be especially problematic for a person with breathing problems.

"A big concern is your heavy smoking," I told her. "Since you've been doing this for decades, the tars from the cigarettes can build up and create a residue in your lungs. Then, this inflammation can result in debris that obstructs your breathing, as well as puts more pressure on your heart, which can contribute to the possible congestive heart failure you experienced when the nurses initially tried to take you off the machine."

"I know smoking has been bad for me," Mrs. Collins acknowledged. "But it's been very difficult for me to quit. Cutting me off from cigarettes is like going cold turkey. That package was for the last few cigarettes I had in my purse when I first came into the hospital. When I started feeling better, I smoked them."

"Not good," I admonished her. Then, I had one more test to explain.

"The last test we want to do is to check your arsenic levels."

Mrs. Collins was surprised, as many people are, since they think of arsenic poisoning from a rat poison, which is used in murder mysteries to kill the victim. But people can be exposed to arsenic through their food and water, and in most areas, food is the main source.

So I gave Mrs. Collins a quick explanation of why the tests were needed, pointing out that: "Arsenic isn't just in a concentrated form as a poison, but it could be in some of the foods you eat, and sometimes in the water, contributing to your cardiac problems. That's why we want to test for that."

But when I got the results a few days later, they were negative, leading me to conclude that the problems with her lungs were as I first suspected—due to the COPD, rooted in her long-term smoking. So the congestion in her lungs and the pressure on her heart was likely to get worse.

Although Mrs. Collins still had some good days where she could breathe on her own and walk around her hospital room and to the day room to sit and talk with other patients, usually even the short walk left her very tired and she was eager to get back to her room. Thus, she was at a baseline, in which she had been weaned off the respirator but was still in a weak and precarious state, which would only get worse. Over the next few weeks, she had fewer good days and more bad ones, and often she had to be hooked up to the breathing machine respirator—the Bi-PAP—as her ability to breathe on her own deteriorated.

It was difficult to present this grim prognosis to her, so I wanted to first learn more about her personally to ensure that she would feel more support from me when I told her what to expect.

"What was your life like before you came into the hospital?" I asked her. "Then, I can discuss the test results, and we can decide where we go from here."

"Very good," Mrs. Collins said and began her story. "I used to live a fairly active life until a couple of years ago. I especially liked to go on hikes and long walks. But then my life became more limited to where I could only walk a few blocks or drive by car. After that, I began to become less connected to the people I knew, because I no longer had much energy to go to group meetings or activities.

"In the last few months, things became worse. I found I was barely able to move at home, even around the kitchen to cook, since I began to experience shortness of breath. I'd have to sit or lie down to relax, so I could breathe better again. Sometimes I even felt like I was choking for a minute or two, although after I stopped whatever I was doing to sit or lie down, the choking feeling would go away. So I couldn't do very much each day.

"Then, the breathing problem became so bad that I had to get a ventilator and get connected to it, or I probably would have died from asphyxiation."

"How long has this been going on before you came to the hospital?" I asked.

"About a month. And I'm sick of it."

She looked at me plaintively. "Will I get better, doctor? What do the tests show?"

The last thing I wanted to do was tell her about her prognosis, since she had been surviving on the hope she would get better for so long. But now she was clearly dissatisfied with what she was experiencing in her life, and she was unlikely to want to continue in this state as her breathing became worse and she had to be permanently affixed to a tube, because there would be no more good days.

Finally, I answered somberly, steeling myself to present her with the worst possible news.

"I'm so sorry," I said, "but the tests show permanent damage and scarring in your heart and lungs, along with continued inflammation and infection. So the best we can do is give you pills to relieve the pain and suffering. But you will continue to grow weaker, and soon you will have to be on the respirator again."

"I've been preparing for the worst," Mrs. Collins said. "And I don 't want to continue to live like this. It's not the way I used to live my life; it's not how I want to continue to live in the world."

I took her hand and squeezed it to show my continuing support, as I began to talk about her resuscitation status, which is always a difficult topic to discuss with patients at the end of their life.

I pulled out a resuscitation document from my briefcase and showed it to Mrs. Collins.

"This document indicates your resuscitation status," I said. "When your children and sister first brought you to the hospital, they indicated that you should be listed as full-code status, which means you want to be revived and kept alive as long as medically possible."

"But I don't want that," Mrs. Collins said firmly, though still very weak. "I don't want to live like that."

"Then, you should be a Do Not Resuscitate/Do Not Incubate type of patient," I explained. "That way if you have an end of life incident, such as not being able to breathe or experience heart failure, the medical team will not try to revive you. It's called being a DNR/DNI patient."

"That's what I want," said Mrs. Collins. "I think it is much better to be in that situation, and I should have been listed that way in the first place. Why wasn't I?"

"Because of the way your daughters and sister wanted you to be listed when they brought you in, and that is the default status. But only patients can opt to be in this DNR/DNI status. Otherwise our mandate as doctors is to prolong life as long as possible."

"Even if it's not a good life?" Mrs. Collins asked.

"Yes, even then. So I need your agreement to change this."

However, while the change could easily be made if Mrs. Collins agreed, she started to reflect on what the close members of her family—her daughters and sister—wanted, although she knew that others in the family would support her decision.

"I'd like to talk to the members of my family, so they will feel comfortable with my decision."

"Of course," I said, although I was concerned that if she waited too long and her breathing and heart problems progressed, she could easily end up in a coma or otherwise be too ill to make a decision or sign any document. In that case, the closest members of her family—her children, who disagreed with her decision and wanted to prolong life as long as possible, would decide.

Thus, to try to work things out amicably with the family, I called on the hospital's palliative care nurse, Julie, to meet with the family members and discuss this situation. She could also use this meeting to discover more about their feelings and concerns.

When Julie arrived at my office and sat down across from me, I described the situation, telling her about Mrs. Collins' shortness of breath, congestion in the lungs, pressure on the heart, potential for cardiac arrest, general weakness and fatigue, and long-time smoking history. I also explained about the family dynamics: "There is some dissension in the family over the resuscitation status. The patient wants a do-not resuscitate order, but some family members do not. So the patient is not sure what to do."

I took Julie in to Mrs. Collins' room, where Mrs. Collins was resting quietly.

"I would like you to meet Julie, a nurse I work with," I explained. "She is here to help make things more comfortable for you."

At once, Mrs. Collins became more energetic and cheerful, as if she was focusing her strength on appearing the best she could be to a new person, almost like she was putting on a performance to seem well, when she was not. But for the few minutes that Julie chatted with her, Mrs. Collins was able to sustain her greater vibrancy. She even told Julie, "I'm feeling so much better now." Still, I felt certain that her statements about her better health were just for show, though I didn't want to say anything to dim her spirits or undercut the way she presented herself to Julie.

Thus, a few minutes later, when Julie came back to my office to discuss the case, her comments reflected her observation that Mrs. Collins seemed better.

"I'm concerned about getting involved at this stage," Julie said, "since this patient is relatively young at sixty-two and looks relatively well. So I'm surprised to see her being a candidate for the palliative care program."

"But that's not how she really is," I explained. "I feel that Mrs. Collins pulled on her last reserves of strength to appear relatively well for a visitor. But I'm sure she will soon sink back into her baseline state, in which her condition is deteriorating rapidly and she is becoming weaker and weaker, while she has problems with breathing and her heart could stop at any time. So I think the palliative care program would work well to help her face what is happening, as well as resolve the conflict with the family over her end of life DNR status."

A key reason I felt so strongly that Mrs. Collins should go into palliative care now is that palliative care helps to improve the dying patient's quality of life by providing relief from the symptoms and stress of a serious illness, as well as improving the quality of life for family members. Such care is provided by a specially trained team of doctors, nurses, and other specialists who work with a patient's doctor to provide this extra support. While it is appropriate at any age and stage in a serious illness, along with a treatment to cure the problem, palliative care is especially appropriate at the end of life to make both patients and family members more comfortable with what is happening.

This care focuses on assistance with a variety of symptoms, including many which Mrs. Collins was experiencing, such as pain, shortness of breath, fatigue, loss of appetite, difficulty in sleeping, and depression. It also helps the patient gain the strength to carry on from day to day, tolerate medical treatments, and better understand the choices for treatment. It is like having a partner who can spend as much time as needed with the patient and his or her family, and the palliative team members are skilled in helping both patients and their families understand their treatment options and goals.

Thus, I concluded my discussion with Julie by suggesting, "You can further discuss this care option with Mrs. Collins and her family. And I suggest your call her primary care doctor, who treated her before she was referred to the hospital."

Julie said she would, and later I met again with Mrs. Collins to tell her what Julie was going to do.

"That's good," Mrs. Collins said. "I'll feel much better if I know everyone understands and agrees with what I want to do. I think my family members are much more hopeful about my prognosis than is actually the case."

"That's true," I said. "It may be that they still remember you from a year or so ago, when you were still active and healthy, and they don't understand the way everything has changed."

Mrs. Collins looked thoughtful, as if she was processing her understanding and acceptance of the situation and was at peace with it. Then, she added: "I realize that there's no way to go back to the way things were. I just wish now I hadn't smoked so much."

I nodded, and she told me: "Thank you for everything."

A day later, I heard back from Julie, who told me she had done what I normally do in helping the patient and family decide what to do about the end-of-life care. As Julie told me:

"I spoke to Mrs. Collins first to be sure what she really wanted and then spoke to the family. I realized that her children had some difficulty with the DNR/DNI decision, because they thought that Mrs. Collins would recover. They felt like she was only sixty-two and had been in good health up until about a year or two ago. So they felt resuscitating her would give her more opportunity to heal and return to her normal way of life.

"Also, one daughter had some religious concerns. She felt like a do-not-resuscitate order would be like assisted suicide, but I explained that it wasn't, since it didn't involve taking any proactive means to end a person's life. Instead, a DNR/DNI order simply meant not reviving a person with special resuscitation techniques after they have naturally stopped breathing, which has ended their life. Also, I explained that Mrs. Collins had explicitly requested that no extraordinary means should be taken to revive her at the end, because she didn't want to live hooked up to tubes keeping her alive. She felt she had lived an active, satisfying life and was ready to go when it was natural for her to do so, rather than being kept alive by artificial means after her natural passing."

I was pleased to hear from Julie that everything had been resolved as the patient wanted and in a way that made her family feel comfortable with a DNR/DNI order, so Mrs. Collins felt more comfortable with the way her life was ending and her family was fully in agreement with her decision. Also, I felt that Julie's palliative care intervention had helped in getting both Mrs. Collins and her family to come together around this very important decision, resulting in us ending up with a very clear and firm DNR/DNI status.

The case also illustrates the problem that occurs when family members prefer to go with their own beliefs and convictions, though they are different from what the patients want for themselves. Ultimately, the role of the physician is to respect what the primary patient wishes, not what the relatives want, though the optimal solution is to work with the family—or bring in a palliative care team to assist—in order to help the family understand that what the patient wants is in the best interest of everyone, as occurred in this case.

Unfortunately, in some cases where there is a difference of opinion between the patient and the family, the family fires the doctor, who is often considered part of the problem rather than being part of the unwanted solution. When this happens, the patient then has a new doctor who may not know anything about the background situation, such as how the patient used to live and what the patient really wants for end-of-life care. In some cases, the patient has had a long-time close relationship with a primary care physician, and it can be heart-wrenching for the patient to suddenly have to deal with a new doctor who understands nothing about the patient. It's also disheartening for a primarily care doctor to find a patient removed from his or her care due to the relatives' unwanted influence and desire for further control when the patient can no longer make these decisions. Fortunately, this didn't happen in Mrs. Collins' case, since by bringing in the palliative care nurse, the situation was resolved to everyone's satisfaction—a real win-win solution in an end-of-life case.

Additionally, I was glad that the palliative care team's involvement helped resolve what is sometimes a cause for confusion and concern: the difference between a DNR/DNI directive and a "do not treat" request. Often patients and family members think these terms mean the same thing, which contributes to their reticence to agree to a DNR/DNI choice. The patients and family members often do not realize that they will be treated without any exceptions or reservations once they are admitted, whether they have a DNR/DNI directive or not, and they will be treated with all the appropriate medications and necessary procedures. In other words, no patient will be short-changed or considered a lesser patient just because he or she has a DNR/DNI status.

While many patients and their relatives may hesitate to choose the DNR/DNI option because they feel the medical team will treat them differently and provide less treatment if they choose this alternative, this is not normally the case. The one time this might happen is when the person's primary care physician is unable to care for that patient in the last days or weeks of life. In that case, a new physician might interpret a DNR/DNI status to mean that he or she should provide a less-aggressive treatment approach, or he or she might treat a DNR/DNI patient less promptly or less completely than a non-DNR/DNI or full-code patient.

But otherwise, both DNR and non-DNR patients normally receive the same quality of care, and I was glad that Julie was able to explain that to Mrs. Collins' relatives so they could feel more confident that there would be no problem in providing her with equal treatment and care.

Finally, as Julie explained to the relatives, not all patients with a DNR status are necessarily at the end of their life. While some patients may be clearly terminal and are actively dying, others who are still healthy have opted to plan ahead, so they will have a DNR/DNI status should they die. Making this option is a little like making a living will well in advance of dying, which can sometimes be many years away. Even so, it helps to have such an option in place in advance of a sudden unexpected death, such as when someone suddenly dies as a result of an accident or event of nature like an earthquake or avalanche. While part of Mrs. Collins' clash with other family members occurred because she had no advance planning in place, such as in a last will and testament, at least the issue was soon resolved after Julie spoke with the relatives and allayed their major concerns. So ultimately Mrs. Collins agreed to the DNR status, because her family members now felt comfortable with that status, too.

7

KEEPING IT SIMPLE

Some end-of-life cases can be much simpler to handle when the patients and relatives are in agreement and there are no other complicating factors, such as a long progressive illness. That's what happened in the cases of Mrs. Kimball and Mrs. O'Donnell.

THE STORY OF MRS. KIMBALL

Mrs. Kimball, in her late seventies, was one of many patients who suffer from chronic obstructive pulmonary disease, also called COPD. Patients with this disease, which is progressive and terminal, have commonly succumbed due to smoking, for much the same reason that many patients who smoke heavily succumb to emphysema and have to remain connected by tubes to portable respirators for much or all of time in order to breathe.

People suffering from COPD frequently experience a persistent cough that produces a large amount of mucus that clogs the throat, and they also experience wheezing, shortness of breath, chest tightness, and other symptoms. Not only is cigarette smoking the leading cause of the disease, but most people who have it currently smoke or used to smoke, as did Mrs. Kimball. Another contributing factor can be a long-term exposure to other lung irritants, such as air pollution, chemical fumes, or dust, which Mrs. Kimball experienced, too, because she lived near several industrial plants, including an oil refinery that puffed smoke all day and night.

Unfortunately, the disease interferes with the air flow that goes through the windpipe into the bronchial tubes or airways in the lungs, which branch into thousands of smaller airways that end in tiny round air sacs called alveoli that are filled with small blood vessels called capillaries. Oxygen passes through the air sac walls into the capillaries, while the waste gas, carbon dioxide, moves from the capillaries out through the air sacs. In effect, the process is akin to filling up the air sacs like a small balloon when you breathe in. Then the air sacs deflate and the air goes out when you breathe out.

But when a patient like Mrs. Kimball has COPD, less air flows in and out of the airways because of a series of problems: the airways and air sacs lose their elasticity, the walls between many air sacs break down, the airway walls become thick and inflamed, or the airways make more mucus than usual, clogging them up, like debris in a sink drain.

Since this is a progressive disease, a patient can live for some time with it, while experiencing more frequent coughing and gasping for breath. So gradually the person has to live a more constricted lifestyle as the disease progresses, because it can be harder and harder to engage in any activity or experience any stress without the symptoms of the disease—coughing and a difficulty in breathing—appearing. Over time, these symptoms become increasingly severe, until the patient becomes more immobile and bedridden.

It was at this point that I met with Mrs. Kimball, shortly after she was admitted to the hospital with significant and progressive respiratory distress, which would either get better or would lead her to stop breathing due to muscular fatigue. Eventually these patients just stop breathing out of fatigue, with death ensuing shortly after since toxic gasses, including carbon dioxide accumulate and lead to a coma, which further reduces the process of breathing.

After briefly introducing myself as the doctor who would oversee her care, I asked Mrs. Kimball: "How are you feeling? What are you experiencing?"

"A lot of pain," she reported, speaking in broken sentences as she needed to rest in between words. "It's hard to breathe and my throat and chest hurt from so much coughing."

"How is the disease affecting your lifestyle?" I next asked.

Her explanation was typical for others suffering from the disease. "I seem to have so little energy, so it's hard to even perform the most basic everyday activities."

"Like what?" I asked.

"Just walking around the house, taking my medicine, preparing my meals, even going to the mailbox to pick up the mail. And it's hard to go to the bathroom or do anything else with a long hose attached to my nose, so I can breathe extra oxygen from the heavy tank I have to carry around."

Her symptoms and behaviors sounded much like what Mrs. Collins experienced in her last year, since they both suffered from a pulmonary disease, with smoking a major contributing factor. But now Mrs. Kimball was making all the choices, since she had no relatives with different views to deal with.

After getting Mrs. Kimball's description of her condition, I looked briefly at the medical records that accompanied her. They described her increasingly severe symptoms, so I realized her condition was now terminal, and it would be only a few more days before she died. She had also requested not to be intubated in the event matters got out of control and she wasn't able to continue to breathe on her own. So now there was no way to halt or reverse the progression of the disease. It was like an enemy army increasingly ravaging her lungs by making her airways and air sacs more inelastic, further inflaming the walls of her airways and further clogging her lungs with increasing mucus.

I gave her a quick rundown of what was happening, explaining the ravages of the disease in laymen terms. "Essentially, you have a pulmonary disease called COPD or 'chronic obstructive pulmonary disease,' which is commonly caused by smoking. Unfortunately, there is no cure, so it will get progressively worse."

Mrs. Kimball nodded, as if she already knew what the prognosis was likely to be.

"Yes, I understand," she said.

"So the best we can do for you now is to help you to be more comfortable and pain free."

I motioned for a nurse to come in, and she set up a large bag connected to a tube with a needle at the end, which she injected into Mrs. Kimball's upper arm, as I explained what was happening:

"We're setting you up with a morphine drip to make you feel more comfortable. You should feel less pain in a few minutes, once the morphine kicks in. This will reduce or eliminate any pain for the next few hours, after which the nurse will change the bottle and add some more morphine."

Fortunately, this case was simple to deal with, since Mrs. Kimball not only had no interfering relatives to placate, but she was a much older patient, so she readily understood and accepted that she had come to the end of her life. Many of her friends when younger were already gone, so her current contacts, mainly from a local senior center, were more like associates—people she saw at center activities, but with whom she had not developed any deep friendships. So emotionally and mentally, it was easier for her to let go, feeling she had lived her life, which had been a full one when younger, and now she was ready to pass on. While her smoking had brought the end of her life perhaps five to ten years sooner than if she hadn't smoked, she still had lived a fairly long life. So she felt ready to accept that life was ending, and I wanted to make it as comfortable and painless for her as possible.

That comfortable, painless end should be the goal when the end of life comes due to a natural disease, such as Mrs. Kimball experienced. It shouldn't be complicated by new technologies that permit resuscitation to extend life, especially when this extension results in increased monetary expenses while the person is hooked up to machines but is barely alive. The quality of life at this point is so low that many patients are only too eager to have their life end. So ideally, as I tell my patients, it is best to meet the end through a much simpler, humane process. Rather than enduring an extended period of pain and suffering before dying, a patient should be treated in his or her last days in the most gentle, loving way possible.

Thus, in that spirit, I told the nurse, "Please continue to check on Mrs. Kimball and change her morphine drip every few hours, so she can die peaceably and painlessly, which is now inevitable." Then I further explained: "Mrs. Kimball doesn't want to be resuscitated, and the progression of her disease has left her no opportunity for going back."

THE STORY OF MRS. O'DONNELL

Sometimes the issue is not who will make a decision, but making the DNR/DNI decision, which was the case for Mrs. O'Donnell. Like Mrs. Kimball, she suffered from a pulmonary disease, where smoking was one triggering and exacerbating factor. But in her case, the problem was complicated by her heart condition, seventy years of age, and extreme obesity of over three hundred pounds due to a long history of eating foods high in starches, fats, and sugars.

When Mrs. O'Donnell first arrived, she was accompanied by her daughter in her fifties, who already weighed around two hundred pounds herself, but was not yet morbidly obese like her mother. As I met with them, Mrs. O'Donnell and her daughter described Mrs. O'Donnell's background. Of Portuguese descent, she had grown up in a family of immigrants; her parents came from Portugal with her older brother and sister, though she was born in the United States. Once school started, she began a lifetime pattern of overeating because as a daughter of Portuguese immigrants, she felt very much the outsider. She found it hard to make friends and became a loner who found solace in eating, especially since her mother was an excellent cook of high-calorie Portuguese food, with such specialties as sweet pastries, potato soup, sausage, rice pudding, caramel custard, and grilled, poached, and fried fish.

So Mrs. O'Donnell grew up loving her mother's cooking. As a teen she was already overweight, and over the years, her weight increased so by her late thirties, soon after she gave birth to her daughter, she had difficulty moving around. In turn, her lack of mobility contributed to her heavy smoking, since it was one of the few pleasures she could enjoy while sitting at home. Eventually, her smoking helped to trigger her pulmonary disease. By the time I saw her, the disease was much advanced and made worse by her obesity.

When I came into Mrs. O'Donnell's room, she was propped up in bed against a pillow, since her weight made it difficult to sit up straight. Her daughter, Imelda, was seated at her bedside, holding her hand for support. After I made my examination, doing the usual routine checks for blood pressure, heartbeat strength, breathing, and other vital signs, I could tell that all of her conditions, especially her weight and advanced pulmonary disease, meant that her situation was terminal.

Mrs. O'Donnell took the news stoically, as did her daughter. "I understand that it doesn't look good, but does this mean I'm going to die?" she asked.

"Isn't there anything you can do now?" said her daughter.

"I don't think so," I explained, turning back to Mrs. O'Donnell. "There are so many problems contributing to your condition." I listed them and continued. "So one of the things we need to do now is address the code for your resuscitation status, according to hospital regulations."

I explained what these regulations meant to help her decide, since the hospital policy is for doctors to encourage patients to make a decision quickly, preferably once the patient is alert enough, competent enough, and willing to decide. However, this is not an easy decision for many patients, since when first admitted and diagnosed, many feel a great deal of stress. They usually come from home, where they have felt safe and secure, to an alien, high-tech setting with sterile walls and strange people rushing by in white coats. So some patients truly feel like aliens in a new world. Then a doctor tells them they are dying, which means leaving all they have known and loved behind forever.

I waited quietly for Mrs. O'Donnell's response, since she stared blankly ahead, as if thinking about what to do, while her daughter held her hand tightly.

"We'd like to know now," I said. "The hospital needs to know what to do if your heart stops for any reason, so we can respect your wishes. If you experience a heart stoppage, we can subject you to numerous painful procedures to keep you alive, which can cause you a great deal of suffering, because as doctors we are pledged to prolong life as long as possible. But if you are only going to get worse, you may decide you don't want to continue to suffer. So if you don't want us to do them, none of these procedures will be done. Thus, this is the time to let us know what you want us to do, so we can proceed according to your wishes."

"I'm still not sure," Mrs. O'Donnell finally said.

"Can't we wait until we know more about her condition?" her daughter asked.

Since neither was ready to decide anything, I dropped the subject, thinking I could tell Mrs. O'Donnell more definitively about her poor prognosis once I got the report about the condition of her heart from the cardiologists.

Unfortunately, the following day when I met with the cardiologists at the lab where they strap a patient into a heart monitor to determine the strength and regularity of the heartbeat, one told me: "We cannot do a complete work up on Mrs. O'Donnell because of her obesity. She won't fit in the straps and the measurement equipment won't reach."

When I met with her to describe the cardiologists' determination and my prognosis, she just joked about it.

"Oh, I've always been heavy, but look how long I lived anyway. So now, maybe I can continue to live much longer than anyone thinks I will."

I tried to press Mrs. O'Donnell for a decision, explaining that "the situation is different this time. All of these conditions together are now terminal."

But she still didn't want to make a choice.

"Give her time," her daughter said. "My mother likes to think on things for a while."

"Certainly, we can wait for a while for you to make your decision," I said, feeling it was hopeless to push for her decision now, though I knew the negative consequences of her failing to decide. If she did not opt for a DNR/DNI status after she could no longer decide for herself, and her daughter didn't make a decision either, the medical staff would make the decision for her—to continue to revive and treat her as long as possible, even if that treatment extended her pain and suffering. Nevertheless, sometimes that's what a patient actually wants, harboring some hope of continuing to return to a normal life, despite the unlikely odds of that happening. So I knew Mrs. O'Donnell should still make a decision quickly, since once a crisis event, such as a stroke, occurred, a patient might not be in a condition to make this decision, though possibly her daughter could act on her behalf as the closest kin to opt to relieve her suffering by making that DNR/DNI choice for her.

Thus, for now, since Mrs. O'Donnell preferred to postpone making a decision, I moved on to discussing what medications she might take to ease any pain while she remained at the hospital.

Yet, while Mrs. O'Donnell had put off making a decision, at least no relatives would interfere with her choice, since her daughter was fully onboard with whatever her mother finally decided, which is the ideal situation. Sometimes patients succumb to what their family members want, since they want to keep peace in the family or don't want to oppose a domineering relative, such as a controlling parent or manipulative child. However, by law, regardless of what family members or relatives think, the only opinion that counts and must be respected by the medical team is the patient's unless that patient is no longer competent to decide.

Fortunately, in Mrs. O'Donnell's case, there was no family input complicating her making the decision. She just didn't want to make it, perhaps because such a decision may suggest that the patient is really about to die, and patients don't want to face that reality, as I sensed was the case for Mrs. O'Donnell. Even though I made her and her daughter aware that a DNR/DNI decision wasn't always made when death was likely soon and might be made like a will prepared years in advance of a terminal condition, she still wanted to put the decision off.

A few days later when I examined her and found her condition much the same as when she was admitted, she still laughed the decision off, saying: "I just don't like to decide anything too soon, since I often change my mind. This way, I can make a final decision once and for all."

However, after a few more days, as her pain increased and she realized her situation would only get worse, she finally agreed to the DNR/DNI status. Thus, while it had been a struggle to get her to make a decision, in the end, she made the right one, since it would avoid prolonging her suffering once her heart stopped and she had truly reached the end.

8

DEATH IN THE ICU UNIT

When patients end up in the intensive care unit, also known as the ICU, they are in a critical state. They are being kept alive by medical means and commonly are unconscious or barely conscious. They are hooked up to various devices that help them survive, until their own body mechanisms respond to begin the healing process—or if not, death can come at any moment.

Such devices might include a mechanism to keep the patients' heart pumping, a ventilator to help them breathe, a kidney dialysis machine to get rid of waste products, and other devices to measure blood pressure, heart rate, and other vital signs. They need these mechanisms to keep them alive because their own organs have been damaged through disease or injury, or their mental facilities aren't functioning to direct their body to perform these functions—even such basic functions as breathing. Thus, they need external breathing support or a mechanical ventilator, which is a highly sophisticated and computerized breathing machine that reaches inside the patent's airway and takes over their breathing.

At the same time, a medical team closely monitors the state of these patients to see if they are still living and determine what interventions, if any, might keep them alive. Also, as needed, a nurse with this team might provide morphine or other pain-relieving medication to keep patients from suffering while in this state, since sometimes patients, when not in a coma, will be aware of their machine-controlled bodily functions and the ravages caused by any illness or injury.

Meanwhile, as a patient remains in this intensive care state, his or her close relatives will often wait nearby to learn what is happening, and many pray for a positive outcome.

That's the situation that Albert faced after he suffered a serious motorcycle accident in which a truck cut him off, and he went flying off his bike and landed in a grove of bushes near the highway. He not only sustained multiple fractures of his arms, legs, and torso, but since he wasn't wearing a helmet, he suffered a serious concussion and partially severed nerves leading from his brain to his spine. As a result, not only was Albert barely conscious when he was brought into the emergency room and transferred to the ICU, but his mental facilities weren't functioning well enough to keep him breathing. So the medical team quickly put him on life support to enable him to breathe and checked his condition frequently to see if he could walk again or would be permanently paralyzed. The team also wanted to determine if he could perform other basic bodily functions on his own, such as breathing, digesting food, and excreting.

While these checks were going on, his father, mother, and younger sister waited nervously in the waiting room, wanting to know his prognosis and what they could do to help the medical staff. As is common in these cases, Albert's primary care doctor was not present, since normally these doctors are not involved in their patients' care in the hospital and commonly do not show up. Rather, they stay in their offices, ready to consult on the patient's past history if a doctor requests this, but otherwise, they leave it up to the medical team to take care of their patients.

I learned about the case soon after Albert was placed in the ICU on life support. The team supervising his case included a cardiologist to oversee his heart condition, since he no longer had his normal heart rhythm and could be subject to a heart attack or more serious cardiac arrest; a neurologist, to assess the extent of his brain injury; a pulmonary doctor, to evaluate the condition of his lungs; and a nephrologist to handle any kidney-related issues, since his kidneys had shut down after his accident. Also, there were three nurses to monitor Albert's condition over three shifts and alert any of the medical specialists, as needed, to intervene. My role as the supervising intensive care physician with a specialty in end-of-life care was to coordinate the work of others on the medical team. I also was there to consult with and advise the family members when a patient was unable to handle his own care, which was the case, given Albert's grave condition.

It was clearly a touch-and-go situation, and as the supervising physician, I had to let the family members know what was going on and give them my recommendations about how to care for Albert. As I walked into the waiting room and saw them sitting on a long couch, they looked clearly upset. The father, Jake, sat up ramrod straight, like he wanted to wall off any emotions, while the mother, Sarah, clutched a handkerchief to her eyes to wipe off her tears. Next to her, Andrea, the younger sister, kept looking up at the clock, as if wishing time would pass quickly and help her brother heal.

I went over and introduced myself, telling them, "I'm Doctor Sepulveda, and I'll be your intensive care doctor. So I want to explain what is happening to Albert and what you can expect. There's nothing much more you can do for him, except to be here when he is conscious and able to receive visitors. Then it will help the healing process for you to come to Albert's bedside, although we can't promise anything, given the severity of his injuries. The medical team is doing everything possible to save his life, but there may not be anything they can do to save him. At this point, we just don't know."

I assured them I would keep them informed and advised them, "You can wait at home if you want. We can call you if we see any signs of Albert waking up, or if there are any other developments."

I suggested that they might return home, since it can be exhausting for families to continue waiting at the hospital; many cases can be relatively prolonged and even last for weeks with little change because the patient has come to a plateau. At this stage, the patient can quickly go in either direction, such as healing sufficiently to be upgraded to a fair condition or experiencing a rapid deterioration and dying within minutes. But, in general, once a patient ends up in the ICU, the prognosis is usually bleak, since about a third of the ICU patients do die and the mortality rate is higher than in any other medical care unit.

I didn't want to burden the family with those grim statistics, since it is always good to keep up hope and make the family members feel better. At the same time, it is best not to paint too optimistic a picture so they don't get their hopes up too far to be unrealistic. If so, it will be even more painful for them when the patient doesn't survive.

"We'll stay a little bit longer tonight, just in case," Albert's father said. "But after that, I guess you're right. There's no use waiting around for hours, when there are no new developments and we can do nothing to help."

After I assured the family members that we would be working around the clock to try to save Albert, I returned to the ICU unit to see what was going on.

When I did, I saw one of the nurses holding Albert's limp arm to take his pulse, while the machines hooked up to him hummed away, as the needles on the monitor went up and down charting the different measures. These included his heartbeat, breathing, and state of mental arousal, also called "mentation," which indicates the level of the patient's ability to think. Meanwhile, the medical team doctors checked with other nurses about other ICU patients to determine what to do to help them.

Despite the growing use of medical equipment that measures and monitors different aspects of a patient's functioning, the medical team doctors still examine and monitor the ICU patients themselves. However, nurses have taken a more active role in patient care, so they take charge on a day-to-day basis. Though they still take direction from the doctors, who are like army generals supervising their troops, the nurses are like sergeants on the front lines providing the hands-on care. At times, the nurses serve as the link between the doctors and the patients, so if I had not met with the family members, the supervising nurse in charge of Albert's care would have done so.

Soon after my arrival, the other doctors on the medical team arrived, and the supervising nurse gave us a run-down on Albert's status. Typically, the nurses give such a run-down two or three times a day, sometimes once a shift, for about a half-hour per patient, so the team members can assess what is happening. Then the doctors can draw on their own specialty in suggesting what to do to continue the patient's care. Or the doctors might point out that we can't do much more for the patient medically, so now it is just a matter of time until his or her death.

In Albert's case, each doctor offered his input in turn.

"His mentation now is minimal," the neurologist observed. "He has suffered an extensive concussion from the accident, including skull fragments that have lodged in his brain, and his brain has undergone a great deal of swelling in response to the trauma. It will be another day before the swelling goes down in order for us to determine if the neural connections have resumed functioning. Thus, he needs to be kept in an induced coma for at least another day, while his functions are maintained by other equipment."

Then the cardiologist provided his assessment. "I agree that his heart can't continue to pump on its own, and a heart pump or potent medications will be needed to maintain this. This procedure will keep his blood pressure within acceptable to normal levels, and hopefully, maintaining this level will not be threatened by various common factors, such as an infection, toxic chemicals in his system, or an overdose. At least, the patient did not have a high level of drugs or alcohol in his system, which could have contributed to the crash by affecting his response rate when avoiding the truck that hit him while he was going at a normal rate of speed."

The nephrologist then reviewed the level of functioning of Albert's kidneys. "They seem to be regaining their functioning, though there was some tearing from the initial impact when his ribs broke from the accident and pressed against his kidneys. While his kidneys still can't function on their own, the lab work shows his kidneys becoming stronger. So it may be that they will be able to function again. Or if they don't, the patient will need a kidney replacement therapy or dialysis for at least a temporary basis, since most patients' kidney function returns as they get better."

Finally, I asked the nurse about the patient's nutrition, medications, and elimination. She pointed to the long tube connecting Albert's stomach to a long plastic bottle half-full of a brownish liquid. "He's being fed intravenously," she said, "and he is being given a morphine drip to prevent any pain should he regain consciousness or which his nervous system might feel though he is not conscious."

The nurse also described the medications Albert had been given. She concluded by explaining what had been done to control any bleeding or clot formation. It was especially important to learn about this, because if any bleeding occurred, blood could readily leak out from one organ system into another. If this occurred, the team had to drain out any accumulating pools of blood, or if necessary, thicken the blood to prevent further bleeding. They might also use medications to strengthen the walls of the stomach, the usual site of unwanted bleeding, to prevent the blood vessels from breaking through. The team also had to avoid the other extreme of clot formation—thinning the blood too much, such as by injecting the patient with a blood thinner to keep the clots from forming or to break up any clots that had already formed. In any case, without thinning the blood too much, the team had to act quickly, since an excessive though sometimes normal thickening of the blood can cause clots to form and travel to critical areas, resulting in the heart stopping, leading to the patient's death. Thus, the team had to engage in a kind of balancing act to prevent clots from killing the patient without overdoing it.

After the nurse's explanation, each team member had to dictate or write up a report, which would become part of the patient's record. These reports could then be used to assess how the patient was doing over time, as well as be used by the hospital if anyone had any questions about the nature of the patient's care. A hospital needs to keep such information to show that the patient received the best possible care, given his or her condition. In the ICU, such records can be particularly important, because about a third of the patients die in this unit, so family members or others might have questions about the patient's death. In particular, they might want to know what the ICU medical team did to save the patient or provide comfort in his or her last days, taking into consideration whether the patient or the family had decided on a DNR/DNI status or not.

After checking the monitor to see how Albert was doing, I advised the nurse beginning the night shift: "Monitor his vital signs closely, since his condition could be acute and immediately life-threatening, or his dying process might be prolonged and slow, such as if he experiences a respiratory failure, which can go on for weeks. But since he's a relatively new patient, we don't know yet. So be alert for any emergencies that threaten his breathing system or cardiovascular stability. Also note if there is any development of a sepsis syndrome."

The nurse said she would contact me about any sudden change for the worse in Albert's condition. Then the rest of the medical team and I got ready to leave for the night. Such an arrangement in which the nurses do the ongoing monitoring is typical in the ICU, where the medical team doctors assess the patients' condition and make recommendations for their care. Then the nurses are the frontline workers, who continually monitor the patients' condition and report back.

Often relatively little changes in a patient's condition over time, and certain conditions can go on for weeks, such as a sepsis syndrome, which is a spreading infection that the medical team needs to stop quickly before it becomes even more dangerous. Stopping this infection is especially critical for ICU patients, since their immune and other bodily systems are already compromised. If not checked, a sepsis condition can easily become much worse, so the goal is to notice the condition in its mild stage and treat it quickly.

Essentially, sepsis is a whole-body inflammation caused by an infection, and the common symptoms include fever, increased heart rate, and increased breathing rate, plus there may be symptoms related to a specific infection, such as pneumonia or a kidney infection. In its more advanced stages, sepsis can cause poor organ function or insufficient blood flow, evidenced by low blood pressure and a small amount of urine. A common treatment is giving the patient intravenous fluids, although septic shock can occur when blood pressure drops even lower despite getting the fluids.

Thus, before I left, I advised the the nurse to be on the alert for any problems. As I told her:

"Besides looking for these early signs of a sepsis syndrome on the monitors and by checking the patient's blood pressure, take a blood culture to confirm this. Then, if the syndrome has developed, we can use some antibiotics and increase the intravenous fluids to maintain the blood pressure. Or we can use medications to raise the blood pressure, although Albert is already on dialysis and connected to a mechanical ventilator."

I was especially concerned because once sepsis develops, it can easily progress to a more severe sepsis syndrome and put the patient into septic shock, which would likely be fatal given Albert's already touch-and-go situation.

"Of course, we'll check carefully," the nurse reassured me. "And I'll call you immediately if I see any signs of sepsis, such as an unusually high or low body temperature, unusually fast heart or respiratory rate, or difficulty breathing."

"Good," I told her. "I'll be back in the morning to see how things are going."

As I left, I saw Albert's parents and sister were still in the waiting room, and I urged them to go home to rest, since the ICU environment can be a very scary place.

"A patient in Albert's situation can remain in the same condition for days if not weeks, and if there is any sudden change in his condition, the nurses will notify me immediately." I pointed to my cell phone. "I have my phone with me at all times, so they can call me, and I will let you know, so you can quickly return."

I also explained why the ICU was not a good place for families to be.

"The whole ICU environment is an uncomfortable one for families to wait it out, because you'll hear a large number of alarms and monitors going off, as well as doctors, nurses, and lab technicians rushing by. So you may become upset because you think the emergency relates to your family member when it does not."

Albert's father had one last question. "You were inside with the medical team checking on Albert's condition. What do you think is the prognosis? We're really praying for him."

I tried to be soothing, though I had little new information to tell them.

"We still aren't sure what the outcome will be," I explained. "Albert had a very serious accident, and so much depends on how much his body can take and of the body's natural ability to heal. The medications we are giving him can help, and he is on a ventilator to assist with his breathing, as well as on a dialysis machine to get rid of excess fluids and toxins. Also, we are monitoring his temperature and blood pressure, as well as taking precautions to avoid any infections while his immune system is low. It's good that Albert is young and healthy, since this will improve his chances for survival, as compared to someone who is older and suffering from any conditions that accompany aging. So I would say his prognosis could be good, but at this point we still don't know."

Finally, the family agreed to leave, and I felt relieved that they didn't have to experience the unnecessary suffering of waiting around and experiencing the sudden rush of a medical team called into action, when it wasn't for their own family member.

As I drove home, I reflected on how different dying can be in the ICU compared to dying on the medical floor. In the ICU, the patient is much more heavily medicated and monitored, and a terminal event can happen very abruptly under a number of circumstances, such as when a patient's body shuts down, despite all the efforts made to treat the disease or injury.

Unfortunately, many times, even though the doctors know that a given patient's condition is terminal, as the major bodily functions shut down, including the brain and heart, many family members can be confused by the continuation of these functions and think the patient is still alive and well, so there is hope for their recovery. Sometimes in the case of a brain injury, it can be easy to show the family members the images from a CAT scan that indicate that the patient has suffered devastating damage to the brain. But sometimes there may be no visible damage though the functional damages are beyond repair, such as when a medically dead brain can appear normal on CAT scan images. But in fact, there isn't any hope of life. The doctors know this, but sometimes when there is no DNR/DNI order in place, the family members might insist on heroic efforts to keep the patient alive, thinking it is just a matter of time until he or she regains consciousness.

Family members are sometimes misled by the stories of individuals who have been in a coma for months or years and suddenly wake up. The difference between the two states is that a person in a coma has a general "brain failure" in which his or her consciousness is severely depressed, often due to some accident, serious illness, or organ failure, so there is a chance that the person can later revive after sufficient healing has taken place. By contrast, a person who is brain dead has suffered from an irreversible cessation of all brain functions, including those of the brain stem, so that person can never wake up. Individuals who wake up from a coma are the rare exception that can keep hope of recovery alive, when normally, once the patient's condition has deteriorated over a period of weeks to far beyond what is normal, there is usually no hope, despite spontaneous bodily responses that might be viewed as signs the patient still aware and can eventually recover. Once the brain is dead, there can be no recovery, although the body can continue to respond automatically, such as to touch or pressure. But these responses are much like what happens when one cuts off the head of a dog, cat, or other animal. The animal may continue to jerk, twitch, and show other signs of movement, but it is dead.

This continuation of automatic responses is not something that one can easily explain to family members when they continue to hope for the best. They prefer to deny reality so they can believe and hope, though sometimes providing them with multiple medical opinions can help explain the absolute irreversibility of the patient's terminal condition. Then the family members can better understand that the best choice is to stop further treatment and remove all life-support equipment, while making the patient as comfortable as possible, normally with morphine and other painkillers. This way the patient can pass with dignity and a minimum of pain, though the process may take a few days or even a few weeks.

Usually, however, patients at the end of life experience a terminal event from which they cannot recover, such as a cardiac arrest or cessation of breathing. In some cases, patients can get slightly better, so it might seem they have a chance to survive on their own. But can they? To determine this, the medical team will try removing their life support. But if such patients fail one more time, that's a strong indication that their condition is most likely terminal, and they should be left without any further life support so nature can take its course in finally ending their life.

In Albert's case, there was no certainty about the outcome. Maybe his body would be strong enough to rally with the help of the support systems that were maintaining his bodily functions, along with monitoring of his vital signs. On the other hand, maybe the damages from the accident were too great for him to pull through. His condition could improve or deteriorate; his prospects for living or dying could go either way.

Meanwhile, the medical team and I continued to do the best we could to help him heal, using the latest medical technologies to support and monitor his condition. Certainly, in this touch-and-go situation, it might not be possible to save a patient like Albert in the case of a sudden emergency overwhelming his system, and there might not be time for the team to pull together the needed defense. For example, in the case of a cardiac arrest, despite the machines pumping the blood through the patient's heart, there might be only a few minutes to get the heart pumping again in order to get oxygenated blood to the brain fast enough to keep it functioning. Within these limitations, the ICU gives the very ill or injured patient a final chance at life even though the patients brought there already have a high risk of dying. At least, the progress of modern medicine has improved a patient's chances of recovery in the ICU, and that's the best we can do.

About an hour later, feeling we had been doing the best we could for Albert, I pulled into my driveway, opened the garage, and drove in, knowing that anything could happen to my car while in the garage, from being stolen to a fire breaking out. Likewise, I knew that anything could happen to the ICU patient, depending upon the strengths he brought to the situation, such as being strong and healthy before his accident, as in Albert's case. Then, once inside the house, I put my cell phone on the bedside table, so I could hear it should I get a call from the night shift ICU nurse, letting me know if there was any sudden emergency due to a change in Albert's condition. In this case, there was nothing more to be done, since Albert passed away later that night.

9

DEALING WITH DEMENTIA

The issue of dementia comes up for some end-of-life patients, usually the oldest patients who have been gradually losing their mental faculties. It also occurs for some younger patients who have a serious injury or illness or have abused drugs, so their brain has been injured or deprived of oxygen for a few minutes.

One problem can be determining whether a patient has dementia, which makes it difficult to explain certain procedures or get an informed consent for DNR/DNI status. Another problem may be not correctly classifying a patient as having dementia, because he or she outwardly seems lucid. But if one spent more time talking to the patient, the signs of dementia would become clear, such as when a patient repeatedly asks the same question after getting it answered. Another sign of dementia that can easily be missed is when the patient makes seemingly clear statements about something but the commonly known facts are wrong (such as claiming to have an experience which he or she didn't have).

The problem of dementia can also trigger many other issues, such as when close family members or relatives don't want to believe a patient with dementia has it. Sometimes family members or relatives may claim that someone is demented who is not, usually because they want to gain control of the patient's affairs or refute a will or other papers signed by the patient. If it is agreed that the patient is demented now, the question can arise about when he or she became demented, since if the person is demented and when that occurred can affect the validity of documents he or she signed, from major purchases and business agreements to a last will and testament.

Thus, the issue of dementia can be a complex one which raises all kinds of questions about if a patient is suffering from dementia, and if so, when did that happen and the seriousness of the condition, because dementia is not a simple yes-or-no proposition. Instead, the condition is commonly characterized by a gradual deterioration of mental facilities, except when the dementia is due to a sudden trauma resulting from an illness, accident, or overdose. So doctors sometimes have to assess the seriousness of this condition by seeing how well the patient understands certain explanations or instructions. Lawyers may get involved when the patient has to sign legal documents or participate in a court case and there is a dispute about a person's level of understanding.

I experienced these complexities in several cases involving dementia, where I had to deal with both patients and their close relatives in order to determine what the patients could understand and decide about their end-of-life care. I also had to determine if the dementia was serious enough, so their family or relatives had to make the decision.

EXPLAINING WHAT TO DO TO A PATIENT WITH DEMENTIA

A key issue is how much the patient understands when symptoms of dementia appear, since the patient should normally make the DNR/DNI status decision and chose whether or not to get certain procedures, such as an operation to amputate an arm or leg due to gangrene when circulation has cut off a limb. But in the early stages of dementia, as in Alzheimer's, it is not always clear what a patient can understand or not. Furthermore, it may be possible to carefully tailor an explanation to the patient's level of understanding, so as possible, a doctor should help the patient make an informed decision rather than turning that decision over to family members or relatives.

This issue comes up because dementia is not a condition that can be measured by quantitative means on a fixed scale; so, for example, a patient might be considered to be only 10 percent rather than 40 percent demented, and therefore able to perform at a certain level of functioning. Rather, it is often unclear where a patient's abilities lie on the spectrum of dementia, particularly since a patient can have good and bad days of higher and lower functioning, and some signs of dementia can seem like momentary and ordinary lapses, such as when someone forgets a name or address. Otherwise, unless the signs of dementia are so clear that everyone knows it, the evidence of dementia can be very ambiguous. But once some signs of the condition appear, a doctor should seek to help the patient understand and make his or own decisions as much as possible.

That's what I tried to do with Mrs. Smith, a "semi-demented patient," in trying to explain the "do not resuscitate" concept, so she could understand it and I could persuade her to opt for a DNR/DNI status while she still could understand enough to make that decision herself. In her case, she was in her early eighties and suffering from a serious case of pneumonia. At one time, she had participated in a variety of social activities and causes as a volunteer, since her husband had been a successful corporate executive and had left her a substantial inheritance. As a result, she could stay in their large stately home and continue to participate in her charitable works. But over the last year, she had experienced growing memory lapses, mistakes in using words, getting lost while driving once-familiar streets, and other signs of growing dementia. Yet she still had many lucid periods and could follow simple, clear instructions. While she was expected to recover from the pneumonia, at her age, the next disease she contracted could well be fatal, so it was good to talk to her now while she still could understand and make arrangements for how to handle her death and dying.

When I went to see her in the hospital, her fifty-something daughter Anna was waiting outside her room. Like her mother, Anna had married a successful business executive, was involved in charitable and society events, and had plenty of time to devote to her mother's care. She also had her mother's best interest at heart in getting ready to make decisions for her when the time came.

"What's the plan and what can I do to help?" Anna asked, after greeting me at the door of Mrs. Smith's room.

"I just want to explain to Mrs. Smith what it means to choose a DNR/DNI status," I said. "I'll try to keep my explanation as simple as possible so that she can decide for herself, though she doesn't have to decide now. It would be good for her to make the decision or for you to understand and agree to what she would like to do when the time comes."

"Of course," Anna said. "That's what I'd like to do, since my mother's wishes are my first priority. We always had a close relationship, and I want to be sure she is as comfortable as possible when the end comes."

When I led Anna into the private hospital room, Mrs. Smith was sitting up, flipping through a popular home and gardens magazine and looking at the pictures. She smiled at Anna as she put down the magazine. As Anna stood at the foot of her bed, I pulled over a chair to sit by her bedside, introduced myself, and tried to explain the situation as simply as possible.

"I will be telling you about a decision you have to make about your care at the hospital. But you do not have to make this decision now."

I paused to see if Mrs. Smith was following me. "Do you understand what I just said?" I asked.

Mrs. Smith nodded. "Yes. A decision to make."

"Good," I said and went on. "Now if anything I say is unclear, you will let me know."

"Yes," she nodded.

"Okay. Now what you need to understand is that we will need to make a decision about your care at some point, so we can respect your wishes. We want to do what you want, not what others want, while you can still make this decision yourself. You understand?"

"Yes," Mrs. Smith nodded, and glanced over at her daughter as if seeking her approval.

"Very good, mother," Anna said.

So I continued, with the next part of the explanation, which was more complicated.

"Do you know what your current DNR/DNI status is?" I asked, since it is set to full code, which means to do every treatment possible, unless the patient opts to choose a DNR/DNI status, or a family member or relative makes that determination when a patient is unable to make that decision.

At first, Mrs. Smith looked at me blankly, since the question was too technical for her to understand, so I tried explaining this in various ways.

However, all she could understand was that "I don't have to answer you now."

At this point, I felt it best to put off trying to explain anything more to Mrs. Smith, since she wasn't ready to understand now, though perhaps later in her more lucid moments she might be. If not, her daughter could take over and make the decision for her.

This example illustrates the difficulties that occur when patients are suffering from some type of dementia in the early stages of the illness where they might still understand what is happening to them and what they need to decide now or in the future, while they still can for themselves. This case also reflects the need to simplify the explanation, so patients might understand enough to decide now or later what to do about their treatment in light of their impending death. Additionally, it shows the importance of having a family member or close relative who is in alignment with the patient's best interests involved, so they can take over if the patient is no longer mentally competent to decide, based on understanding what the patient would likely want if he or she could make that decision. Obviously, in some cases, family members and relatives have their own agendas, which can lead to battles over what the patient really wants or is in the patient's best interest. But at least here, Mrs. Smith and her daughter were in a close and loving relationship, so they were clearly on the same page over what to do for Mrs. Smith when the final opportunity to make that decision arrived.

This conversation with Mrs. Smith also illustrates that it is not necessary to go into all of the details about the meaning of a DNR/DNI status with a patient with dementia. Such a patient cannot understand all the complexities about what might happen without options for this status, such as receiving drugs to reduce pain, electrical shocks, needles to the heart to get it going again, CPR, and intubation. Obviously, for a patient who can barely understand a simple explanation, a more detailed discussion of the medical details would only lead to more confusion. So the more humane thing to do is to present a summary of the situation in a sentence or two, which the patient or an observing family member or relative can readily understand.

A few days later, Mrs. Smith was still not able to make any decision, but I was glad for this earlier dialogue to give both Mrs. Smith and her daughter something to think about to help them opt for a DNR/DNI status, when Mrs. Smith or her daughter needed to make that choice and sign the necessary documents to make that status happen. Now I just had to wait until they were ready for me to give my explanation to Mrs. Smith again or until the decision had to be made by Mrs. Smith or her daughter, once her condition was terminal and her death only a few days or weeks away. Her dementia status at that time would determine whether she would make the decision or her daughter would make it for her.

DEALING WITH A PATIENT WITH DEMENTIA WHO SEEMED NORMAL

A big problem in dealing with patients with dementia is they can seem outwardly normal in their everyday appearance and conversation. They may dress in ordinary business clothes and go to business meetings, and they may seem fine when exchanging ordinary pleasantries, such as at typical business networking meetings, when people first meet, describe what they do, and exchange business cards. However, if one pays closer attention to the person's speech content and reasoning, their comments can indicate that something is off.

For example, in speaking, they might repeat questions that were just answered, because they don't remember that they asked the question or don't remember the answer. Such an exchange might even seem like an ordinary conversation, because often at such meetings, normal people aren't paying attention or are thinking about how to reply, so they don't recall how someone answered a question. But this could be a sign of dementia if there is a pattern of repetitive questioning and a failure to remember the answers.

As another example, someone at a meeting might not remember meeting someone before, even if they went out for a further coffee meeting or dinner somewhere. But normal people who are meeting a lot of people at these events could easily forget a meeting if the person didn't feel this was a potentially profitable business connection. So again, the evidence of dementia would be in a repeated pattern of forgetting meetings and conversations.

Still another sign of dementia is when a person's speech shows a pattern of non sequiturs—responses that have little or nothing to do with the topic of conversation and might often be flights of fancy. Standing alone, such responses might be an example of creative thinking; but multiple disconnected responses, particularly if combined with other possible indicators, such as repetitive questioning or forgetting previous meetings, might be indicative of dementia, too.

In ordinary social situations, people don't often pay attention to these kinds of cues when a person looks normal enough, especially if they have known this person for some time and he or she has seemed fine in the past. So past acquaintances might be likely to continue to regard that person as normal based on their previous impressions, since people naturally carry over their past characterization of someone into the present unless there is a reason to change. Moreover, the condition of dementia can creep up so gradually that people may not recognize it. Even the person exhibiting these signs may not be aware of suffering from dementia at first. But a physician or other medical practitioner looking for these signifiers of dementia may recognize the condition and diagnose how serious it is.

I had this experience when I met with Michael, now eighty-two, who had been a successful businessman. He had been a top-level corporate executive involved with sales and marketing, so he was well versed in how to speak in a compelling way to others in the company and prospective clients and buyers. Likewise, at business networking events, conferences, trade shows, and other events, he had always been a commanding presence. Even after he retired in his mid-seventies, he continued to attend local networking events and was involved on the boards of several community organizations. Thus, when he first began to show the symptoms of Alzheimer's in his late seventies, no one noticed. When I first met him in the hospital because he had a painful left foot due to poor circulation, he had no awareness of his deteriorating mental condition. But I became aware of his cognition problems when he first came into my office to describe what was wrong and what he hoped the hospital would do for him.

"Tell me what's wrong," I began.

"It's my left foot," he said. "It's very painful, and I think it may be because of poor circulation, since a few weeks ago, I was admitted for poor circulation in my other leg. But they operated and then everything was fine."

Operated! The fact that there was an operation was a warning signal that this had been a serious condition. Plus I was surprised that he minimized the seriousness of what happened. So I probed with more questions.

"What kind of operation?" I asked.

"They had to take off a toe," he said.

"Why?" I pressed.

At this point, he paused and got a faraway look in his eye, as if he had to think carefully to retrieve what this operation was about, even though it had happened only a few weeks before. Certainly, this was information he should know immediately, but as the seconds ticked by, he was trying to search for a memory, which could be a sign of memory problems.

"Why did they have to remove it?" I asked again.

Michael jerked back to attention and looked down at his shoe, as if that would help him remember.

"Oh, yes," he said finally. "I know what it was. My toe was turning brown and green, so they had to get rid of the colors."

"Do you mean gangrene?" I asked, knowing that gangrene could be a result of poor circulation, and that a typical sign for it was the skin turning a brownish green. However, it was odd that Michael was referring to the colors of his toes resulting in an amputation, rather than using the common term "gangrene." So this was another sign that he could be experiencing a memory loss for ordinary, though less-used words.

I made a note on my notepad to check further on Michael's mental condition.

Then we had some further discussion about his past medical history before he had this current problem. I pulled out a hospital admission form to make notes, so anyone treating him in the hospital would see them.

"Tell me a little more about your other recent medical treatments," I said.

"Why?" he asked.

I thought it an unusual question, since commonly admitting doctors or medical staffers ask these questions, since they need to know a range of information about allergies, negative reactions to medications, previous diseases, and past injuries to know the patient's overall physical and mental condition. Often patients are asked to fill out these forms by a receptionist or nurse, after which a doctor reviews them, though generally it is better when a doctor or other medical professional talk to the patient while filling out the form, since they can be more accurate and provide more detail to describe the patient's past history. A reason for this better input is that patients often fill out these forms as quickly as possible, so they leave information out. I like to fill out these forms myself based on a patient's responses, since this gives me a chance to more fully assess the patient and recognize any gaps or unusual responses, so I can ask further probing questions.

That's what I did with Michael, though mostly, in response to my questions, he had trouble remembering what happened when. While many patients may have this difficulty, they usually can come up with more detail after some thought. But in Michael's case, a lot of information seemed to be missing because he couldn't remember or didn't want to tell me, though I suspected the former, since Michael otherwise seemed eager to cooperate. He just seemed to have blanks in his mental cabinet, so he couldn't remember many incidents of medical treatment.

Still, as he talked, I was able to learn much about his medical history. Among other things, I learned that he had a long history of medical problems and multiple hospitalizations, in part due to a long history of tobacco abuse. But because most of these hospital admissions occurred at different hospitals, we had no access to those records, only the record of the hospital where Michael was now. So we had to depend on Michael's limited memory of any medical encounters for the last fifteen to twenty years. At least he was able to talk about the highlights of his long history, which helped me realize that his odd responses and limited recall of major past events could be a sign of gradually increasing dementia.

"I don't know," he said finally. "I guess if I looked in my datebook for the last fifteen or twenty years, I'd find more times when I saw somebody in a hospital for some treatment. I don't remember. But I'm here now and I'd like to get my toe taken care of and move on."

I said I would help, telling Michael, "I'll have to get this information to the surgical staff and they'll contact you to set something up."

"Okay," Michael agreed, seemingly satisfied with that arrangement.

Then, because of his age, I wanted to talk to him about his code status in case anything happened to him while he was undergoing still another operation, even if he expected it to be routine. But he looked at me blankly, when I tried to explain about the "resuscitation" and "do not resuscitate" status.

"What's that?" he asked, so I tried to put the arrangement in more simple terms, much as I did with Mrs. Collins, who already had the beginnings of dementia.

"It's whether to revive you and continue to treat you if you have an end-of-life or terminal condition that can't be or is unlikely to be cured."

Michael laughed oddly, like he thought the idea was absurd. "I just have a problem with my toe, so why think about the end of things now?"

Thus, I concluded that it didn't make any sense to continue the conversation to try to persuade him. Michael seemed to think he was fine, or at least he wanted to feel all was fine, in spite of his long history of medical problems, most of which he had forgotten about. So I figured I could wait until later to ask these questions, assuming he was still competent to answer them. If not, I could always direct my questions to one of his family members who would be taking on the responsibility for caring for him, or I could find an elder-care facility to care for him once he could no longer do so himself. Given his apparent medical history and apparent dimming mental capacity, I suspected that might not be long in occurring.

It wasn't. A few days later, the day before Michael planned to arrange for the operation on his toe, I was called from the hospital at 1 a.m. to hear: "He just had a respiratory arrest." Apparently, this problem was caused by the painkillers he had been taking to relieve the intense pain in his toe. Thinking more pills would provide even more relief, he took enough of the pills to cause him to stop breathing—much like an overdose of many other drugs might result in a similar cessation of breathing.

As a result of the call, I quickly called the hospitalist, a doctor whose primary focus is the general medical care of hospitalized patients, to tell him about Michael's condition. The hospitalist then arranged for Michael's transfer to the ICU. Normally in such a painkiller-overdose scenario, the patient could be given an antidote to reverse the chemical effect of the drug, so Michael could wake up and then be observed to make sure he was continuing to recover. But if a patient took more than one type of drug, this chemical reversal wouldn't be possible, so the patient would spend the night connected to a breathing machine, which would breathe for him while the medication wore off. Then the tubes would be removed and he would return to his initial status, which in Michael's case was being in line for the operation on his toe.

Unfortunately, further complications ensued. While Michael was hooked up the breathing machine, his heart stopped for a couple of minutes and his blood pressure dropped to nothing, so his blood wasn't circulating to transfer oxygen to his brain. As a result, he was already suffering from the initial symptoms of dementia, such as memory lapses and inappropriate responses to questions, this reduced oxygen to his brain would make any of these symptoms even worse.

I learned about these problems when I got another call from the hospital an hour later to report what happened to Michael. So I headed back to the hospital to see what I could do, both to help the patient and to talk to his family members, whom the hospital also called with the grim news.

I arrived at about 3 a.m. and went immediately to be by Michael's side and help the hospitalist get him breathing again. While I was Michael's primary care doctor, the hospitalist worked with a medical team in the hospital to provide this critical care, whereby each doctor provided input based on his or her area of expertise. My role was primarily to show my support for the patient just by being there, when he was conscious enough to recognize my presence and let the family members know what was going on, as the hospitalists and specialists on the team worked on keeping him alive.

The team members had to repeatedly stimulate his breathing over the next three hours, since again and again, he stopped breathing, and again and again, they massaged and pumped his chest to start his heart going again. But even when Michael resumed breathing on his own, the signs didn't look good because he began to have episodes of posturing, in which a person becomes stiff in a "posture" where his arms are bent toward his body, his wrists and fingers are bent across the chest, his fists are clenched, and his legs are held out straight. The condition is called "posturing" because the person looks a like an actor trying to assume a stiff posture to show he is angry and ready to strike out at someone. But medically, posturing is a sign of severe brain damage that is likely irreversible.

Meanwhile, when Michael began to breathe on his own for a while, I went to the waiting room area, where his wife and two of his sons in their fifties were sitting nervously, waiting to hear how he was doing. As I started to explain that "Michael has been having trouble breathing on his own and may have suffered some brain damage from the times when oxygen was cut off from his brain," his wife interrupted me.

"That's absurd. Michael was a completely healthy eighty-two-year old man. He was walking around and fine until yesterday."

But I knew Michael was not completely healthy because of his long history of medical problems, even if his wife didn't know about them or was trying to deny their importance. So I tried to explain with a simple description of Michael's dire situation.

"Whether or not he seemed fine or whether or not he had a history of medical problems doesn't always matter. Even though a person is in good physical condition and exercises every day, he could suddenly experience a medical crisis.

"A poor medical history or a current crisis such as a drug overdose could make a sudden unexpected condition contributing to death more likely. But a sudden death can happen to anyone anytime. So it's hard to predict what will happen tomorrow."

His wife still remained certain that Michael was going to recover, that this was just a temporary, quickly reversible condition.

"He'll be fine soon," she kept insisting. "He's always been so healthy and able to bounce back after an illness. It doesn't matter if he's eighty-two. He's always been very active and alert, so he'll be fine."

Again, I tried to convince her that he wouldn't be. "You have to understand. Michael has had two cardiac arrests in two hours, and he's still connected to a machine that is helping him breathe. He is additionally showing signs of major brain damage, such as holding his body in a stiff, abnormal posture with his hands clenched. Plus his blood pressure is very low. So this is really a very critical situation."

This time Michael's wife looked at me with a steely glare, as if she was angry for me telling her these things, which she didn't want to believe.

"But he's always come back despite the odds of recovery in the past. He's a real survivor, and he's a physically strong, active man for his age. He's even participated in some marathon races in the city recently, and he came in with the first third of the contestants."

"I know," I sympathized. "I'm sure it has been different in the past for Michael. But now Michael has experienced some irreversible consequences that started with the overdose of painkillers. These caused some complications leading to his whole system shutting down. And his low blood pressure and lack of breathing for a time have led to an insufficient supply of oxygen to his brain, resulting most likely in severe and permanent brain damage."

Michael's wife glared at me in a stony silence in response to my further attempt to get her to understand the gravity of Michael's situation. Her anger directed toward me seemed like a case of blaming the weather on the weatherman; in this case, me, the doctor. This desire to deflect blame onto the doctor, hospital, or other treatment facility often happens in these end-of-life situations because family members and relatives would like someone other than the patient to blame for his or her death.

Michael's ability to conceal his dementia in his conversations with others, including his family, contributed to making his death seem like an unexpected occurrence. And his actions contributed to that perception. To the very end, he was able to present an image of a healthy, high-functioning eighty-two-year old, when behind the façade, both his body and mind were failing.

Now his wife wanted to believe in the image he presented, not the truth behind it. For her, the image was the reality. So, for now, in the face of her rising anger, I didn't feel I could do much more to help. I had to let her growing awareness of the situation settle in.

Thus, I stood up, not knowing what more I could say about Michael's condition, and told her: "I have to go back to the ICU again to check on your husband's condition."

Then I walked down the corridor toward the ICU. It was a relief to leave Michael's wife in the waiting room with her sons, since I was exhausted from all the explanations, along with the intense critical care manipulations I and the hospitalist performed to keep Michael alive.

This time on my return to the ICU, the hospitalist told me that Michael was finally stable. Though still on the breathing machine, at least he had no more episodes of posturing or sudden drops in his blood pressure, and his temperature was back in the normal range.

Now that it was about 6 a.m., I turned supervising Michael's care and coordination with the family over to the next critical care team, led by a supervising doctor and other medical specialists, so a new set of eyes could assess Michael's condition and report on the results to his wife. As I explained to the team leader:

"The wife really wants to believe her husband is going to be okay. But if she hears about his grim prospects from someone besides myself, this will help to show her the objective truth about the situation. She needs this knowledge, because she and her sons show a complete lack of understanding about what the situation really is. They don't want to believe that Michael is not really going to be okay again."

With that, I left the hospital, got into my car in the parking lot, and drove home. Fortunately, as I learned when I woke up the next morning, after each of the critical care team doctors had multiple meetings with the family, the wife came to finally recognize the medical truth of her husband's condition. Then she accepted finally that her husband was not ever going to be okay again.

WHEN A SEEMINGLY NORMAL PATIENT WITH DEMENTIA AGREES TO AN OPERATION RESULTING IN COMPLICATIONS

Another complication is when a patient with dementia who seems normal, much as in Michael's case, consents to an operation, which he or she could normally choose to make. But then the operation has complications, leading to questions in retrospect about the patient's ability to give consent in the first place, since the family later revealed the patient had a diagnosis of dementia.

If this explanation of the case sounds complicated, that's because it is, since it can be easy to fail to diagnose dementia when a patient outwardly appears to be functioning well. In such a case, medical personnel not particularly trained to recognize the signs of early-onset Alzheimer's or other types of dementia don't recognize this. That's why any agreement by a very elderly patient or by a patient whose behavior raises suspicions of having dementia may be better off if checked with the family members, who by then might have assumed—or be in the position of assuming—decision-making power.

In such a situation, if the patient's mental condition is in an assessment limbo, no operation should be ideally done without the family input, though it was done in Mr. Johnson's case, as he seemed normal for his age. The operation was done because he had an emergency situation and he seemed to be able to communicate and "consent" to the surgical and anesthesia teams without raising any suspicion that he might not be cognitively able to consent to such a procedure.

Unfortunately, the actual process of declaring somebody incompetent for any reason, including dementia, is a complicated and difficult process involving psychiatrists, lawyers, judges, and expert witnesses, and it normally takes several weeks or more to decide.

In many ways, Mr. Johnson's case was similar to Michael's case in his presenting symptoms. As the owner of a small store, he continued to play an active role in managing it and meeting with customers, much like Michael continued to go to business networking events after retiring as a successful corporate executive. Mr. Johnson was also in his eighties, and he came in with a problem in his lower leg, where he had very poor circulation, which endangered his life, since a superimposed violent infection could kill him by producing septic shock. Furthermore, like Michael, he had a wife who was monitoring his situation closely, though she wasn't in denial about the seriousness of his condition, like Michael's wife.

Mr. Johnson was also seemingly normal because he was able to conceal his symptoms of dementia from others, mainly because he had a type of dementia where he had bouts of lucidity, and that's the front he presented to the public. By contrast, when he wasn't lucid, he tended to withdraw from socializing with others, as if he knew something was wrong and didn't want others to know it. Thus, in these lucid periods he seemed very much himself and he could fool others with his seemingly normal speech about his work, business, and the state of the world. Nevertheless, as demonstrated in Michael's case, a trained professional could recognize the common failings that pointed to his being in the early stages of dementia, such as when he occasionally slurred his words, chose the wrong word, experienced some memory gaps for recent events, and forgot familiar names and faces. When these slips happened, Mr. Johnson generally just laughed about them, and whoever he was talking to followed his lead, thinking the slip just a momentary lapse and not an indication of some serious problem.

After I met Mr. Johnson in his semiprivate room, I explained that I was the hospital physician in charge of his case, which meant that I would be meeting with the medical team providing his care and with any family members and close relatives.

"Good to meet you, doc," he told me in reply. "I'm glad I have someone watching over me. You're like a guardian angel making sure I get the best care possible."

I smiled back and made some quick notes about the guardian angel reference. Was this a perfectly harmless metaphor for someone caring for him, or could it suggest a problem since it was an unusual reference?

Then I went to see the surgeon who saw Mr. Johnson and decided to operate on him. In his opinion, performing the emergency operation was absolutely advisable to clear the arterial blockages he found building up in the arteries of Mr. Johnson's leg. Importantly, he had gotten Mr. Johnson's standard consent to perform the operation. As he told me, as I sat across from him in his office:

"Mr. Johnson was having a serious buildup of plaques and other blockages in the arteries of his leg, which could lead to him losing his leg at any time. So, I operated using a thrombolysis and bypass procedure, which involves blasting the clots into small pieces and bypassing critically narrowed sites."

I fully agreed that an operation seemed in order.

"And we did get the appropriate consent from Mr. Johnson himself to go ahead," the radiologist said proudly, showing me the agreement form Mr. Johnson had signed acknowledging the operation and understanding the risks and benefits of it.

So everything seemed fine, since Mr. Johnson had "appropriately" consented to the procedure. But then everything went horribly wrong, since soon after he was in his room resting from the operation, the blood flow through his leg was restricted and did not resume as it should, resulting in a subsequent operation to amputate his leg, which sometimes occurs under these circumstances.

Then Mr. Johnson's situation became even more complicated. When I spoke to his wife in the waiting room and explained what had happened and that he had needed another operation to amputate his leg, she was already upset about the decision to operate on him in the first place.

Mrs. Johnson was livid. "Who gave the medical team permission to perform the operation in the first place?" she fumed. "You didn't have my approval."

That's when I learned that Mr. Johnson had been diagnosed with early-stage dementia, possibly with Alzheimer's, though the physician who diagnosed this condition wasn't sure. Just in case, the doctor had started Mr. Johnson on taking Aricept, which is the most commonly used medication to treat dementia, and this medicine was part of Mr. Johnson's home list, which indicates the medications he had been taking at home.

Eventually, his wife suggested that a "leg transplant" might help, since the arteries wouldn't be blocked, though a transplant was not an option, and transplants are generally never performed as an emergency or if there is an ongoing infection.

In short, all of these complications following the procedure are not unusual when vascular surgeons and radiologists perform an operation to open the patient's already severely compromised circulation, and subsequently a lack of circulation to the leg can trigger a systematic reaction and collapse.

Unfortunately, due to his overall deteriorating condition, Mr. Johnson went into a respiratory and short cardiac arrest, whereby his heart suddenly stopped pumping blood and he stopped breathing. Immediately, a medical team with a doctor and several nurses rushed into his room and administered CPR to give him oxygen and put pressure on his chest wall to get his heart pumping again. But a few minutes later his heart and breathing stopped again, and this time the medical team wasn't so fortunate. The initial operation to improve the circulation to his leg triggered a multisystem organ failure, and this breakdown led to substances from the dead tissue in his leg entering his bloodstream and traveling to his brain—resulting in the multiple organ failure that lead to his demise.

If Mr. Johnson had not been suffering from dementia, the doctor's decision to go forward would be fine, since the medical team had done the best they could under the circumstances. They had obtained consent based on believing from their observation that Mr. Johnson had an acceptable level of understanding and ability to consent to the surgery. But muddying the situation is the ruling under HIPPA regulations, as provided by the Health Insurance Portability and Accountability Act of 1996 that doctors must always deal directly with the patient; they should only involve family members, relatives, or others in making a decision when they are in doubt about the patient's capacity to make his or her own decisions. Yet the question of whether there was or should have been any doubt opens the door to legal arguments, pro and con.

This case illustrates the kinds of issues that can occur when a patient is suffering from dementia. However, in the early stages, this dementia may not be obvious, because outwardly the patient can appear normal or in some cases even experience periods of lucidity where his or her mentation is normal. Thus, such cases can be a special challenge for doctors and other medical personnel involved in end-of-life care, since a determination of the patient's mental status and what the medical team should know about it affects whether a procedure has appropriately been approved and whether the medical team or hospital has any liability for what happens when things go wrong. After the fact, the determination of these facts can go either way, as the question of who is liable for what hangs in the balance.

THE FAR-REACHING EFFECTS OF A DEMENTIA RULING

The question of whether a patient is suffering from dementia can affect other determinations when a patient dies in the hospital and family members and relatives battle over the patient's estate. To help answer this question, doctors may be asked to give their opinion about whether the patient is suffering from dementia or not.

For the hospital, the issue of dementia affects care in two ways, as previously noted. One way is in determining the patient's DNR/DNI status, since whether the patient is judged mentally sound or not affects who decides on this status. If the patient does not have dementia, a doctor will look to the patient to make that decision, since this status is normally the patient's choice even when the patient and his or her family and relatives disagree as to what to do.

However, if the patient is deemed to be suffering from dementia that has progressed far enough that the patient is unable to knowingly make that DNR/DNI status determination, the option to choose this status passes to the next of kin, unless the patient, while still sufficiently of sound mind, has previously made a will or designated a proxy to make decisions for him or her if the patient can no longer do so. Then the family member, proxy, relative, or other party specified in that document will be the one to make the decision.

The other way that the patient's dementia status can affect end-of-life care is in how the nurses and other staff members treat that patient while providing that care. For example, the nurses and doctors may be especially careful in giving instructions to the patient with dementia or asking what he or she needs or wants, such as by providing an additional dose of painkillers to reduce the patient's pain. Or if the patient has garbled speech or otherwise has difficulty making his or her wishes known, the medical staffers might spend more time trying to communicate with and understand what the patient is saying. They might even bring a drawing board, so the patient can draw what he or she wants or needs.

The big complication that can often occur is determining whether a patient is suffering from dementia, and if so, if the dementia is serious enough so the person can no longer make an informed decision about something. Presumably, a trained doctor can make this determination by giving the patient a series of tests to ascertain his or her level of awareness, understanding, and performance. But these tests are not always accurate, since in the early stages, some patients are at least partly aware of their growing mental decline and can seem to be fully sound of mind by giving seemingly lucid answers to the questions. As a result, they can evade an accurate diagnosis of their real mental abilities and therefore not be considered to have dementia. Or because the symptoms of dementia can come and go, a patient may seem more or less alert at different times of the day or on different days. Furthermore, different medical experts on dementia may have different determinations for when a patient is suffering from one of the dementia conditions, based on the patient's presenting symptoms, as in the case of a patient with Alzheimer's. Moreover, different assessments may be made by doctors in the hospital and doctors who have seen the patient outside the hospital, such as when a family doctor who has known the patient for many years makes this determination versus a medical specialist who sees the patient for the first time.

An example of this difficulty in determining when a patient has a serious enough dementia to be unable to make their own decisions is illustrated by the popular film *Still Alice* starring Julianne Moore.[1] It tells the story of Alice, a successful linguistics professor afflicted by Alzheimer's disease. The first signs of the disease occur when she is teaching a class and forgets some words. Later, as she jogs through the campus, she gets lost on a familiar path because she forgets where she is. When the doctor gives her some memory and perception tests, he diagnoses that she has the early stages of the disease, and soon after that she is retired from her job at the university. Yet she can still function for a while, and many people are unaware that she has the disease. Gradually she experiences other losses of abilities, including the ability to communicate as eloquently as she once did. But the film makes the point that despite these losses, she still is "Alice" who responds to the love of her family members. But at some point, she has lost the ability to think sufficiently to make her own decisions and she has to be cared for by others.

Likewise, it can be hard for doctors to make a determination of dementia, as well as agree on when a condition of dementia has gone far enough so that the patient is no longer mentally competent to make decisions about his or her DNR/DNI status, if not already decided, or to make choices about other treatment procedures. Then someone else has to decide, as determined by the patient's legal papers about granting power of attorney to someone else in the family or based on a legal determination about who should take over this function in the absence of clear instructions from the patient about who should do this.

Further complications can arise after the patient dies, based on whether the patient was determined to have dementia and who made this determination. Making matters worse, even more complications result when the patient's family members and relatives disagree about the patient's condition and which family member or relative should take charge when the patient is no longer competent to choose, if that patient has not left clear instructions on who should do this. And sometimes the patient's instructions can be challenged by warring relatives, who have different views about whether or not the patient was competent to make those instructions, much like relatives can challenge the patient's competence to make a will.

While such questions about the mental competence of a patient to make choices may depend on the diagnosis of dementia by a doctor, they can turn into legal questions when the diagnosis of one or more doctors is challenged by the patient's family members or relatives who are in a position to assume responsibility for care or inherit the patient's estate after his or her death. This kind of dispute generally does not occur in lower- and middle-income families, since the main concern is doing what is deemed best for the patient, whoever makes the decision. But such a dispute can at times occur in higher-income families where the patient has a substantial amount of money in his or her estate, since the outcome of the battle over whether the patient has dementia and when he or she can be deemed incompetent to make decisions can affect who gets the money and how it is distributed.

While I have not faced any of these issues in my practice, some other medical practitioners have, and I wanted to provide an example of what might happen and how a doctor might get involved in dealing with the patient's family members and relatives, as well as with the lawyers they bring in to represent their separate interests in the matter.

Take what happened to Edward R. At one time, he was a wealthy banker and venture capitalist with a large family of several sons and daughters, including two very young children with his second wife and several stepchildren from his second wife's previous marriage. Additionally, he had several adult children with his first wife, whom he had divorced a few years before. At one point, Edward had drawn up a will during his first marriage leaving everything to be divided between his first wife and children, with half of his estate to go to his favorite charities. But shortly before his final illness, a cancer that progressed into a brain tumor in the last months of his life, Edward drew up a new will leaving most of his money to his new wife and their two children, with a smaller amount to his stepchildren, and nothing to his favorite charities.

The situation of the two wills was ripe for dispute by the ex-wife and the current wife and their children, as well as by the charities that were left out of the second will. The outcome depended on the determination of whether the patient was competent to change his will when he did. In turn, that determination depended on the doctor's assessment of the patient's competency, based on whether he had dementia or not and whether this dementia had progressed to the stage where he might be deemed no longer competent.

In Edward's case, there was a further complication in that different family factions had sought different medical determinations at different times as to whether Edward was competent or not when drafting both his will and his instructions to opt for a DNR/DNI status. Now even his DNR/DNI status was being challenged by family members, who wanted Edward to remain alive as long as possible while the issue of which will was valid was resolved. While one doctor claimed that Edward was competent to draw up the second will and chose not to be resuscitated when the time came, the other doctor claimed that Edward was not competent to draw up the second will or make a decision about the DNR/DNI status, so based on that determination, Edward's first family wanted to reject the DNR/DNI option. They even wanted to use the option to choose that status as a bargaining chip in the negotiations to get Edward's second wife and family to work out a compromise, whereby the funds could be distributed between the two wives and all of the children. And by now, Edward's dementia had progressed so far that he could not determine himself what to do. So in the course of developing their cases for the two warring families, the lawyers called on the doctors who made the determinations about the patient's dementia and mental competency to explain how they reached their determinations. In this way, the lawyers sought to challenge the doctor whose view they disagreed with in order to support the view of the doctor who supported their side.

Ultimately, I'm not sure what happened in this case, since as in most cases where lawyers are involved, the dispute was resolved with a settlement between the families out of court about how Edward's dementia affected the validity of the different instructions and wills. But the case illustrates the way a determination of dementia can become complex, since it is a progressive disease and a patient can have good and bad days as the disease progresses. So doctors seeing the patient on different days can reach different conclusions about the patient's mental competency, and some patients can be wily in answering questions to suggest they are mentally competent when their answers appear lucid, even though factually incorrect. But doctors who don't already know the patient and family may not know this, so they can be fooled into diagnosing the patient as not having dementia when the patient really does have it.

For a time, as the disease progresses, a determination of whether the dementia has progressed far enough, so the patient is no longer competent to make decisions, can go either way. It is as if the patient is in limbo between being competent or not, much like someone looking at a half-full glass of water might describe it as half-full or half-empty. In much the same way, one doctor might consider such a patient to be still competent while suffering from early-stage dementia; another doctor might consider the patient to no longer be competent; and still another doctor might not be aware that the patient has dementia at all.

While this determination of competency might contribute to deciding on the patient's course of treatment and DNR/DNI status, in some cases this determination might have legal ramifications when there is sufficient money involved and family members and relatives disagree about how this money should be distributed based on the patient's previous instructions and wills. A doctor can only determine to the best of his or her ability whether a patient has dementia and to what degree at a particular time. Then these other decisions can become the province of lawyers and judges, based on determining the accuracy of a doctor's diagnosis. Unfortunately, there may be no clear lines, since medicine is part art as well as science. So the doctor's interpretation becomes grist for the lawyer's mill; and it is eventually up to the lawyers to negotiate and the judges to decide.

10

FAMILY, CULTURE, AND RELIGION

Family values, culture, and religion can also play a part in making end-of-life decisions, especially when patients and family members disagree about what these decisions should be. One result can often be tense discussions as family members become very emotional in defending their choice, when this is not what the patient wanted, though often the patient is too sick to decide anything now. So my role becomes meeting with the family to try to work out what to do.

These issues can arise for all kinds of reasons. Sometimes the family has unrealistic expectations of what medical science can do, and they want to believe the patient will recover when the situation is clearly hopeless. In other cases, family members have difficulty understanding the situation. Sometimes they have preconceived but incorrect ideas about different alternatives. Some families have unresolved issues and anger based on past experiences, so family members may find it difficult to be at the hospital to make decisions for a patient from whom they are alienated. Sometimes family members' choices are influenced by religious beliefs that differ from the patient's. In one case, a family member wanted to extend the patient's life because she wanted to continue receiving social security payments from her father, even though the decision would prolong her father's pain and suffering by delaying his inevitable death.

This chapter illustrates this range of situations and options in dealing with families, whose choices are informed by their own culture, religion, and values.

FAMILIES WITH UNREALISTIC EXPECTATIONS

Sometimes when families have unrealistic expectations, it can be hard to show them how and why they are wrong. They can be so set in their beliefs that they want to deny that the patient's condition is really hopeless; they are so emotionally invested in maintaining their false belief of recovery that it can be difficult to convince them otherwise.

That's what I experienced when I dealt with the family of Mr. Malvani, an eighty-six-year-old man who was previously in the hospital because he had a carotid disease, in which a blockage prevented the artery from bringing blood to his brain. To try to get rid of this blockage, a surgical team operated, but there were complications because a clot formed after surgery and either partially or completely blocked the blood traveling to his brain, resulting in a stroke—a common result when a clot causes a blockage in the blood flow.

For a time, Mr. Malvani's family cared for him at home, but his condition got worse. He became weaker and soon returned to the hospital, with virtually no hope of recovery. The prognosis was that he would become weaker and weaker and could even suffer another stroke should further surgery be attempted. It was also likely, given his fragile condition, that he would not recover from the surgery.

Though Mr. Malvani was still mentally competent and aware enough to understand the situation and decide on his DNR/DNI status, his daughter Joy decided to become the family spokesperson. However, it quickly became clear that she had unrealistic expectations about what could be done medically to save her father. She presented a list of demands, like a queen issuing a proclamation, and she readily argued down anyone who dared to disagree with her. I found her the most disruptive, arrogant, demanding person I had ever met. It was like she had grown up as a princess who was used to getting her own way, with everyone at her beck and call to fulfill her wishes. It was my job to calm her down and explain what the medical team could do given her father's condition.

As I sat across from her, her two brothers, and her mother, the patient's wife, I started my explanation. But Joy quickly insisted, "You need to provide my father with better care. You say he can't recover from his stroke. But I know if the surgeons operate again to remove the blockage in his carotid artery, the blood will start flowing again and his brain will heal. So he can recover."

Though Joy was completely wrong in her ideas about what could be done, I knew I had to use extended diplomacy to get her to realize the truth. At least her two brothers disagreed with her, while the patient's wife remained silent, as if not to take sides. So I felt the brothers might become my allies in my effort to show the daughter that she was wrong, while doing so in a way that she could still save face. I felt a little like a politician having to think of the best strategy to respond to her attack.

"We certainly want to do all we can to help your father," I began. "But unfortunately, some medical procedures you are asking about are technically impossible due to your father's age and condition."

"Bulls**t," she responded angrily. "My father has always been very healthy and active, and he always ate a very healthy diet until he suffered a blockage in his heart."

"But he is eighty-six," I stated. "If he was younger, the situation might be different."

At this point, the two brothers chimed in, as if to rescue me, and I felt relieved by their input. I listened quietly for a while, since I thought it best to wait until the fight between the three family members played itself out.

"You should listen to the doctor," the brother Terry said.

"Yeah, you don't like to listen to anyone else. You always think you're right," the other brother Alex said.

"So you think you know better," Joy shot back. "I'm just trying to do what's best for our father."

"But it may be too late," Terry replied. "You heard what the doctor said about his condition."

The battle went on and on, until it seemed that the family members had finished expressing their anger to each other.

Finally, in a moment of calm, I commented to Joy: "If the surgeons operate again, there is the possibility of a cardiac arrest and your father flatlining, which would most likely be an irreversible condition. In a cardiac arrest, the heart stops, and there are only minutes to get it started again. Given the damage to your father's heart from a previous heart attack and his carotid disease, which has already restricted the blood supply to the brain, restarting his heart again would be highly unlikely and much further damage would be inflicted to his brain."

Joy glared at me, as Terry sought to defend my assessment with an apt comparison.

"Look, what the doctor is saying about this situation is like what happens to a car engine at the end of the car's life. When it breaks down, you can't repair it again."

Joy was still not mollified, though a little calmer. "Well, I just want to do everything possible for our father to try to bring him back."

But I was convinced that Mr. Malvani's condition could not be reversed. So her reaction was completely emotional and irrational, and the rest of the family seemed to understand that. Even her mother, Mr. Malvani's wife, nodded her agreement with Terry's assessment of the hopeless situation.

Finally, to bring some peace, I told the family: "I'll ask Mr. Malvani one more time about his wishes for his future care. You have to understand: according to the laws about these decisions, the only thing that counts is the patient's wishes, when the patient is still able to make these decisions, which your father is."

Finally, after more heated discussion and more questions to me, in which I explained that "The patient's physiology is really near the end, and there nothing more we can do for him medically," the room became very quiet. It was like everyone was emotionally exhausted from the hour of arguments and questions back and forth.

"I'll go talk to the patient and see what he wants," I said, glad I could leave this very conflicted family.

But when I spoke to the patient things became even more complicated, since Mr. Malvani commonly deferred to the wishes of his demanding daughter.

"I understand it's my decision to make," he said, as he sat in bed propped up by several cushions. He was also hooked up to tubes that helped him breathe and kept his heart pumping. "But if my heart flatlines, I want to defer to my daughter and whatever she wants to do."

"Of course," I said. "It's your decision and you have the right to choose whatever option you prefer."

As Joy came out of Mr. Malvani's room and returned to the waiting room where her brothers and mother were waiting, she walked with a swagger and smiled broadly like she was gloating, since she had won over the rest of the family after all. But any seeming victory was short-lived, since her brothers soon began yelling at her again, continuing the family conflict.

However, I decided to leave their conflict alone and check on another patient. After all, it was their battle; my own suggestions had little influence, and I could only recommend and advise. So if the patient wanted to defer to his daughter, even though I thought he was wrong, that was his choice to make, and he reaffirmed that the next morning when he told me again:

"I understand what you are trying to tell me about my neurologic condition and the code status, but I still want to defer to what my daughter wants."

So that was that. Since his daughter wanted him kept alive as long as possible, she rejected the DRN/DNI status and insisted that he be transferred to a teaching hospital, so that is what we did.

TAKING BACK THE OPTION TO CHOOSE FROM THE FAMILY

Paradoxically, another elderly patient, Mrs. O'Brien, wanted to defer to her daughter, but after I explained her options and what choosing the DNR status really meant, she took back the right to make the decision herself. Here's what happened.

Mrs. O'Brien, in her mid-fifties, had been my patient at the hospital for about three years. I met her when she came into the hospital as an unassigned "service patient," which meant that the next doctor in rotation to handle new patients would take her on, and that was me. I saw her at her bedside where I normally see and examine patients and do a short initial interview to decide what to do. She lay in bed wheezing and coughing, with a tank of oxygen by her side. At once I realized she had a bad case of COPD—where one's lungs become more and more inflamed, which obstructs the breathing passage, making it hard to breathe. Other symptoms include having shortness of breath, especially during physical activities, wheezing, experiencing chest tightness, and a chronic cough that produces clear, white, yellow, or greenish sputum.

After listing the classic symptoms that she experienced and she believed were due to "a lifetime of smoking," Mrs. O'Brien went on to explain:

"I'm not doing too well now, doctor. These symptoms have been going on for several weeks, and I feel like this could be the end, since I'm having so much trouble breathing and I cough so much. I feel like I could simply stop breathing, or I could cough so much that I choke to death. So now, because of this damn disease, my life consists of watching TV from the couch, and just about the most exercise I can manage is to click the remote control and go to the bathroom. I sometimes even need assistance to get up and walk there, so sometimes I need to ask my neighbor to help."

Initially, I had thought there was some medical hope for Mrs. O'Brien, so I prescribed some drugs to reduce the inflammation to help her breathing and stop her coughing. So for a while, she could move around outside the house and go shopping, and she carried her oxygen container with her, with clamps on her nose so she could breathe. She even began eating again, though now to excess; she put on about five pounds a week, so after three months she was up about fifty pounds.

"Eating is my hobby. It makes me happy, so I'm very happy now," she said.

But after a few months she was back in my office, sitting across from me with her daughter, since now her COPD was even worse, due in part to her continued smoking, though I had told her to quit. Now I saw no hope of recovery. Though Mrs. O'Brien was still mobile, walking around with her oxygen tank, the inflammation and coughing would become even more severe, so it was time to break this news to her and talk about her death.

As soon as I broached the subject, she told me firmly: "I will defer to my daughter." Her words echoed the response of Mr. Malvani, but her family conditions couldn't be more different, since her daughter was an only child and willing to carry out her mother's wishes whatever they were. Another big difference is that Mrs. O'Brien had no large family with members who had different agendas, so there was no fight over a will or instructions to a successor. Rather, my role was to successfully explain the situation to the daughter, so she would do what her mother wanted. Thus, as I sat by Mrs. O'Brien's bedside, her daughter seated nearby, I explained how the law works and what would be best for her, based on what she told me about her attitude toward her life.

"I understand you have been enjoying what you have now, but you know it won't last, since your shortness of breath and coughing will only get worse. So the right thing to do is to make your own decision now. It can be very hard for your loved ones when you defer to them, since they are going through a very difficult time of their life, too, seeing a loved one suffering. So it's best if you can decide for yourself, while you still can, about how you would like things to end."

"Oh, I see," she said. "Now I clearly understand it's my own responsibility."

Her daughter nodded. "That's fine, mother. I agree you should decide for yourself too."

With that point of contention resolved, I went on to explain that the DNR or "do not resuscitate" status meant that if she was found unresponsive and in a flatline situation, nothing would be done to provide any treatment. "So we'll let you go in peace," I concluded.

"That sounds fine," Mrs. O'Brien agreed, since she now she found it easy to make her own decision. "Yes, that's what I want."

I pulled out one of my DNR forms, handed it to her, and she said she wanted to take it with her.

"I just want to show it to the rest of my family and let them know what my decision is."

Her daughter nodded her agreement. "This way everyone in the family will feel they have been a part of the decision, even though my mother has already made it. We just want to make sure everyone else is in peace with it; so they don't feel like they have been given an ultimatum that this is the way things will be."

"Of course," I agreed.

I pointed to a few short tear-off instructions with the words "DNR/DNI" on them.

"These are instructions that you can carry with you to make others aware of your DNR status, such as if you have a heart attack or suddenly pass out, say while you are shopping. Just cut each of these off and put them in a plastic container or envelope; then you wrap these around your wrist. So, if someone finds you after you have a heart attack or pass out and are no longer breathing and your heart has stopped beating, they will know that you don't want anyone to do anything to revive you. But if your heart is still beating and you have a pulse, they will know to provide you with all the standard care available or seek medical health, just as in any situation where you are still alive with a hope of recovery. The DNR status only applies when a recovery is normally not possible."

Again, both Mrs. O'Brien and her daughter were appreciative for this additional information.

Finally, I wanted to clarify one more point—when the family would make the DNR/DNI decision, though they could do so in keeping with the decision that Mrs. O'Brien had already made.

"Based on your decision, Mrs. O'Brien, the medical team will treat you for all other diseases. The only time your daughter or other family members will be asked to make a decision for you, if you haven't made one already yourself, is when your ability to make decisions is impaired due to brain damage, such as if you experience another and more serious stroke. Then it's up to the medical team to respect your original decision, irrespective of your surviving family wishes. But hopefully, any decision your family might make will match your own. You can even write up your own instructions now, so your family will follow them should that time come."

Later, after I left Mrs. O'Brien and her daughter's room that day, I felt good that not only had Mrs. O'Brien made the right decision to have a DNR status when the time came, but her daughter was fully onboard both with her mother making the decision and with the decision her mother made. At the same time, I recognized that both Mrs. O'Brien and her daughter wanted to include the rest of the family in knowing and accepting her decision so they could feel a part of the process, though Mrs. O'Brien was the only one making that decision. In this way, Mrs. O'Brien and her daughter felt more comfortable knowing that the rest of their family understood that she was dying, and they accepted how she wanted to end her days.

NEGOTIATING THE FAMILY TRIANGLE TO DECIDE WHAT TO DO

In some cases, it can feel like being caught in a triangle when two family members have different ideas about what should be done at the end and when the patient's prognosis is uncertain after undergoing surgery. Then the choices can go back and forth, prolonging the patient's pain and suffering for weeks or months, and the long process of deciding is not in the patient's best interest since the likelihood of a recovery is virtually nil. Yet the hope of recovery fuels the effort to extend life in the face of daunting odds.

That was what happened for Mrs. Byrne, a woman in her seventies who had gynecologic cancer, which is cancer of the female reproductive organs, including the cervix, ovaries, uterus, fallopian tubes, vagina, and vulva. Before she became ill, she had been fairly active in local community activities and had a close relationship with her two daughters who lived nearby and with her son who lived in another state.

Unfortunately, one of her daughters, Cynthia, was determined to find a cure for her mother and remained optimistic in spite of medical opinions to the contrary. As a result, Cynthia had arranged for her mother to have surgery about four months earlier, although the medical team said it was unlikely to produce a good outcome. But Cynthia insisted, so Mrs. Byrne agreed to placate Cynthia rather than because she wanted the surgery. As a result, the surgeon removed many of the organs in her pelvic region, including her ovaries, uterus, and fallopian tubes.

Unfortunately, one of the complications of this removal is the formation of other wounds in the same area in the form of fistulas, which are tunnels containing stool from the intestines that extend all the way to the abdominal wall surface. When this occurs, there may be no cure.

Still, Cynthia wanted the surgery for her mother, and after Mrs. Byrne spent a few months of healing, including a prolonged stay in the hospital, Cynthia took her mother to a nursing home. But Mrs. Byrne felt that the nursing home wasn't properly caring for her for various reasons, such as the room being too small and a lack of immediate service. So Cynthia brought her mother back to the hospital, where I saw her one more time.

I first met with Cynthia at Mrs. Byrne's bedside, where she told me how she felt about the situation.

"I want to see my mother cured, and I'd like her to have the highest level of care possible."

I tried to dissuade her from continuing care.

"Your mother has already had some surgery four months ago to remove the cancerous organs, but she hasn't been healing well and the cancer has already returned. So the only possible option is to remove even more tissue to completely eliminate any remaining cancer cells. But doing so is likely to be impossible, since the new wound will be so large that it will never heal. Moreover, due to this operation, your mother will be left with really big holes in her reproductive area, which will be impossible to fill with any surrounding tissue, since this will already have been removed during surgery. Additionally, your mother has been going through a great deal of pain and suffering for months now without any signs of improvement of her wounds."

"But I want the doctors to do everything they can. I want the best for my mother now, especially since I feel I failed her before by not getting her in better condition."

I tried to reassure her and point out that she was not to blame.

"Don't blame yourself for anything," I told her. "How can you be responsible? You live apart; your mother has been independent for years. And this disease could strike anyone and can be hard to detect."

"That's all true. But I should have been more careful that she was eating well. I should have noticed when she looked paler and had less energy, so I should have recommended that she see a doctor sooner. That's why I feel so guilty and want to be there for my mother now."

"These were decisions for your mother to make. So you shouldn't blame yourself for anything."

Cynthia leaned back, a little less tense, though I still felt she might be blaming herself and feeling she needed to cure her mother to absolve herself.

But before our conversation could continue, Mrs. Byrne's son, Will, arrived. A few minutes later her husband, sister, and brother-in-law came, too, to see how she was doing. I led them into her private room where she was sitting up, with several vases of flowers scattered around, giving the room a sunny, festive air. After greetings all around, I asked Mrs. Byrne:

"What do you want to do about your future treatment?" I asked. "Your daughter and I were talking about an additional surgery to remove the cancer that returned, though I recommend against any more surgeries, since the cancer has progressed so far and has returned."

Mrs. Byrne smiled wanly at Cynthia, Will, and her sister and brother-in-law.

"I can just go with the flow," she said. "I can do whatever my daughter, son, and other relatives here tell me to do."

Will immediately jumped in, firmly stating that he wanted to do what Cynthia wanted.

"Let's see what modern medicine can do. It can work miracles these days," he insisted.

"But it's your decision," I reminded Mrs. Byrne. "And sometimes people have an unrealistic idea of what is possible because of what they see in the medical TV shows."

Mrs. Byrne smiled sweetly at me. "I know. But I'm fine with whatever they decide."

Thus, I continued my discussion with her family members in my office. Again, I emphasized the futility of further surgery or any hope for a cure.

"So the best thing is to reduce her pain and suffering now," I said. "We are proposing to use some injections. But these narcotics are only used to dull the pain, not like using a narcotic for recreational use, which is illegal. In your mother's case, her wounds are so severe and painful that she needs this. Otherwise the pain would be excruciating, especially when the nurses try to clean the wounds to heal them. It's very painful to do this, because this open tissue is like what's left after a burn."

At last Cynthia agreed with me that we should determine the best way to reduce her mother's pain, and the husband, sister, and brother-in-law went along, after Will first objected to using narcotics, asking: "Aren't they supposed to be illegal?"

"Not in a hospital for medical use," I explained.

So now everyone was in agreement. The nurses gave Mrs. Byrne a series of injections later that day and in the morning to dull the pain. The next day, Will returned a little sheepish and now was much more reasonable.

"I'm sorry I was so set against narcotics yesterday," he said. "I guess whatever you think is most humane, do that. Some medical team members suggested that a hospice might be a humane option for my mother's lasts months."

But while Will seemed quite reasonable now, the next problem was Mrs. Byrne's husband when I next met with her, as her sister and brother-in-law sat nearby. When I asked her: "What do you want to do about your further treatment?" he jumped in with his own view.

"I think we should reinitiate the treatment and refer my wife back to the surgical team that performed the original procedure in the big university hospital. They will already be familiar with her case and can remove any further cancer that has developed."

I tried to convince him otherwise. "But the outcome has already been unsuccessful after several months, and this will just mean more pain and suffering."

"That'll be worth it, if that operation will get rid of the cancer and cure her."

Again, Mrs. Byrne deferred to whoever was making the decision, so I felt I had no more options. I had to prepare the necessary paperwork to transfer her back to the tertiary care center, so the surgeons there could evaluate her and consider performing additional operations, or most likely making no intervention at all.

But just as I was about to turn in the transfer paperwork at the reception desk, Will appeared. Now he had a more humane opinion of what to do with his mother.

"I don't think my mother should go to that care center and have another operation," he said. "In fact, this morning, my mother met with a very dear friend, and she asked her friend not to allow anybody to move her to this other center, which would only increase her pain and suffering. Now I understand what she has been going through, and I agree. She should only be given whatever painkillers are necessary so she doesn't continue to suffer. I don't think the doctors and surgeons can do anything more to help her now."

Thus, as they say, "All's well that ends well." Though Cynthia continued to blame herself for failing to take proper care of her mother in the early stages and wished that more could be done to reverse the cancer, Mrs. Byrne and the rest of the family was united in the decision to focus on care and comfort by placing her in a hospice for her final days. There would be no more operations that were almost certain not to succeed. Instead, Mrs. Byrne would have painkillers to ease the pain and could relax until her death several months away.

"BUT WE DON'T UNDERSTAND"

Occasionally, the family members of the patient, as well as the patient, have difficulty understanding the different choices about treatment the patient or relatives have to make, if the patient can no longer make these choices.

That's what happened for Sophia and her son Derek, who was the last of her living relatives in the area, since she had outlived them all or they lived across the country and chose not to visit in her last days. Initially, Sophia, in her early sixties, came to the hospital with syncope, which involves a temporary loss of consciousness and posture, so she experienced a recurring series of incidents where she fainted or passed out, sometimes at very inconvenient times. For example, she would be shopping and would suddenly fall in front of the counter with the items she wanted to purchase. Usually, the store owner would be so concerned that he would let her take whatever she was going to purchase for free, so her blackout spells actually generated a substantial profit because she took home so much free merchandise. But other than that upside, she dreaded these incidents, which could occur at any time. She also found her blackouts very embarrassing, especially when she was with friends, who had to grab her and deal with the mall and store personnel for several minutes, before she could rouse herself, sit up, and say: "I'm okay."

After hearing about her experiences, I described the condition she might have and asked her some questions to determine what was causing the problem, since this could be a temporary condition rather than an end-of-life condition.

"Blackouts are usually related to temporary insufficient blood flow to the brain, because when the blood pressure is too low, your heart doesn't pump a normal supply of oxygen to the brain. That could happen for a number of reasons, such as if you have been under emotional stress or your blood pools in your legs after you suddenly changed your body position. These blackouts might also occur if you experience overheating, pain, dehydration, heavy sweating, exhaustion, or prolonged coughing, or they could be a side effect of some medicines."

Sophia thought for a while and then replied: "No, I don't think they're because of any of those causes. I don't feel under much stress now, since I recently retired as a teacher and feel more relaxed, because I don't have to deal with a lot of young kids. I haven't done any extensive exercising or sports activities. And I haven't been sick with a cold or anything like that recently, so I'm not taking any special medicines—mostly I'm just taking some vitamin pills."

Thus, there appeared to be no obvious reason for her syncope condition, leading me to suggest some blood tests, X-rays, and other lab work to see what might be wrong.

Finally, after several days of testing and waiting for results, I discovered the culprit. Sophia had a valvular lesion—a lesion on one of the large valves from the arteries leading to the heart, suggesting the possibility of further cardiac disease.

"We might be able to repair this lesion," I told her. "So we'd like to perform a cardiac catheterization, which involves checking your heart from inside by using catheters and dye to study your valves and coronary arteries. Then we can assess the possibility of replacing the valve with one made of a synthetic material."

Sophia looked at me blankly, like she didn't fully comprehend what I was talking about, but she agreed.

"I guess you know best," she said.

However, after the cardiologists performed the cardiac catheterization and evaluated the options for replacing the valve, they discovered that Sophie had an extensive tumor from her chest area to her pelvis, and there was a large balloon-like mass in her groin. After that, they closed her up and considered what might be done next. Could the extensive tumor be removed by surgery? Or would the patient be likely to die of the surgery? And if surgery was not to be done, what should I as her doctor tell her?

It was at this point that a failure to understand Sophia's serious condition became a problem, both in dealing with Sophia and with her thirtysomething son, Nathan. I met with Sophia in her semiprivate room and Nathan joined us, since I called him as her nearest relative.

Sophia smiled wanly as I sat down at her bedside and Nathan stood nearby. After I glanced at the chart at the foot of her bed, I could tell that a number of other doctors—her surgeon, his assistant, and several cardiologists and oncologists—had stopped by to check on her condition, and they described the extensive damage of the tumors to her system and her difficulty in accepting this condition. So what could I do? I felt I might be able to build on what the doctors had done before to support my recommended treatment—no more surgery and the use of painkillers to make the pain at the end bearable. Though Sophia might not want to believe it, she had to know the truth.

"I'm very sorry to be the bearers of bad news," I told her. "But what the other doctors have told you is true. The tumor has spread throughout your body from your heart to your pelvis, and there is no way we can operate to remove that much tissue without you dying on the operating table. Given the size of the tumor, you have about two to three months to live. I'm so sorry."

"But I don't understand," Sophia responded. "I've just been passing out and having trouble breathing."

"But all of your bodily systems are connected. So the tumors have caused your blood to get blocked as it goes to the brain. Your blood doesn't get there fast enough, and that's why you've been blacking out."

"Then can you do something to make the blood go faster, like giving me some pills to thin the blood?"

"That won't work because of the tumors," I began, when Nathan began asking the same questions over and over with a slight variation in wording, as if he, too, didn't want to acknowledge the true health state of his mother.

"So why not thin the blood? . . . How can my mother have tumors in her pelvis that cause her blackouts? . . . Why wouldn't an operation to replace the valve in her heart solve the problem? . . . Can the surgeons put in another one? . . . What about natural herbs to shrink the tumors?"

His questions went on and on, and I felt exhausted trying to answer them all.

Finally, the meeting at her bedside ended with Sophia saying: "I don't want any further treatment now."

"We should get another opinion at another institution," Nathan said.

I quickly agreed, since I hoped this added input would convince him of the seriousness and irreversibility of his mother's condition.

Soon after that meeting, Sophia decided she wanted to go home, and Nathan agreed she should.

A few hours later, Sophia checked out with the aid of her son, though the herbal remedy she tried didn't work and the second opinion echoed my own. Now it was time to finally acknowledge the inevitable—Sophia was going to die within a few days or weeks, and we could do nothing more, except make her last days as comfortable as possible and reduce the pain.

WHEN RELIGION AFFECTS THE FAMILY DECISION ABOUT TREATMENT

Sometimes the patient's and family's religion complicates the decision about how to treat the patient and handle the final days. Both the patient and family members may wrongly believe their religion requires them to do everything possible to maintain life at the end, despite any suffering for the patient. They can't, they believe, *not* take such actions.

That's what happened for Duong Do and his family, who had emigrated from China over fifty years ago. They still maintained their family traditions and followed the teachings of Buddhism. Among other things, they believed in following certain right-living practices contained in the Noble Eightfold Path. The system is fairly complicated, but essentially the eight factors are: Right Understanding, Right Intention, Right Speech, Right Action, Right Livelihood, Right Effort, Right Mindfulness, and Right Concentration. The family members felt it important to apply these principles to the end of Duong's life, which meant doing everything possible to maintain his life, until it was ultimately the time to let go.

Unfortunately, at eighty-three years old, Duong had been experiencing numerous medical problems. Among other things, his kidneys failed, so he had been on dialysis for ten years, and he had many chronic conditions. One was a heart condition called "atrial fibrillation" in which an individual experiences an abnormal heart rhythm characterized by rapid and irregular beating, which at other times is accompanied by heart palpitations, fainting, shortness of breath, or chest pains. The disease also increases the risk of heart failure, dementia, and stroke. In addition, Duong had been blind for the past five years and was largely bedridden because of all these conditions. However, he had the support of a large and loving family, who came over regularly to visit and assist with his day-to-day functioning, from preparing his meals to carrying him to the bathroom as needed.

So Duong was essentially living in a day-to-day end-of-life situation, where he could die from any number of conditions at any time, though his family wanted to do everything possible to keep him alive for as long as possible. They considered any death to be a transition from one stage of life to another, so they felt it would be wrong to disrupt or speed up this transition, rather than letting it occur naturally. Duong's son explained the circumstances to me, as seven children and grandchildren and Duong's sister and brothers sat across from me in my office:

"Because of our religion, we regard this as a go-go-go situation, so we have to let Duong keep going, going, and going, as long as he can live."

I tried to explain that a DNR status didn't mean withdrawing care. "You have to understand that Duong has a terminal condition and is very near death. Since he can no longer make this decision for himself, it is up to you. So I hope you'll understand that a DNR status doesn't mean we will not care for him as long as we can. We will continue giving him the nutrients he needs by tube to stay alive, as well as the painkillers to relieve his suffering."

But the family members seemed not to understand what I was saying and were determined to follow what they believed they should do according to their traditional Buddhist practices.

"That's not what we want to do," said Duong's oldest son. "We want you to keep treating him as long as he is still alive."

As the family filed out, Duong's daughter remained in the back to ask me a question.

"Are you saying Duong is no longer alive, when you stop the treatment?"

"Yes. His body is essentially dead after he goes into cardiac arrest for several minutes, and trying to resuscitate him at this point just extends the pain and suffering for a few more days."

"Oh, I see," said the daughter.

"So can you try to explain this to the other family members? Otherwise, I am very worried about his last days. He will only suffer needlessly."

Though his daughter tried, her explanation didn't make any difference. About ten hours later that day, in the early evening, Duong did go into cardiac arrest while about a dozen family members were visiting him. A loud whistle went off, alerting the staff that Duong's heart line on the monitor had flatlined, indicating he was in cardiac arrest, and suddenly a half-dozen nurses and a doctor appeared with tubes and defibrillators. If Duong had a DNR status, no one would have come in, and he would be allowed to die quietly. However, since he had full-code status, the medical team put the defibrillators and other equipment on his body and began pounding and pumping.

After a few minutes, Duong jerked several times, yelled in agony with each jerk, and began breathing again. After that he lay in bed breathing heavily and moaning slightly, still suffering, as a nurse gave him morphine to numb the pain.

In the morning, I went in to see Duong in the ICU, where he had been moved for close monitoring. His older son, the daughter I had spoken to, and eight other family members were still there, and they were clearly shaken by what they had observed.

"I didn't realize how much pain he would experience," said the oldest son.

"I didn't know they would have to break several ribs to resuscitate him," said a second son.

Finally, the family members agreed that the nurse should administer medications only to reduce the pain.

"Then if he dies under those circumstance, we're all okay with it," said the eldest son. "Though we hope he will survive long enough for some other relatives to arrive, so they can pay their respects."

"The medical team will do all they can to do that," I said.

Later that day, I made one last check of the patient, noting that his overall condition was quite dismal. As I wrote in my journal notes for that day:

"He is on every medication that we have available to keep his blood pressure and heart going. His blood pressure is still on the low side. He has received plenty of fluids through his veins. However, he is suffering from a buildup of fluids throughout his body, because his kidneys are not functioning to make urine. So now he is literally drowning from within."

Then I left, feeling I had done all I could and pleased that his last relatives might arrive before his final demise, which they did. Once they were all there, in keeping with their Buddhist practice, they shared some last prayers over his bed, hoping he would find happiness in the other world and that he would come back to a better place.

WHEN A DEATH DRAWS BACK AN ESTRANGED FAMILY

Normally, a family draws together when a family member is dying, because the family members want to express how much they have loved that person before his or her passing. Also, family members can reinforce their family connections and gain support for their feelings of loss and grief.

But sometimes this isn't the case when the patient has become estranged from his or her family for some reason. As a result, family members may not come to see the patient in the hospital, hospice, nursing home, or home where he or she is in the final stages of the dying. Or only a few may come reluctantly, because they are the heirs and arrive to help wrap up affairs.

That was the case for Betty Austin, a forty-five-year-old patient in the ICU for end-stage liver disease due to cirrhosis of the liver—the result of over a decade of alcohol abuse. At one time, Betty was married and had three children before her divorce at twenty-three due to her drinking and her husband discovering her ongoing lesbian relationship. He left her and took sole custody of the very young children, whom Betty saw only a few times over the years. Soon after he left, Betty and her girlfriend entered into a marriage commitment, later formalized after gay marriages became legalized. Meanwhile, Betty continued her heavy drinking and increasingly used different types of drugs, from marijuana and ecstasy to heroin, to get high. Under the circumstances, her own parents disowned her because they disapproved of her lifestyle and behavior, including the drinking, drugs, and the lesbian marriage. As conservative Christians, they felt Betty was living in sin and would eventually pay for her sins. When she was diagnosed with cirrhosis of the liver, they felt this was her just desserts for the way she had decided to live.

When I first saw her in my office after her liver condition had flared up, she was suffering from tremors and other symptoms of alcoholism, which included confusion, disorientation, coma, a large belly from fluid accumulating around her liver, jaundice, weakness, malnutrition, and an emaciated appearance. In short, she looked and felt like a mess, and she was looking for some pills to feel better. Rather than prescribing anything, I warned her to stop or at least cut down on the alcohol and drugs. Then I told her about her code-status options.

"Well, don't resuscitate me if I go into cardiac arrest," she replied. "But help me breathe again if I have a reversible state."

I agreed, and left her with a warning: "Get into an alcohol and drugs support program to help you stop drinking and taking drugs. They are only going to kill you."

"Sure, doc," she said, smiling slyly, so I knew she had no intention of stopping, and I felt it only a matter of time before she was back.

That's what happened two years later, when Betty entered the hospital with trouble breathing and was transferred to the ICU.

She was extremely sick and was hooked up to a BiPAP machine when I went over to her bedside. She recognized me immediately from our previous discussions.

"So we meet again, doc," she said, smiling wanly. "Like you said, it was only a matter of time. But I couldn't quit drinking and taking drugs. I liked the feeling of escaping reality and getting high too much. So here I am again. And I know it's worse."

"Yes, it is. Much worse," I told her.

I had arranged for the medical team to put her in the ICU so I could monitor her closely. At least the BiPAP machine could keep her breathing, though she was very weak, couldn't eat, and had to be fed by a tube. She made no final decision on resuscitation at this time, and unfortunately, after two days, she slipped into a deep coma. At that point, the BiPAP could no longer keep her breathing because her airway could easily be blocked by secretions or vomit, and she would not be able to defend herself, so she would choke to death.

Since she was now comatose, I felt the only option was to contact her family members, even though she had been estranged from them for many years and had broken up with her wife. So the only family members remaining were her three children from her first marriage and their marriage partners.

"Your mother is near death," I explained. "Since you are her only kin left, I'd like to talk to you about the final arrangements."

The next day, her two sons, their wives, and a daughter and her husband sat in my office, and I began by explaining the situation.

"The situation is essentially terminal. Although your mother is only forty-five years old, she is about twice her age medically because of her past medical problems including diabetes, severe malnutrition, pulmonary disease, liver cirrhosis, and a chronic state of edema or water retention."

They looked at me in stunned silence, since this was the first they had heard of their mother's condition in many years.

"We didn't know," her oldest son finally said. "She's been out of touch with us for so long, living her own life."

"Maybe she could still be helped since she's only forty-five," said her daughter.

"But despite her age, her condition is really terminal. There are so many medical problems that can't be fixed," I said.

However, they were still reluctant to let her go in peace.

"Let's try to save her," her oldest son said.

"Do whatever you can," her daughter said.

As a result, I agreed to let her remain in the ICU. Yet, after three days, she was still in a coma and one of the intensive team doctors came to my office and asked me: "Should we intubate her or not, since she is actively dying?"

I knew we needed an answer. The issue, however, was the extremely controversial idea of stopping care because of medical futility versus prolonging her suffering to satisfy family members. I met with the family members again to let them know, "This is medically futile. We can't do anything more."

Yet the older brother, speaking on behalf of the rest of the family, questioned my prognosis, since they wanted to proceed.

"How certain are you that our mother will die of her condition?"

I responded with my usual answer to this question. "If I could read the future, we would know definitively what the outcome of any procedure would be. But the opinion of the half-dozen doctors who have seen her is that there is no hope she will survive. We believe we should proceed with mechanical ventilation as needed, but do nothing more, which were her wishes when she still was able to make her choices known.

"She said she wanted to end her life with 'dignity' if she had a cardiac arrest. Also, you need to understand that the two key issues are the continued operation of her heart and her lungs. Her heart could still be beating, but her lungs have become so diseased that no medical therapy can treat this. Even if we attach her to a mechanical ventilation machine, there is no hope that she would come back. I think if your mother was alive and well, she would want to be taken off any supporting medical devices to die in peace."

Yet for all my effort to convince the family, based on both the medical assessment and the patient's wishes, they remained unconvinced. But why? Why were they so interested in taking charge of their mother's situation when they had been estranged from her for years because of her heavy drinking and drug use? Why assert themselves so forcefully now and in opposition to what their mother wanted and the unanimous medical opinion about what to do?

It was hard to know why, but I believed they resisted their mother's request to die in peace without further treatment, because they may have felt some guilt for her condition, since they hadn't intervened earlier when she might have gotten the needed support to end her self-destructive, addictive behavior. Instead, they had each walked away, not approving of their mother's behavior and feeling embarrassed by it. But perhaps now that their mother was dying, they wanted to aggressively act to save her even if it was too late to do so.

Anyway, for whatever reason they acted as they did, I couldn't do anything more. Despite my recommendations and the opinions of a half-dozen doctors, they chose to push for continued intubation. Since they were now in charge of the medical decision making, that's what was done. Though this choice was against Betty's more realistic wishes when she was well and still able to decide for herself, now her fate was in her children's hands, and they wanted to keep her alive as long as they could, even if she was in a coma and the medical team had to keep resuscitating her to keep her body functioning. At the same time, the team kept giving her painkillers to prevent her body from experiencing any pain, until mercifully, she finally died. After that, her children went home feeling they had done their part to give their mother the chance of coming back, though medically I and the other doctors who reviewed her case thought this was impossible.

WHEN A FAMILY MEMBER'S PERSONAL SITUATION AFFECTS A CHOICE

Normally, even when they are wrong, family members make choices about whether to resuscitate a dying patient or not based on what they think is best for the patient. Altruistically, they try to put their own wants and needs aside. So commonly they defer to what the patient wants in accordance with their cultural or religious values and beliefs.

However, in some rare cases, a family member may put their own needs first in making an end-of-life decision, to the detriment of the patient. That's what happened to Mr. Thompson, an eighty-something veteran. His daughter Kim initially brought him to the hospital for a recurrent urinary tract infection. When the first-line doctors examined him, they discovered that he had a major stroke that led to his weakness on one side, making it difficult for him to stand or walk without leaning on someone for help. Moreover, the examination showed that he had the beginning stages of dementia, Parkinson's disease, and another stroke, which affected his ability to think, speak, stand, or walk around, as indicated on his medical charts. As a result, Mr. Thompson couldn't understand any question about resuscitation or DNR status. He couldn't think clearly or understand anything said to him aside from the simplest instructions such as "Stand up," "Sit down," and "Go to your left or right."

Thus, after he and Kim sat down across from me in my office, I turned to Kim, expecting her to make the decisions for him and gave her a quick rundown of the medical findings.

"So your father has multiple problems," I concluded. "And his strokes have prevented him from understanding the choices that are available after his condition becomes terminal, which is likely soon because of his many medical problems. So I recommend the most humane approach to reduce his pain and suffering at the end is by not resuscitating him after a cardiac arrest."

Kim quickly agreed. "Yes, I think that would be the most humane approach to his care."

But everything changed when Mr. Thompson was later admitted for having seizures and trouble breathing. Soon after, his thinking further deteriorated so that he could no longer even remember his own name or recognize his daughter. As a result, a team of nurses and orderlies strapped him to a gurney and rushed him to the ICU unit, where he was placed on a ventilator.

Kim stood with me in the hallway, watching him go in. Then I led her back to my office to discuss his case.

I pulled out his file from my desk drawer, and as I flipped through it, I saw the DNR order from Mr. Thompson's previous admission.

"We already have this DNR on file," I said, "so everything should be set. We'll do everything we can to care for your father. But we won't resuscitate him when his time comes."

I thought that would be the end of the discussion, but suddenly, Kim argued that his DNR order should be changed back to full code. Later I found out through the social service that she had said, "If he dies, I will become homeless."

"You can't be serious," I said when I confronted her, and she gave me a document to indicate that she had the authority to act as a proxy for her father, as she was his only direct heir because his other children and wife had passed away and he was quite alone. But could her document supplant his original DNR order?

"You have to recognize this," Kim said. "I had a lawyer friend draw this up for me when I realized that once my father died, I would be cut off from receiving any pension and welfare money. So this is a request to change the DNR to a full-code status."

Though the document did give her that power, it was a shock to have Kim tell me this, since it was the opposite of her father's wishes and not in his best interest to reduce his pain and suffering. Rather, it was in her interest to keep him alive for her own monetary gain. I felt the request not only unethical, but it brought into question her ability to be her father's proxy because proxies are supposed to act in the patient's best interest.

But what if she was acting to the patient's detriment because her proxy status enabled her to do something contrary to the patient's best interest? Certainly the initial DNR order from her father was the most humane way to approach his end-of-life situation. But barring a legal challenge, Kim was the proxy if Mr. Thompson no longer had the mental ability to make any choice. Unfortunately, in this situation, Kim was in control and the DNR order was changed to full-code status, since the hospital was not about to initiate litigation over this change even if it was against the patient's best interest.

As Kim left with the DNR order changed, the whole incident left a bad taste in my mouth. I felt what she had done was completely unethical and she should no longer have the right to be her father's proxy. But regardless of how I felt or how other doctors who knew about the situation were likely to feel, there was nothing we could do. Kim had the legal power in this situation unless challenged, and since no one was going to challenge her, there was nothing more to do. It was unfair, but for now, I and other doctors could do nothing more, since we were not about to mount a legal challenge due to the high expense of what could be lengthy litigation lasting for years.

WHO'S IN CHARGE?

Sometimes a lot of confusion can arise over who is giving the instructions about end-of-life treatment when the patient gives unclear instructions about his or her resuscitation status, and different family members have different ideas about what to do and are present at different times. In this situation, it becomes uncertain what to do and how to determine the legal status of the different requests.

That's what happened for Betty Murphy, a fifty-something woman, who was active in local society events from charity balls to teas in elegant restaurants. Then she got vulvar cancer, a cancer of a woman's external genitalia, which are composed of the skin and fatty tissue that surround the clitoris and the openings of the vagina and urethra. Betty had several operations to remove the cancer, but it kept recurring.

Now she was back with a urinary tract infection that spread through the bloodstream, so she had become septic, meaning that the infection had spread throughout her body. Initially, I had treated her with antibiotics to fight the infection, and she had gotten a lot better. But she still faced the danger that both the infection and her cancer could return and be terminal. So I had to prepare her for this eventuality and determine what she wanted to do about her resuscitation status at the end.

I met with her in her private room, where she sat in her bed, her mother seated to one side and holding her hand sympathetically.

I began by asking her: "Have you decided on your resuscitation status?"

When Betty answered, she at first was very clear in opting not to be resuscitated. But her family members had different views from what she stated and from each other.

"My mother and father already signed the do not resuscitate orders," she began.

However, Betty's daughter Nicole, a young mother in her thirties, quickly jumped in.

"No, that's not what you should do. I'm in the room now, and I'm much closer to my mother than her parents are. So you should do everything to bring her back."

Betty looked surprised, but didn't say anything, as if she was afraid to get in the middle of the battle between her daughter and her parents.

I tried to sort things out after I finished checking Betty's vital signs with my stethoscope and looked at the monitor graphing her breathing and heart rate. I took Nicole into one of the conference rooms to discuss her mother's situation. But before I could say anything, Nicole presented her position like she was performing her regular job as a management consultant.

"Look, if my mother's heart stops and she stops breathing, I want you to do everything to bring her back. It's my role to oversee her care now."

I tried to explain the legal position surrounding the DNR/full-code options. "Then we have a problem. This is an unusual situation, because we are bound by law to go by the patient's wishes. And in this case, Betty's living husband has the same wish, that we don't resuscitate her. "

"But he's not here, and if I'm present in the room and he isn't, then I have the right to make the decision."

"No, that's not correct," I said. "It does not matter who is here. The patient's wishes are our orders. All we need is the patient's verbal request, and we follow-up what the patient wants with a written order. Then we execute the plan on the patient's death, and others have to respect the order. But to be sure, I will check into the legal status."

So for the moment, Nicole's efforts to change the order were stayed, and she quietly nodded. "Okay, I'll wait for a legal opinion before I do anything."

However, before I could do any checking, over the next day, Betty's condition deteriorated and she had a cardiopulmonary arrest; both her heart and breathing stopped. Moments later, the doctor on call called me and described his dilemma.

"I'm not sure what to do. I thought the patient is DNR and DNI, and that's what's documented on her chart. But her daughter was present in her room when her cardiopulmonary arrest happened. She invoked her ability to make the decision, and she said she wants the full code to proceed. So we did start CPR, because otherwise, Mrs. Murphy would be dead, and there would be no way to discuss whether to treat her or not."

I had to think for a moment because I wasn't clear about what to recommend at this stage: the cardiopulmonary resuscitation had already been going on for a while, so who had the power to make this decision was immaterial at this point. Normally, Betty's husband would be next in line to decide if she couldn't, and his directive was in keeping with what Betty's parents wanted. But he wasn't in the room when the emergency happened; the daughter was. So the question was what to do. My first inclination was to respect the patient's wishes, as provided in the documentation provided by the husband, since the parents supported this decision, too. But since the daughter was present and the husband was absent, it seemed like she now had the power to rescind the DRN/DNI status and insist on going full code, though legally that was not the case. In a practical situation like this one, a doctor may start the resuscitation until matters are clarified. Then, assuming the patient has chosen a DNR/DNI status, it is a matter of gently stopping resuscitation and executing the patient's real wishes over what relatives otherwise may want.

Meanwhile, as the medical team continued to use CPR to keep Betty alive if possible, I tried to explain to Nicole that it was possible to use a more humane approach regardless of who had the legal authority. But the daughter was adamant. "No. I'm here now, and I want everything done that can be done for my mother."

Thus, with time running out on the ability of the medical team to resuscitate her mother, I decided the most sensible thing, whether Nicole had the power to make the decision or not, was to order the medical team to continue the resuscitation effort. That would possibly reduce the hospital's liability for not resuscitating a patient when a DNR order was replaced by an order to go full code. On the other hand, the hospital could legally be liable to a charge of assault and battery by subjecting a patient to unwanted resuscitation if the patient had a DNR/DNI status. Thus, it was a very tricky situation from a legal perspective as to whether to honor the patient's request for a DNR/DNI status or the daughter's claim that as the proxy she had the right to order a full-code status. Medically, the best possible option seemed to be to keep Betty alive through resuscitation as long as possible, since once she died, any conversation about what to do would become moot.

Accordintly, I told the on-call doctor to continue with the resuscitation plan for now, and he rushed off to advise the medical team to do so. The result was that Betty was revived successfully, woke up long enough to let her daughter know she appreciated her being there, but the following night died. And this time, the attempt to resuscitate her didn't work, so in the end, whether the DNR order was in place or not, she died peacefully a day later, and Nicole seemed to feel comfortable with that outcome. She had done her best to save her mom, but ultimately, she couldn't do so because the power of the disease and infection was too great.

Meanwhile, I tried to get some clarification on what to do in this legal limbo where relatives have different ideas about what to do and patients can no longer express their own wishes. How does the medical team determine who is really in charge, so they know what to do? It would seem like the best solution is to have a detailed, informative meeting to explain the medical realities to the family members who are in line to decide when the patient cannot. This way they can better understand what modern medicine can and can't do.

Unfortunately, many people have a vision of doctors performing medical miracles, so they need to understand that in the face of a very severe illness, injury, infection, or other medical problem, medicine can only do so much. In most terminal cases, doctors can only be successful in about 10 to 15 percent of the resuscitation cases where patients are revived in order to heal from a serious condition, or in my experience a cardiac arrest, where a patient has "died" according to the usual criteria for death, but then is revived. But in the vast majority of cases, any attempt to resuscitate the patient will only prolong his or her pain and suffering, so the most humane thing is not do anything and let the patient die in peace.

Despite all of these medical and legal considerations, it's up to the patient or the next family member in line to make the actual determination of what to do. The doctors can only recommend and do what the patient or the family member wants. If the situation is confused so there is no obvious clear legal path, as in Betty's case, the most conservative legal choice seems to be to go with the full-code option. This way at least the patient can still survive in case the full-code option is the appropriate choice, whereas if the DNR option is chosen and the legal determination is that the patient should be full code, that option is not possible after the patient has died. On the other hand, should the full-code option be chosen and should the legal determination be that the DNR choice was the correct one, at least any hospital liability is limited to an assault-and-battery charge for causing the patient additional pain and suffering. Any litigation or penalties are probably unlikely, since the hospital has chosen the more conservative response in a murky legal situation. Thus, where the legal status of who should decide is unclear, attempting to resuscitate the patient might be the best path to choose when the patient experiences another cardiac arrest and stops breathing.

Ironically, this kind of transgression of a DNR order happens every day because the first responders do not normally know what a patient's DNR status is, so they do what they know how to do, which is to resuscitate the patient if possible, since the alternative is death.

SUMMING UP—THE PROBLEM WITH DEALING WITH FAMILIES

As the previous discussion has shown, the families of patients can create many complications in deciding what to do about a patient's treatment. The major problem comes when one or more family members have different opinions about DNR/full-code status than the patient or than other family members. So there can be an extended period of discussion, debate, and conflict over what to do.

While doctors and others on the medical team may recommend choosing the DNR/DNI option as the most humane approach possible in the face of a terminal, irreversible condition, they can only recommend. Ultimately, it is up to the patient or, if he or she can't choose or prefers to defer to a family member, up to that family member.

However, complicating matters is the question of which family member has the right to decide when they disagree. Complications can ensue because this right can hinge not only on the closeness of the family member to the patient, but whether that person is present when an emergency occurs due to the patient's heart and breathing stopping.

What is the correct lineup in determining which family member has the power to decide when the patient can't decide and family members disagree? And what happens when patients change their mind about what they want or about which family member should act as a proxy when they can no longer decide? Ultimately, as they say in law school, it depends on many different factors. As best they can, doctors have to work through these complications with the patient and family members in deciding what to do.

11

A LACK OF UNDERSTANDING

Often the major reason that patients or their families have trouble making decisions about what to do is they don't understand what happens at the end of life and the different choices available to them. Often they think there is a simple distinction between life and death, but there are stages of dying, where differences exist between brain death due to irreversible damage and the heart stopping leading to a cardiac arrest, which can result in death in minutes. What can be confusing is when there is no longer any brain function so the person is brain dead, but the person's body still survives and will continue do so if further nutrition is provided by tubes and breathing is enabled by ventilators. At this point, whether or not the individual still experiences pain is uncertain. But a morphine drip is usually included along with nutrition and a ventilator to make sure there is no pain or suffering. But is the patient still surviving or dead at this point? And does the patient or family want the patient to be kept alive under these circumstances?

Sometimes it can be hard to get the patient or family to understand these distinctions, especially when a decision of whether to continue treatment or not must be made under very difficult circumstances. It is a time when patients and their families are experiencing a great deal of fear and anxiety. Still, I try to explain the options and make my recommendations as best as I can at this difficult time. This lack of understanding played a major part in making the following cases especially difficult to deal with.

I DON'T KNOW WHAT IT ALL MEANS

A good example of how this lack of understanding can interfere with a patient making an informed decision is the case of Florence, an eighty-five-year old woman, suffering from chronic obstructive pulmonary disease (COPD), which involves growing damage to the lung. As described in an earlier chapter, this condition, like asthma, makes it hard to breathe. The symptoms can get progressively worse over time.

When I met her, Florence was living in a retirement community with the regular assistance of a home healthcare worker, supported by her social security. She also survived on regular checks from her daughter Cherise, who lived in California, and they mainly stayed in touch with phone calls every two weeks. Otherwise Cherise was living a separate life, so Florence now lived mostly on her own. Though at one time, Florence went to occasional events, such a night at the movies or a bridge game with other women in their eighties, for the past year she had difficulty walking, so she could no longer do her own grocery shopping or go to group activities. Instead, she mostly lay in bed or watched TV from her couch.

About a week before I saw her, her home-care aide brought her in for an apparent emergency. Florence suddenly began gasping for breath while watching TV, fell off her chair, and held her throat. The facility care worker rushed over to administer CPR and called the hospital emergency room, which dispatched an ambulance. By the time the ambulance team arrived, Florence was stabilized and breathing, though with a gravelly heaving sound that indicated that her breathing was labored and could stop at any time.

The paramedics soon took Florence in the ambulance to the hospital, where she was assigned a semiprivate room. As she settled in, the supervising nurse set up a monitoring system with a camera mounted on the wall to observe and record her through the night. This way, the medical staff could watch over her from time to time to make sure she experienced no incidents of respiratory arrest in the night or if she did, help her breathe and help hem plan how to deal with her problems in the future.

For a time, Florence rallied, and after two days of seemingly normal breathing, the hospital doctor on call examined her and checked her breathing and pulse. After seeing the results, he proclaimed that these COPD symptoms seemed to be under control and sent Florence home.

However, a week later, her symptoms worsened, and her home healthcare worker sent her back to the hospital.

This time, when I examined her, it seemed that her end of life was coming soon, and it was unlikely that she could leave the hospital given her serious condition. So it was time for an end-of-life conversation, which she never had before.

As soon as I began to describe the options, she looked at me blankly.

"I don't understand any of this," she said. "I don't know what you mean by CPR or respiratory management or any of the other terms you mentioned. I thought I'm either alive after a coughing fit or if I don't breathe soon enough, then I'm dead."

I tried again, explaining in simpler layman terms.

"If you choose to be resuscitated, the medical team will spring into action if you stop breathing to get you breathing again. But if you can't breathe on your own after a certain time limit they will try intubation, which means placing a tube into your trachea, which is your main breathing pipe. This tube can be connected to you as long as you need it, until you can breathe on your own again."

"Then I guess intubation is okay if that's how it goes," she said.

But she didn't understand— or want to understand—the inevitable progress of the disease even if she was kept alive. She didn't understand the difference between using intubation to prolong a person's life by keeping him or her breathing, so healing could take place in an earlier stage of the disease and using intubation in a situation where the disease was so advanced and the person's physical condition so poor that healing wasn't possible. But that is one of my responsibilities as physician dealing with end-of-life issues—to help patients understand that their life really is at an end, so they can best prepare to face this in a way that reduces their own pain and suffering.

I continued with my explanation of the cardiac resuscitation process.

"This is different from keeping you breathing," I said. "Cardiac resuscitation is designed to get your heart beating again. It usually involves powerful electrical shocks, where a doctor or paramedic uses a defibrillator that sends an electrical current into your heart to stimulate it. In addition, the doctor or paramedic will perform chest compressions by pressing down on the middle of the chest about two inches, one hundred times a minute. Unfortunately, once someone is in their fifties or sixties, this process can result in a number of broken bones and ribs, since the bones become more fragile over time.

"During this procedure, the doctor or paramedic may sometimes insert a large needle into the heart or press down to compress the heart to remove any excess fluid that has accumulated around it. In some extreme cases, such as if the heart stops in the middle of heart surgery, the surgeon can manually squeeze or massage the heart to get it beating again."

"Wow! That seems like it would be so painful," Florence said. "So I don't want you to do that on me."

Finally, I told her about the modified DNR system.

"Essentially this involves two types of resuscitation, since the heart and breathing stop separately, except in a cardiorespiratory arrest, when they stop together. When the heart stops, you stop breathing within seconds, whereas when you stop breathing, you may have a couple of minutes before the heart stops.

"When someone stops breathing, such as in a drug overdose, it can be easy to restart the breathing without any complications, unless the cause for it to stop is irreversible, such as a serious lung disease that has damaged the lungs. So if you choose a modified DNR, you could be resuscitated if just your breathing has stopped. Very often these efforts to restart the breathing work, because any intervention can occur over several minutes. If the heart stops, this means death within two to three minutes, since the blood stops getting pumped to the brain. But with a breathing stoppage, one has a few minutes to an hour or two, so the medical team has some time to react and plan what to do to bring you back."

"Oh, I see," said Florence.

"So that's why," I continued, "it is best to leave it up to the medical team to decide what to do. That's why it's so important to intervene early to prevent these events from happening, and not use any CPR that involves compressions and electrical shocks."

As Florence pondered over my comments, I thought about the way science and research have provided the best combination of techniques to use, so well-trained teams can apply them. However, I felt these techniques are too complex to explain to a patient with little knowledge about these procedures. For example, in a full-blown code resuscitation, the efforts to restore the respiration through intubation and ventilation also require efforts to restart the heart, which include chest compressions, electric shocks, a complex array of medications delivered by IV, and sometimes needles injected into the heart to remove any excess fluids that have collected there. But I felt that since Florence had already chosen to have a modified DNR to resuscitate her breathing, she didn't need to know all these details.

Finally, Florence nodded, "That's fine, " though the gazed look in her eyes suggested she was on information overload after my detailed explanation. At least she had agreed to what I suggested.

"Good, " I said, making a note in my notebook of what her treatment plan would be, as Florence reaffirmed her choice.

"I know this is all very confusing, and I'm not sure I understand everything, but I feel like you really know what's best in my situation. So that's what I'd like to do. I'd like to keep breathing as long as possible. But I don't want any heroics once it looks like it's really over. I don't want to experience all of that pain and suffering, if that's what it takes to bring me back. And for what? I'll still be lying in bed connected to all kinds of tubes. I had a pretty good life when I was younger. But now I feel I'm done, and I guess I'm ready to go."

"You've made a good choice," I reassured Florence, and I left, feeling pleased at taking the time to help her understand her choices and what would happen. By doing so, I had helped her come to this decision, so she could die in peace.

I DON'T HAVE ENOUGH INFORMATION OR HAVE INCOMPLETE INFORMATION

In some cases, patients or their families feel they don't know enough to choose, even though I have given them a description of their various options. In some cases, they feel confused because they have obtained information from other sources and are bewildered by the multiple streams of information, so they are not sure what to do.

The experience can be a little like driving along a freeway when you see several exits within a few yards of each other and different signs with arrows pointing in different directions. But you may be unsure which arrow points to which sign, while traffic is piling up, so you feel stuck, unable to make a quick decision though you have to do something.

That's what happened with Mrs. Harris, an eighty-nine-year old woman, who had been sick for many months. At one time, she worked as an elementary-school teacher and was active in PTA activities, and after retiring, she volunteered in a number of local community programs for young kids. She also had a close relationship with her daughter and son. But once in her eighties, she found her world contracting as she lost the energy for participating in volunteer community programs. Also, the friends she used to go to lunch with began to move to retirement homes or died, and she increasingly lost touch with relatives due to deaths in the family. By the time she became increasingly ill after she turned eighty-seven, her only family left was her daughter, since her son had died in an auto accident. So now any decisions for treatment were up to her and her daughter Pam, who wanted to carry out her mother's wishes.

When I first Mrs. Harris in the hospital, she had been admitted for a large myocardial infarction, which is essentially a heart attack that occurs because of the irreversible necrosis or death of the heart's muscle's tissue due to not enough blood flowing to it. As a result, she was suffering from congestive heart failure, where the heart's pumping ability is lower than normal. In her case, her heart which used to pump at a normal capacity of 55 to 60 percent now pumped at only 30 percent capacity. This led to a slow-down in the blood carrying oxygen getting to her brain, resulting in her lessened ability to stay alert or think clearly. Plus, she had extra fluid in her lungs due to her poorly functioning heart and her taking antibiotics to combat an infection. Making matters worse, she had kidney failure, leading to a buildup of waste products in her body that contributed to her feelings of weakness, shortness of breath, and general lethargy and confusion.

I recommended some rest and medications to help her kidneys work again and to get her heart to pump more quickly and normally. Then I gave her some extra water pills to take to get rid of the extra fluid. After that, I sent her home with her daughter Pam, who had brought her to the hospital, since I thought that the treatment was all she needed to recover, although her age meant recovery would take longer than for someone younger with the same problems.

However, two weeks later she was back in the emergency room. When I came to see her again, things looked truly dire. Basically, her condition was a failure to thrive, perhaps because she had become so isolated from social activities due to her illnesses, so her condition was even worse. Not only was she failing to eat enough because of her lack of appetite, but she had lost about ten pounds and was beginning to look gaunt and emaciated. In addition, she was weak, barely able to sit or stand, and her temperature and blood pressure had dropped—all signs that her body might be shutting down.

So now, instead of just suffering from an acute myocardial infarction and kidney failure, her major problems from two weeks earlier, Mrs. Harris was in an end-of-life situation. But when I looked at her emergency records, I discovered that when the medical team met with her after I saw her, one team member had given her the wrong information about the DNR/DNI options. So she had chosen the wrong DNR/DNI status, as frequently happens, since many medical practitioners aren't fully informed about these end-of-life options. As a result, she had opted for a DNI status only, which means "do not intubate." But this choice meant that even if her heart was still beating, she shouldn't be given the needed respiratory support of putting a tube through her mouth into her airway and providing the needed oxygen to keep her breathing if her breathing stopped. Without this support, she would most likely die within minutes from poor or no oxygenation. Instead, if she was only opting for one choice, she should have chosen a DNR status, which would mean not resuscitating her if her heart stopped beating.

But when I spoke to her about correcting this error, she complained about how confused she was.

"I just don't have enough information or incomplete information about this DNR/DNI situation, so I don't know what to choose. So please talk to my daughter about what to do. She chose the DNI status for me, since she thought that was the best thing to do."

However, when I spoke to Pam in the waiting room, Pam felt equally confused.

"It's so hard for me to make a decision now," she told me. "I feel like this decision for my mother carries all the moral, medical, legal, religion, and family responsibilities with it. It's such a burden.

"I chose the DNI status because we have a number of doctors in the family who made some recommendations, but it became a little bit too technical for me to understand. So I wasn't really sure what they were recommending. Also, I was trying to take into account what my mother wanted, and at one point she said she wanted to be progressive, so she wanted the full CPR and mechanical ventilation if needed. But then I thought maybe I should choose the more humane approach."

As I listened, I realized she was totally confused, either because she didn't understand herself or because a local doctor, unfamiliar with end-of-life procedures, had been confused and therefore had given her the wrong information, which made no medical sense. So I tried to set her straight.

"Unfortunately, that's the opposite of what you should do," I said, "since there's no way to successfully perform CPR without providing oxygen, and if you try to provide oxygen without intubation, that won't work very well either. So what you really want to do is to provide the oxygen and intubation to try to get your mother breathing again, but not provide more aggressive resuscitation techniques to restart the heart. Therefore, it doesn't make any medical sense to choose a DNI status if you want resuscitation. And a full resuscitation will only extend your mother's pain and suffering. That's why I recommend that you choose the DNR status, so once your mother's heart stops, that's the time to let her go."

"Thanks for the clarification," Pam said, and she proceeded to amend the paperwork for the DNR/DNI status.

As I left, I was glad I could help the daughter combine the patient's wishes to do what was possible with an understanding that an extended meaningful life was not possible, so the best thing was the DNR alternative to bring about a more peaceful end. Now they both had a clearer picture on which to base their decision, and they agreed with me about what to choose. In fact, the next morning, the nurse working with the family told me that they had decided to choose both the DNR and DNI status. This way there would be no need to try to revive Mrs. Harris's breathing when her respiration or heart stopped, and until then, the medical team would use the standard treatment only. In this way, they would make her end as comfortable and peaceful as possible instead of trying to artificially keep her alive. She could end her life in a more natural way.

IT'S COMPLICATED

A big problem in helping patients choose the best treatment option is the number of choices available if they are choosing a modified DNR option. The choice can be relatively clear-cut when there are only a DNR/DNI, don't-resuscitate-or-intubate option, or a full-code resuscitation. But a modified DRN opens up a range of possibilities that not only confuse the patient, but the medical team as well. Adding to the confusion, the patient and family are in a high-stress, emotional situation because of facing death, while the medical team may be under time pressure when an emergency strikes and they have to act quickly in the face of uncertainty of choosing the best option under the circumstances.

I faced that issue when I was dealing with Therese, a woman in her sixties, who was suffering from a chronic pulmonary disease triggered by her heavy smoking.

For now, the question was what to do about her already-chosen modified DNR status. Therese was still in the early stages of the disease, though like most sufferers, she had both symptoms: a chronic bronchitis, involving a long-term cough with mucus; and emphysema, involving damage to the lungs over time. As a result, she had recently taken to carrying an oxygen tank with her, though she was still able to go out, such as to go shopping or drive her car on errands around town. But increasingly, she found her energy flagging, so she couldn't do all the things she used to do. That's why she had come to me to prepare for the inevitable time when she or her family members would have to choose what to do about her treatment.

"At least I know I don't want the full DNR treatment when my time comes," Therese said, almost in a lighthearted, joking tone, since she was still in fairly good spirits. "I know that means do not intubate, which involves connecting me up to all of these tubes so I look like a pincushion. So I definitely don't want that. When it's time to go, it's time to go."

"Then let me explain about the other options," I said, glad that Therese was alert and open to trying to understand in a calm rational way, whereas many patients or their families are already very upset and emotional. When this is the case, they find it hard to listen or understand and are easily confused by the details and technical jargon used to explain these highly technical procedures to those with limited knowledge about serious medical conditions, including those with higher educations.

"First," I told Therese, "it's important to understand that we can deal with the stopping of the heart and the breathing through separate procedures. So we have different statuses for them. A DNR deals with the heart pumping and the techniques used to get it pumping again, while a DNI deals with respiration and the intubation that can help you breathe again."

Florence tapped the side of her oxygen tank and took a deep breath. "Sure, I can understand that, doc. If I suddenly stop breathing, with a DNI status, you can't try to get me breathing again, such as by using one of those breathing tubes and respirators."

"Exactly," I said.

I continued explaining the different options possible under a modified DNR status.

"You can also have a DNR status without the DNI option, meaning that we would act to help you breathe again. If necessary, that could include putting you on a ventilator."

"Okay. That sounds fine with me."

"Plus there are other options to a full DNR status," I told her. "I know it can be quite complicated to explain to patients who don't have a medical background. Even medical students have trouble with all these alternatives. But let me try, so you can make an informed choice."

"Glad to know. I like to know these things. I used to be a stockbroker and then was involved in real estate, when I was more active in business. There's plenty of detail to deal with in those fields."

"Good," I said. "So let me go on. First, there are the three options you said you don't want, though your initial choice can be changed if you change your mind. One is using antiarrhytmics, which are drugs that suppress abnormal heart rhythms, such as an atrial fibrillation, which is characterized by rapid and irregular beating and sometimes heart palpitations, fainting, shortness of breath, or chest pains. Another condition that can occur is atrial flutter, which occurs in the upper chambers of the heart and is similar to atrial fibrillation. Third, you might experience ventricular tachycardia, which is a rapid heartbeat due to improper electrical activity of the heart, or you could experience ventricular fibrillation, which occurs when the muscles in the walls of the heart quiver rather than contract properly, leading to cardiac arrest. Finally, the heart can go into pauses and stop for short periods of time. You can also experience electric rhythm without actual heart mechanical activity—another form of cardiac arrest."

"I didn't realize there were all these things that could go wrong with the heart," Florence said. "But I don't want any of those drugs if my heart isn't beating properly."

"Then you probably don't want the option of using the medications, known as antihypotensive agents that raise reduced blood pressure, which can occur for many reasons. One is when you develop a major infection or heart attack, your blood pressure drops and you feel faint. Another time your blood pressure might drop is when you have an accident and suffer a major blood loss.

"The purpose of these agents is to raise the blood pressure by various means, such as constricting the arteries and veins or increasing the speed and strength of the heart in pumping the blood. Some of the drugs that may be more familiar to you may be epinephrine, dopamine, and levophed."

"Well, I don't want any of these drugs, which should simplify your choices." "Good," I said. "The results of these drugs are uncertain, and they are unlikely to provide more than a short-term fix for a few hours or days when you are suffering from the ravages of a serious disease like the end stages of a chronic pulmonary disease. These drugs are only effective when the low blood pressure is due to a temporary and short-term condition, such as an ill-advised fast."

Florence nodded again, and I went on.

"The third option that you turned down is CPR, which normally include chest compressions. But there are other options, which include electric shocks and a rarely used procedure of injecting needles directly into the heart to remove extra fluids that are internally compressing the heart. However, it is very hard to explain each one of them and what to use when, since only well-trained doctors and medical practitioners can decide the best approach based on the circumstances at the time. It's best to leave your choices open, so the medical team can choose what to do at the time.

"You might consider making these choices like selecting a la carte dishes at a very expensive restaurant, where each part of the meal is selected separately and has a different price. At least some restaurants make it easier by creating a combo dinner, with one or two choices for additions or changes, such as whether you prefer fries or a salad."

"I know what you mean," Florence commented. "I sometimes have gone with friends to Chinese restaurants, where everything is listed separately on the menu, and it can take us twenty to thirty minutes to place an order."

"That's how it is with choosing a modified DNR option. It can be very difficult for both the patients and the medical team to decide on the particular details, because they are beyond what patients and their families normally discuss or understand in end-of-life planning. And medical schools generally do not cover this topic. It's hard enough to discuss how you want to die, and thinking about this becomes even more complicated and emotionally upsetting with all these alternatives."

"That's absolutely right," said Florence. "I'm trying to be calm, collected, and rational and do this planning well in advance, and already I'm feeling completely confused."

"Which is only natural," I said, thinking about how even the computers have made the choice process more complicated, since feeding information into the computer about a patient simply generates a list of complicated ways to add the different options together. Then the doctor or medical practitioner has to choose among these combinations.

"So what I'd like to suggest," I continued, "is for you is not to select the modified DNR option, as it is too difficult to specify what you want to choose or not. Just let the doctor or medical team handling your case make the specific choices of exactly what to do at the end."

That's what Florence decided to do, feeling relieved that she had finally made a choice—the straight DNR and or DNI status and not the always messy modified DNR status.

BUT IT'S NOT WRITTEN DOWN

Sometimes the source of a misunderstanding is not passing on information, resulting in misinformation about what a patient wants to do. Commonly, the diagnosis and prognosis for every patient is recorded on the chart at the foot of his or her bed, and the determination about a DNR, DNI, or modified DNR status is included on this chart. Therefore any nurse or doctor who cares for the patient can know what other doctors and nurses have done, so if the doctor who wrote up the original record isn't available, others can proceed based on this information. But sometimes this information doesn't get communicated to other doctors and nurses, who have to act quickly in response to an emergency, so the wrong procedures are done.

That's what happened to Mr. Armstrong, a man in his mid-eighties, who had once been a successful businessman before he retired to enjoy a leisurely time for golf and travel. He became ill after experiencing a series of heart attacks, perhaps because of his increasing weight due to eating rich foods and living a more sedentary lifestyle. When I met with him in his semiprivate room where he was propped up in bed, I gave him the usual explanation about the different end-of-life options.

He listened for a while silently, as if pondering the options I had mentioned. For a few moments, I worried if he understood what I said well enough to make a decision, since his mentation was becoming questionable. At times, he seemed very present and attentive, much like he was still a CEO making the everyday big decisions about how to run his company. But at other times, his ability to think seemed to wane, either because he wasn't paying attention or because his neural connections weren't processing information as quickly as before. Thus, I wanted to be sure he really understood what I had told him, so he could make a reasoned decision.

"Did you understand what I just said, Mr. Armstrong?" I asked.

He looked up, and his body stiffened, as if he was coming to attention like a soldier who was lost in thought during a training exercise and was called back to attention by a drill sergeant.

"Yes, I heard you," he said. "And I know what I want. I don't want to be resuscitated. It seems so painful. Why prolong the agony? We all know I'm going to die very soon. So I'd rather go quickly when my time comes."

"Very good, Mr. Armstrong," I said, and I noted his request on his chart. "I'll take that as your wish, and it has been so noted."

Yet while I duly recorded his request on the chart, a formal order based on that request was not recorded right away, since I was uncertain about his mental abilities and didn't want to record a formal order until I could discuss the options with his family. Later, that lack of a formal order caused problems, because his request did not get conveyed to his family, who wanted to do all they could for him, and they thought a full-code resuscitation would help him last longer.

Unfortunately, the day after I spoke to Mr. Armstrong, he had a cardiac arrest when I was not at the hospital.

A nurse called me immediately on my cell phone to let me know what had happened, and I replied that "Mr. Armstrong already told me that he had requested a DNR status, but that was not formalized, as we needed to involve the family given his limited mental capacity."

The nurse took a moment to look at the chart. "I see," she said. "But there is no formal order for it, and his family was here earlier this afternoon. Before he experienced the cardiac arrest, they saw that his mental state was waxing and waning. So they said they wanted a full code to do everything possible to bring him back. I told the family about the DNR request. But they insisted that they wanted him to be full code, so I wasn't really sure what to do."

"But the patient wanted . . . ." I began.

"I know," the nurse said. "But there was some question about his mentation. Maybe his decision could be questioned. So I thought the best and most peaceful way to proceed was to continue CPR and keep the family happy until we could discuss this personally in a few minutes after I drove back to the hospital to meet them."

Knowing this resuscitation was not in the best interest of the patient, since it would only prolong his pain and suffering before his likely death within a few days, I called his wife's cell phone number and spoke to her. Since his wife and three daughters were at the hospital already, I arranged to meet them there.

When I arrived, they were in the waiting room looking very teary-eyed.

"They have him in the ICU and are trying to resuscitate him now," the wife told me.

"We want to do the best we can for him," said a daughter.

I pulled out a copy of Mr. Armstrong's chart, which I had brought with me from his bedside.

"I know you seem to love him very much and are very concerned for his well-being. But I want to explain what a resuscitation really involves, and why this isn't really the best thing to do for him now. And it's not what he wanted."

I pushed Mr. Armstrong's chart across the table.

"You see. He said he wanted not to be resuscitated."

I then explained why that choice was the best thing for him under the circumstances, because of all the damage a cardiac arrest does, and because a resuscitation effort can make the damage even worse.

"So you see, a cardiac arrest is not the same as a heart attack, which many people can recover from, since a heart attack just pauses the heart for a little while and it can be restarted again. But a cardiac arrest stops it completely and causes extensive damage, especially to the brain. So any recovery is unlikely, especially given Mr. Armstrong's past history of heart attacks. The resuscitation would mean that he would be likely to have broken ribs to restart his heart, and then he would be kept alive on tubes, only to succumb within a few days, maybe even sooner."

After that explanation, Mrs. Armstrong and her daughters agreed that the most humane thing would be to place Mr. Armstrong on DNR status immediately and let nature take its course overnight.

As I left, I saw the family hugging and crying softly behind me, and I felt glad that I could help them understand what really was the best thing to do. And later that night, Mr. Armstrong expired peacefully after being terminally extubated upon his family request.

Later, when I thought about what happened, I realized the importance of communicating the order with the patient's wishes to the rest of the team, not just writing it on the chart, because the doctor obtaining the DNR agreement, in this case myself, might not be present when the patient has a cardiac arrest. So without an official order from the doctor taking the patient's request, the medical team would do everything possible to resuscitate the patient until they had information to do otherwise. On the other hand, this kind of situation happens on a daily basis in the hospital, as it is never an emergency to have a full DNR or other order in the chart at all times, because a full code is the default order, and because it may take days of family meetings to achieve a final decision.

In this case, the family wanted to do everything they could to help Mr. Armstrong. But once the family members understood that he couldn't survive in spite of any procedures, they were willing to accept the patient's original determination. In turn, this case illustrates how important it is for everyone—patients, their families, and the medical team members—to fully understand what resuscitation really involves and when it can help versus when it is both ineffective and hurtful to the patient. Then everyone involved can better understand the most humane and medically sensible thing to do under the circumstances.

REASSURING THE PATIENT AND FAMILY THAT THIS IS THE RIGHT THING TO DO

At times, the process of dying can extend over several months, so decisions about treatment made early on can be forgotten, and when the specter of death actually looms, patients or their families can forget what they originally decided. Thus, it can help to remind and reassure them that they are doing the right thing when the time comes. Usually, everyone is highly strung and emotional at this time, because someone loved will be going away forever. But such reassurance can help them feel more support in this time of emotional need, as well as reinforce their original choice as the best thing to do.

This kind of reassurance was important for the family of Mr. Simpson, a sixty-something male who worked on a series of low- and semiskilled jobs, from factory work to being part of a road crew. He was never married or had kids, so he lived alone for most of his adult years. Unfortunately, he enjoyed going to bars when he wasn't working and often drank heavily. He did so because he liked the sociability of being around other drinkers in a bar with loud music and flashing lights, and because he wanted to forget his otherwise usually lonely existence.

When I first saw him in the hospital in his last weeks before his death, he was suffering from hepatic encephalopathy, a type of abnormal brain function, which is usually transient and due to liver malfunction. As in Mr. Simpson's case, the amount of brain activity often declines over time. As a result, he had increasing difficulty in paying attention, a poor memory, and he found it harder and harder to perform everyday routine activities. For example, he slept longer and longer hours, was very lethargic when he got up, and often forgot routine activities, so he would leave pots unattended on the stove until alerted by rising smoke, or he would forget to turn off the bath water until he saw the water flowing under the bathroom door into the living room.

As a result, his landlord wanted Mr. Simpson out, afraid he might burn the house down or cause a flood. To stave off an eviction, Mr. Simpson's only surviving relative—Judith, a sister in her fifties—put him in a nursing home for a few months. As his conditioned worsened, she placed him in the hospital.

Unfortunately, Mr. Simpson had all kinds of medical complications because of his heavy drinking and poor diet. Sometimes he did not get enough sleep, and he fed himself a mix of uppers and downers to compensate for his poor nutrition and low energy.

Thus, his list of medical problems was like a menu of the many common diseases that one might get from not properly caring for one's health. Among other things, he suffered from a urinary tract infection, urine retention from an enlarged prostate, bleeding from his stomach region, and diabetes. He also experienced a growing problem of kidney failure.

For a short time, Mr. Simpson had successful dialysis treatments and returned to a nursing home. But a day later, he was back in the hospital with symptoms of pneumonia and an intestinal infection and colitis, an infection of the colon, in which the bad bacteria in the intestinal tract multiply and take over from the good bacteria that keeps us healthy by fighting off the bad bacteria. The result was he had a severe case of diarrhea, which made it difficult for him to eat anything and caused him to become increasingly dehydrated.

Thus, given all his problems and his difficulty in understanding anything, I met with his sister Judith and explained his conditions that made a recovery impossible. I concluded by reassuring her that we would make him as comfortable as possible in his last hours.

"I assure you, he will be treated as best we can, if he has any possible reversible condition. But if that isn't possible, which seems likely in this case, we'll let him go in peace when his time arrives, whether it's due to an abrupt cardiac arrest or a slower respiratory problem where he stops breathing."

"Thanks for explaining all this," Judith said, as she signed the DNR/ DNI order.

A few days later, I got the expected call from the nurse on duty to tell me that "the patient's not doing well," and she briefly explained why. "He's continued to be on dialysis and treated for his intestinal infection. We also put him on nutritional supplements and checked him regularly. But there is no way for him to recover and return to normal again."

"Just keep monitoring him," I said.

A few hours later at about 10 p.m., I got another call to say Mr. Simpson had reached the point of no return.

"His body is shutting down, and he is going to die in a few hours," the nurse said.

Around midnight, the nurse called again to say the end was a few minutes away.

"His blood pressure is continuing to drop," she said. "So his systolic count is between the 50s and 60s, and his diastolic count is between the 30s and 40s."

Given that the normal systolic count is about 100 to 120 and the normal diastolic count is about 70 to 80, I knew his blood pressure would keep falling, and there was no way to bring it back up, given his myriad medical problems. So I asked the nurse to call his sister.

"I'd like to let her know that the moment of his death is here, and there is nothing else we can do about it."

I wanted to call now that things had turned critical to have another chance to reassure her, as I would other family members, that Mr. Simpson's certain death was coming very soon and there was no point for the medical team to revive the patient, which would only torture him in the last hours before death. I couldn't help but think that even prisoners about to be executed have a more humane end, since they are given injections to knock them out so they don't experience pain in their last moments. By contrast, any last-ditch efforts to resuscitate a patient might include electric shocks, a needle to the heart, and compressions that might break the ribs, only to prolong the patient's moment of death, while increasing the agony the patient might feel if conscious.

When Judith answered, I told her what was going to happen, just as she and Mr. Simpson had previously requested.

"It's only a matter of time," I told her. "Maybe an hour or two. He's unconscious now in the ICU, and like we discussed, we're going to let him go peacefully. That's the most humane and loving things to do, and I wanted to reassure you that what will happen. I'll call you again to let you know when he finally passes."

"Thank you for telling me," Judith said, relieved by my call.

About two hours later, Mr. Simpson did peacefully expire, because there were so many things wrong with him that his major systems—from his kidneys to his heart to his brain—gave out. In turn, my reassuring call to Judith helped her understand that she and the medical team had done the right thing in letting Mr. Simpson go peacefully.

I began thinking about the importance of sharing this understanding as I pulled out a death certificate from my desk drawer. It had only three lines to write down a summary of the cause of death, such as a heart attack, pneumonia, or other infection. But in a case like Mr. Simpson's, the situation was much more complicated because multiple conditions led to his eventual death. So three lines were not enough to tell the whole story, though at least I could explain further in the discharge summary, which I would later dictate into the system to explain the full sequence of events that led to Mr. Simpson's demise. Not only does the patient and family need to understand the situation to come to a proper DNR/DNI determination, but the whole medical staff and anyone else reviewing the case needs to fully understand what happened and why.

A CASE OF DENIAL

Denial can sometimes be the reason for a lack of understanding. The patient or family doesn't want to acknowledge a dire situation, as if by denying it, the problem will go away. It is like putting on rose-colored glasses to make the dark gray clouds that are threatening a storm disappear.

That was the experience I had with Mr. Potter, in his early fifties, who had Stage IV cancer of his esophagus, meaning that the cancer had spread to other organs, including his liver, which is critical for survival. Among other things, the liver filters and processes blood as it circulates through the body, and the proteins in the liver called enzymes metabolize nutrients, detoxify harmful substances, and make blood-clotting proteins.

Mr. Potter had lived a fast-paced lifestyle that contributed to his problems. A top sales executive, he frequently jetted to meet with company heads and go to conferences all over the United States. As part of his job, he drank a lot and smoked at least a pack a day, supposedly to calm him down. But he woke up to cups of coffee with his breakfast, drank several cups at luncheons and conferences, and often smoked both cigarettes and cigars in smoke-filled rooms with other executives to hammer out a deal. The last thing he wanted to hear was a diagnosis that would slow him down.

As he told me when I met him at the hospital, "Look, doc, I gotta get out of here and fast, since I have a big conference to go to and I'm expecting to close a deal. I can't do that on the phone. I gotta press the flesh, so get me out."

But I saw all kinds of danger signs that suggested he was headed for a quick fall if he didn't change his toxic way of life, though he didn't want to hear any of that.

So initially he was playing whack-a-mole with the different symptoms that popped up, rather than trying to find the root cause and deal with that. For example, the month before I saw him he had come in for chemotherapy to treat the spreading cancer. He imagined that he would have a few injections of chemicals and they would kill off the cancer cells; then everything would be normal again. But after a month of chemotherapy, he was back in the hospital because his nose had been bleeding on and off for two days, and his overall blood level had dropped about 33 percent, so it was much thinner because the platelets, which prevent bleeding, drop significantly due to the chemotherapy. With the reduced platelet count, the blood gushed from his nose.

"We have to give you more blood to build up your blood level," a nurse told him.

So the medical team gave him a transfusion in his upper arm, which seemed to work. Soon he was back up near his normal, also called "baseline," and he felt that was all he needed to do.

"Thanks. Now I'll be fine," he told the two nurses on duty, and he gathered his briefcase, preparing to leave.

When I encountered him in the reception area, I urged him to stay for a few tests.

"We need to understand what's really going on," I said. I glanced at a copy of his file and looked up. "Look, you've had a really serious condition—cancer of your esophagus that spread to other organs. And you had chemo. Since your blood level went down, that's why you bled so much. So we should do some tests to see what's going on."

Mr. Potter tried to get away.

"But I feel fine now. Maybe I didn't eat enough and that pushed my blood level down. After all, I was so busy with meetings, I forgot to eat anything."

"That could be one factor," I said. "But if it's something else more serious, you'd want to know, wouldn't you?"

"Not really," Mr. Potter said in reply. "Sometimes what you don't know can't hurt you. Or too much curiosity they say killed the cat."

Mr. Potter was trying to be droll to avoid having to know. Though I couldn't think fast enough to come up with a witty retort, I did think of some good reasons he should know.

"There are plenty of reasons why it's to your benefit to know something. For example, if you were buying a house, you wouldn't buy something blind without inspecting it, because there could be some major hidden damage. So it's good to know some of this basic information about your health so you can take the necessary precautions or start the needed treatment."

Finally, Mr. Potter reluctantly agreed, and I did a screening test to check his blood for its ability to coagulate and form clots and how long it takes. Such a test can help determine a person's risk of excessive bleeding. I also felt it important to check Mr. Potter's blood's ability to clot, because he had experienced a bleeding nose for a few days and had a low blood level, which suggested his blood could have become unusually thin.

To conduct the coagulation test, the nurse first took a blood sample as with most blood tests by injecting a thin needle into a vein in his arm. Then the nurse sent the sample to the hospital lab for testing and analysis, with the results expected back the next day. Also, I decided to do an ultrasound test on his legs to see if he had developed any clots, which sometimes occur when there are other disturbances in the blood, and often cancers cause or increase the risk of forming clots. In this test, an ultrasound scanner sends a high frequency sound to capture live images from inside the body. This way a doctor can see problems with organs, vessels, and tissues and look inside the blood vessels without needing to make an incision.

After we finished the tests, Mr. Potter headed home, thinking he was fine and he had aced this "stupid test," as he called it.

But the next day when the results came in, I felt vindicated. Mr. Potter had not one but two coagulation disorders. One disorder was his overly thin blood due to a low number of the platelets which prevent bleeding, causing his bleeding from his nose. The other disorder was the two clots he had in his legs.

I called him to tell him the news, and he showed up to my office.

"Unfortunately, you have two problems with your blood at the same time. One is the blood loss because your blood is generally too thin. The other is that there is too much abnormal coagulation, so you have excess clotting, and if a clot becomes large enough and gets free, it could go up your blood stream into your heart and cause a lung embolism or major pulmonary artery obstruction, or worse, lead to a cardiac arrest."

Mr. Potter began to protest. "But that sounds crazy. How can there be such extremes? How can my blood be both too thin and full of too many clots?"

I tried to explain. "It's like free flowing water, which can suddenly come together to form concentrations of fast raging water. Then that turns into rapids on the rocks."

Mr. Potter laughed, not wanting to take my warning seriously. But just before he tried to leave, I took a reading of his heart rate with my stethoscope. This result confirmed how dangerous his condition was.

"Your heart is beating at two hundred beats a minute, which is very high," I said. "So you could easily have a heart attack."

I rushed him to the emergency department down the hall, where the doctor there listened to his heart, got a reading of his pulse and blood pressure, and hooked him up to a cardiac monitor. As the doctor there advised, he was admitted to the hospital to get his high blood pressure and heart rate under control.

While he was recuperating in the hospital, the doctors discovered a large ulcer on his esophagus, which was the site of his original cancer.

"We can't manipulate it or use surgery to get rid of this," I told him. "It's too large to remove at this site. So we'll have to try some more pills and injections, and see if they will shrink the cancer."

"Then I'll be fine again, doc, right?" he said.

"I'm not sure. We'll have to see how the medication works," I replied.

But now that his situation seemed even more dire, Mr. Potter didn't want to believe the potentially grim prognosis. He seemed to think that if he could get involved in other activities, he would be fine, not realizing that his energy to participate in these activities was more and more diminished.

He kept up his resistance to understanding and believing over the next few days, when he invited his wife and daughter to the hospital, and a few uncles, aunts, and cousins joined them. Oddly, rather than talking about his own progress, he acted more interested in showing off the different equipment used to test and treat him, such as the blood-pressure machine and cuff which measures his vital signs and the ultrasound machine that checked for blood clots.

Later, when I tried to explain the problems with his blood, recurring cancer, and extra fast heartbeat, he laughed everything off and told his family members and relatives not to pay serious attention to what I had to say.

"He's just trying to scare everyone with this double-edged sword of coagulation disorders causing the blood to thin and clots to form. Then he talks scarily about how my heart has gotten out of rhythm and I might have terminal cancer. Take your pick. The doctor makes it sound like I could pop off any day with a cardiac arrest, rather than realizing I just need a few days to catch up on my rest and then I'll be fine."

It was frustrating listening to him trying to deny the medical reality, while others seemed to go along with him. But then I reminded myself how jokes and humor are often tools of denial to laugh away the horror of something very serious if acknowledged for what it is. And here Mr. Potter had found a support group in his relatives.

In turn, that denial of reality meant that he and his relatives supported a full-code status, so if his heart stopped, he wanted the medical team to connect him to all sorts of machines to try to bring him back from the dead and prolong his life. He even made a joke about that, describing how the doctors were like mad scientists who hoped to connect him to all kinds of gadgets to pull him back from the brink. But obviously, the scenario they were contemplating was unlikely to happen soon, since, he claimed, he was going to be fine.

At least Mr. Potter wanted to think so, but the reality was that very soon he would be back in the hospital for what was likely to be a terminal condition leading to death in a few days, because he wasn't about to change anything in his lifestyle that was leading him to an early grave. Furthermore, it would likely be a very painful last few days because he wanted to go full code, so the medical team would do everything they could to bring him back from the brink. As a result, he did remain conscious enough to experience all that agony for a few more days, until finally the inevitable happened and he fell over the brink. Yet because of his denial, he trapped himself into this outcome, like a prisoner of his own body who couldn't get away.

THE COMPLICATIONS OF TECHNOLOGY

Another reason that patients and their families can have trouble deciding on their treatment options is that modern medical technology has become so complicated that many people don't understand what can be done. Or they may have unrealistic expectations of the power of technology to heal what it cannot. Sometimes, too, patients and their families get misinformation from friends and associates or from what they see in the movies and on TV. Making matters even more complicated, a disease can progress in time through multiple stages, and these are affected by the age and health of a particular patient.

Thus, it can sometimes be very difficult to explain to patients what their options are and make recommendations, especially when a patient has a chronic condition that gets progressively worse and they have been in and out of a hospital or other treatment facility. These circumstances make understanding their case and deciding on the optimum treatment plan even more complicated. Under the circumstances, it is easy to see why different doctors may have different assessments and recommendations for a case. When patients bring past opinions into the mix, that adds still another layer of complications.

I had this experience with Mrs. Armstrong, a woman in her mid-sixties, who was admitted to the community hospital where I worked. Previously, she had been cared for at a clinic in a nearby town, due to lower-cost considerations. But now that her condition had worsened, she had come to the hospital.

After she was processed through intake, I met with her to learn more about her condition. I had nothing in writing about her long medical history, since she had come to the hospital without telling anyone at the clinic she was doing so. She sat across from me wearing a prim pantsuit, looking very thin and about ten years older than her age, as she occasionally leaned over to breathe in and out of an oxygen tank she carried with her. After she described her previous work as an administrative assistant in a payroll office, where she worked, which she did until she had to stop working due to her illness, she gave me a quick rundown on her condition.

"They told me at the clinic that I have a chronic pulmonary disease, or COPD as they called it, and emphysema, which is why I have to use an oxygen tank at home and when I go out. I also got some pulmonary medications I'm supposed to take each day."

She pulled out a half-dozen small pill bottles to show me. Then, nervously, she pulled out a bottle of Ativan, one of the drugs used for anxiety.

"I take this, too, because I'm so anxious about my condition. I'm so afraid that if I go to sleep, maybe I'll stop breathing and die. I used to smoke because that helped to relax me, but I had to stop because the doctors at the clinic said that was making my condition worse. They said it wasn't a good idea to smoke around oxygen, too, since a spark from the cigarette could ignite the oxygen in the tank and cause an explosion. So I feel even more anxious without my smoking. And I have so many questions about what will happen."

I tried to reassure her, telling her, "I'll be glad to answer your questions after I examine you, so I can tell what was wrong."

As I examined her, she gradually revealed more problems that made her case more complicated, which made it even more difficult to explain what could be done to treat her and why. It was hard for Mrs. Armstrong to understand, especially since she had a limited education. Moreover, the strange hospital environment made her more anxious and interfered with her ability to concentrate and comprehend information about new procedures, some involving new and sophisticated technologies.

When such cases become complicated medically and require modern technology that can often be hard for patients and families to understand, making it difficult when they have to sign agreements and waivers for these procedures to be done. That came up in my discussions with Mrs. Armstrong, as she described how she was feeling pain all over due to falling and banging up her body against the furniture.

She raised her pant legs and pulled up her sleeves to show me the abrasions on her arms and legs.

"Also I have a pain in my chest," she added.

I asked her to breathe a few times as I listened with my stethoscope. Suspecting she might have a clot in her lungs, even a tumor given her chronic pulmonary disease, I suggested we do a CAT scan, which is the usual procedure for detecting when people have internal injuries or obstructions. These show up in the scan, which creates a series of images that show slices of the body, which indicate if there are any abnormalities.

As soon as I mentioned doing a CAT scan, Mrs. Armstrong had some questions, since she was not familiar with this high-tech procedure. So I tried to explain as I did with many patients when I was recommending one of the new procedures now possible with modern technology.

"A CAT or CT scan is a type of computerized tomography scan, which combines a series of X-ray images taken from different angles. It uses computer processing to create cross-sectional images, or slices, of the bones, blood vessels and soft tissues inside your body. A CT scan provides more detailed information than plain X-rays. So it's very good for detecting internal injuries, since it can visualize nearly all parts of the body."

"That sounds fine," Mrs. Armstrong said, and then she revealed that she had had throat cancer due to her past history of smoking, making a CAT scan even more useful, since patients with throat cancer are more likely to have clots in their lungs.

But when I told her that "we use an intravenous contrast material made with iodine to create a contrast between the different organs and structures in your body," Mrs. Armstrong immediately objected.

"I'm allergic to iodine," she said.

So I decided to use an alternate procedure—an ultrasound that usually detects a clot outside the chest cavity or in the liver. Though an ultrasound is not as sensitive and precise as a CAT scan, it would still give a fairly accurate reading in certain areas of the body. But since the ultrasound equipment was new to Mrs. Armstrong, this required another explanation.

"Essentially, an ultrasound is a device where we project sound waves at your body, and they move through at different rates of speed, depending on what's there. If they encounter a denser cluster of cells, the sound waves will move more slowly, such as if they detect a clot of blood or unusual growth in your blood vessels, such as in the liver. Unfortunately, there is no other accurate way to look into the lungs, except for a ventilation perfusion scan."

Mrs. Armstrong looked at me with a bemused expression, indicating she didn't understand.

"I know this gets complicated," I said. "But basically this scan uses two radioactive tracers. One goes through the vessels in your lungs and the other goes through your breathing pipes. A doctor can make a diagnosis of what is wrong by contrasting and comparing the two sets of tracer images."

"I guess you can do that," Mrs. Armstrong agreed, and I was glad my explanation was enough to gain her agreement.

But as it turned out, the ultrasound showed that Mrs. Armstrong had a number of cancer lesions in her liver, which was a surprise to both of us. These lesions made her case even more serious, since these were an indication that her earlier throat cancer may have returned and was spreading. Thus, this was no longer a case of only dealing with her pulmonary disease but with an end-of-life issue, since she might have perhaps six months to a year to live. This was one more thing for Mrs. Armstrong to understand and accept. But making it more difficult for her to do so was being in a new environment with a new medical team, since she had come directly to the hospital on her own because it was in her community, rather than going there as a referral from a clinic in another city.

Adding even further complications to the case was Mrs. Armstrong's next revelation, when I commented that she appeared so thin that she might be malnourished.

"I don't really eat very much," she acknowledged. "But I can't, because a couple of years ago, I had a major stomach bleed with blood dripping from some ulcer lesions in my stomach into my intestines. So the surgeons had to remove most of my stomach and left just a small pouch. Then they put a small gastrostomy tube they called a PEG tube from my stomach through my abdominal wall and outside of my body, so that's what I get fed through each day. I have a home care worker who has been coming each day to help me do this."

I was amazed to hear her tell me this. For now, on top of all her other problems, these ulcer lesions on her stomach were one more factor leading to her end of life, sooner rather than later.

"This stomach bleed makes your case even more serious," I told her. "It suggests the cancer is even more pervasive than you thought coming here."

Mrs. Armstrong stared ahead wordlessly, as if all this new information about her serious situation was too much for her to comprehend. But now that it was clear nothing much more could be done to heal her, I wanted to tell her about some treatment options that would at least help to make her more comfortable in her last days—the CPAP or BiPAP machines.

I began by describing the CPAP machine. "This will help with your breathing at any time you need it, so you don't have to feel anxious about your breath stopping. The CPAP, which stands for 'continuous positive airway pressure,' is a small machine that supplies a constant and steady stream of air. It comes with a hose and mask or nose piece, so you can attach the hose from the machine to you. It has sensors that can detect your respiratory patterns—when you breathe in and out. Then, it feeds the right amount of pressurized air to you to help you breathe. Since it's small, you can use it at home."

Mrs. Armstrong seemed relieved by my explanation, and I was glad I could make a complex new device understandable. Otherwise, I could see how patients might easily be lost in this sea of new equipment, much like customers getting the latest computer upgrade and software might be lost without a salesperson to guide them through the process. Now I felt a little like this salesperson telling Mrs. Armstrong about all the great new products available to her, and I was helping her choose which was the best for her situation.

I went on with my explanation to describe what a BiPAP machine might do and how it differed from the CPAP machine.

"Still another device to help you breathe better while you sleep or if you need it during the day is the BiPAP machine, which stands for Bilevel Positive Airway Pressure. It's very much like the CPAP machine, since it also provides you with pressurized air through a mask into your airways. The big difference is that the CPAP machine deliver a steady, continuous stream of pressurized air set to a single pressure, although some CPAP machines can start with a lower pressure and gradually build to a higher pressure. That way the pressure is more comfortable and tolerable in the beginning. Then, it builds to the desired setting through the night or over the next few hours.

"But sometimes patients find the constant singular pressure hard to exhale against, since they have to force their breathing out against the incoming air. But a BiPAPs can adjust to your rate of breathing by increasing or decreasing the air pressure, since it has two pressure settings: a prescribed higher pressure for inhalation and a lower pressure for exhalation. So these dual settings allow you to adjust to your individual needs.

"In any case, we can try out these different machines and the different settings on the BiPAP, so you can decide which you prefer."

"That's a lot of information to absorb," Mrs. Armstrong said.

"I know," I said. "But you should understand the different alternatives. They can really help you if you don't want a machine invading your body but just need some help with your breathing for a short time, such as when you go to sleep at night or if you are having a hard time breathing during the day."

At this point, Mrs. Armstrong looked thoughtful, while remaining silent, as if she wasn't quite sure what to do, since I had now presented her with two alternatives to help with her breathing, in addition to my explanations about CAT scans and ultrasound devices. Now she needed some time to think about what to do.

Finally, Mrs. Armstrong replied, turning any decision over to me, since my explanations had convinced her that I knew about the different options and was in a better position to decide for her. As she told me:

"Please, you decide, doctor. While I appreciate knowing what you told me, this is all so complicated and confusing, I'd prefer to let you decide what's best. You know the different options and now you know about me. So, please. You choose."

That's what I did. After using an ultrasound to detect the lesions in her liver, I arranged for her to be put on the BiPAP machine as needed. I thought this the best choice for her, since it could be adjusted more precisely with different settings for her breathing in and out, whereas the CPAP could only be set to one pressure.

"So we'll get you started on this," I said. "Then, if you can come in next week, I have more options to tell you about, such as what medications to take and what treatment you want in the future."

"That sounds good," she said.

We arranged for a future appointment, and I planned to explain the other options available courtesy of modern medicine then.

The next day, I saw Mrs. Armstrong again, and I first wanted to figure out which medications to give her to adjust her blood pressure and heart rhythm. I began by reviewing the CAT scan without contrast and ultrasound and I asked her: "How are you doing on the BiPAP machine? Did it help you breathe and sleep at night?"

"Yes, it's fine. I'm more comfortable now," she said.

The next step was determining her current blood pressure and heart rhythm. To do so, I asked the nurse on duty to come in and check her blood pressure, which she did by first placing a cuff around Mrs. Armstrong's upper arm, tightening it, and measuring the upper systolic and lower diastolic pressures with a machine, about the size of a postal scale. It whirred for a few seconds, calculating the results; then, it showed them on a monitor.

As I wrote down the notes, the nurse did a manual check to verify the accuracy of the results from the machine, using an arm band connected to a hand pumping device. Since the results were close, showing Mrs. Armstrong had a fair but nearly poor pressure of about 155 over 100, I thought she would benefit from a drug to lower her blood pressure. This would reduce her chances of further medical problems, such as a stroke, heart attack, or cardiac arrest, which are linked to a high blood pressure. Had her blood pressure been too low, I would have changed some of her medications to raise the pressure. Though I knew Mrs. Armstrong probably only had a few weeks to a few months or less before the inevitable end due to her many medical problems, I wanted to make her last days as comfortable as I could.

I pulled out my notebook pad and wrote down some prescriptions which Mrs. Armstrong could take to any pharmacy, including the one in the hospital, which was more convenient, though a little bit more expensive as an in-hospital pharmacy. I explained what I was prescribing so she could understand what to take and why.

"First, I'm prescribing some hydrochlorothiazide, which is a water pill that can help to reduce your blood pressure. Just take one of these 25 mg tablets each day, and you can take them with meals if that's more convenient for you."

I flipped my pad to another page and continued.

"Then, since it seems like your heart may be speeding up at times and not slowing down, so it's not as rhythmical as it should be, I'm prescribing a medication called metoprolol to smooth out your heartbeat. It's best when your heart beats regularly, because that way the oxygen that the blood carries is more regularly pumped to your brain and other parts of your body. While some slight variation in this rhythm might not be harmful, if the heart goes too fast or too slow, either can be dangerous."

"Thanks for the explanation," Mrs. Armstrong said, and I was pleased I could help her understand, since commonly people don't think about these things. They take much of what goes on in the body for granted until things start to go wrong, at which point each part of the body that is causing problems becomes the focus of attention.

"There's one more thing to think about which could go wrong with your heart," I said. "It's the situation in which the heart falls completely out of rhythm in what doctors call an 'arrhythmia,' which means your heartbeat is irregular. It may or may not be beating too fast or too slow; it is just beating out of your heart's normal rhythm. For example, you may feel like your heart skipped a beat, added a beat, is 'fluttering,' or suddenly speeds up. Or you might not notice anything, since some arrhythmias are 'silent.' Depending on the situation, arrhythmias can be an emergency to deal with right away, or they may be harmless."

"How do you know?" Mrs. Anderson asked.

"By taking into consideration your medical issues and the situation as a whole. If you have a lot of medical problems, like in your case, an arrhythmia might be very serious. It could be a warning that things will get worse, so we want to monitor any type of arrhythmia you have carefully and take action right away. Plus medications can help smooth out your heartbeat's rhythm. On the on other hand, some arrhythmias are not serious and temporary, such as when someone feels their heart skip a beat when they are surprised by something. Or someone may feel their heart beat much more quickly or erratically after strenuous exercise, such as at the gym. But if this irregular beating starts while you are mostly sedentary or lying in bed, that is a cause for concern, since something happening your body is triggering this erratic beating, not some external event that is usually temporary."

"And in my case?" Mrs. Armstrong asked.

"It depends," I said. "It depends on the situation and how ill you are at the time. I know these different approaches to dealing with your blood pressure and heart can be quite confusing to you, as it is to many patients and their family members. And all this confusion can be very stressful. That's why it might be better for you to leave a lot of specifics to me and the medical team."

Mrs. Armstrong nodded appreciatively. "Certainly, I understand. It really is confusing. There is so much to think about, and it is better to leave that to the medical professionals. So should I take these now?" she asked, pointing to a few pills I had given to her.

"Yes, so we can keep your body functioning normally as long as possible. Now, we want to treat whatever life-threatening conditions occur, using whatever medications seems to be best under the circumstances. So you might still enjoy many more months of relatively pain-free living, and the drugs I'm prescribing can help. But at the end, we can choose to stop if and when you want us to."

"Okay," she said, indicating that she understood and agreed with my explanation.

I decided there was one more major topic to go over with her—her choice of a DNR/DNI status. Would she prefer to be resuscitated no matter what with a full code, "do everything you can" approach? Would she rather have the monitor turned off to let nature run its course until the end? Or would she prefer some modified DNR status, in which the medical team would use some resuscitation methods but not others?

"Now we have one more big decision to make about your DNR/DNI status. Let me describe what that is, and I'll give you my recommendations. Then you can decide."

As Mrs. Armstrong listened quietly, I began my explanation as I have for hundreds of patients. In the end, Mrs. Armstrong agreed that she wanted no special heroics to extend her life.

"Just let me go when it's my time quickly and painlessly," she said. "That's all I ask."

That's exactly what happened. A few months later, when Mrs. Armstrong could no longer walk around with her oxygen tank and was confined to a hospital bed, where she had difficulty standing and walking even to the bathroom, her heart suddenly started beating erratically. Minutes later, after she seemed to be going into multiorgan failure, with her kidneys and then her lungs shutting down, she stopped breathing, too. So per her instructions, we did nothing, and in a few minutes, she peacefully expired. Despite their complexity, I had been able to explain the many different end-of-life procedures, so she was able to rationally decide what she wanted us to do—which was to do nothing, since she had chosen the DNR/DNI status—and that's exactly what we did—nothing at all.

12

LEGAL CONSIDERATIONS

The different procedures we follow as a hospital and I follow as a doctor are shaped by the federal and state laws and regulations affecting end-of-life care. Besides providing our expertise about what treatments should be provided under what conditions and when to apply the DNR/DNI or modified DNR conditions, our choices are shaped by the laws that affect what we can and cannot do.

Recently, a movement to permit individuals to end their lives painlessly with the assistance of doctors providing prescriptions for pills has been gathering ground, with four states now making this individual choice legal and others considering this option. This approach to the end of life is sometimes called "compassionate choice. " Most recently a woman in California, Christy O' Donnell, who had terminal cancer, spearheaded a campaign to make compassionate choice option legal in California, and this legislation, called the "Medical Aid in Dying" bill just passed.[1] This movement raises a number of legal and ethical issues, although it is not yet discussed at my hospital by the doctors in the area, so I will discuss those issues in this chapter, too.

This chapter features the range of legal considerations that come up in guiding our practice and our response to patients or their families, who may not recognize these considerations or take issue with them.

DECIDING WHAT TO DO IN LIGHT OF LEGAL RESTRICTIONS

In making a decision about how to best treat a patient, the first concern is to do what is best for the patient, given that patient's condition and the patient' s right to choose between a DNR, DNI, or modified DNR status. The basic requirement is that a doctor and medical team have to do everything possible to maintain life, which includes resuscitating a patient, even if the patient's condition is terminal and resuscitation will only lead to more pain and suffering until the end, though we can legally do all we can to minimize the pain and suffering. However, if a patient signs a DNR, DNI, or modified DNR form, that gives the medical team the power to not resuscitate or intubate the patient or to use only those methods of resuscitation requested by the patient.

However, that agreement can become complicated as the patient's situation becomes more complex, so it isn't always clear what the patient wants when the patient seeks to change his or her initial status or when the patient's family members question whether the medical team is properly carrying out the patient's wishes. One problem is that sometimes what is best medically can conflict with the legal restrictions. Another problem is that the uncertainty over whether a patient's condition is really terminal or not can affect whether a DNR/DNI status should be applied or whether the medical team should do all it can to revive the patient, because his or her condition may not be terminal.

Those complexities were well illustrated in the case of Jenny's death. A woman in her sixties, once a marketing executive before she got ill, Jenny had a lawyer son in his forties who wanted the best possible care for his mother and had the money to pay for it. When she first came to the hospital suffering from bronchitis, she expected to recover fully from what at first seemed like an ordinary case of a very severe flu, with coughing, chills, and a high fever. At the time, Jenny had originally chosen to be DNR/DNI, a commonly accepted status, since it is designed to alleviate everybody's worse fears of dying painfully over time. The option is not subject to any controversy when it is invoked immediately after a cardiac and respiratory arrest, since everything occurs very quickly and patients pass away within a few minutes, without any attempt to either resuscitate them or connect them to tubes to help them breathe.

But in Jenny's case, things got complicated after she developed pneumonia, which resulted in a mucus plug logging the airway in one of the main stems leading to her lungs. Such a plug is usually due to the secretions from the lungs coagulating together or to a tumor blocking the airways, which may or may not have been previously detected. In Jenny's case, the problem began with her complaining about her breathing difficulties when I met with her in her semiprivate hospital room, where she had gone to recover from her bronchitis.

"I suddenly find I can't breathe for a few seconds, and then I can," she told me. "This problem has been going on for two days, and it's really scary that these periods when I can't breathe might get longer and longer."

After I examined her by checking her usual vital signs, such as her rate of breathing, pulse, heartbeat, I noticed she might have some extra fluid or edema in her body, so I told her:

"I'd like to suggest some diuresis, a water-elimination procedure, to get rid of what appears to be extra fluid in your body. We can reevaluate daily, and see how it goes."

However, the situation continued to worsen, and two days later she complained that her episodes of not being able to breathe were lasting longer.

So later that day I brought in a pulmonary specialist for another opinion. As Jenny sat up, he tapped around her shoulders and chest and peered down her throat with an endoscope, a long, thin, flexible hose that enabled him to see into her lungs. The endoscope also contains optical equipment for taking photos or short films and can be used to take biopsies, clear the airway, and stop any bleeding. After he finished making his observations, he turned to me to give his verdict.

"I think her lung has been collapsing throughout the day from this mucus plug that is interfering with her breathing."

Meanwhile, as we discussed her case, the situation became even more life threatening. Jenny began gasping for air.

"Please, please. Help me breathe," she begged.

To avoid a ventilator and tube, the lung specialist recommended a noninvasive alternative using the BiPAP. A respiratory therapist soon joined us with a BiPAP machine. He strapped the mask tightly around her face so that air would move in and out with her breathing and she would take in more air with each breath.

"How does that feel?" the lung specialists asked.

Initially Jenny nodded and replied, "It's fine. "

But within a few minutes, she began to feel increasing stress, due to a growing sense of claustrophobia from this heavy mask around her face. Finally, in desperation, she pulled off the mask.

"I'm sorry, but I can't stand wearing this," she gasped.

"But you have to relax with it. And it'll be fine," the lung specialist told her. "Just imagine that you are floating underwater, and this mask is enabling you to breathe."

For a few minutes, Jenny put the mask back on and imagined herself as a scientist with a spear and she saw schools of fish swim by, which seemed to relax her. But as the mask steamed up a little, she became very afraid and desperate again, and pulled off the mask.

"I can't do this," she gasped.

At once the lung specialist and I had a quick meeting, and we decided to intubate her by connecting her up to a mechanical ventilator with a tube down her throat. Although she already had signed a DNI agreement to indicate that she didn't want to be intubated at the end of her life, she had also given her son the power to make decisions for her if she could no longer make these decisions. We figured that recovery was still possible and reversed the DNI part of the DNR/DNI order. Legally we felt we could do so, since her son Adam was part of the team making the decision, and he agreed with this approach since it would give her a chance of overcoming the problems with her lungs and breathing that brought her here.

In any case, the legal DNR/DNI document she had signed would apply whether she recovered or not, because normally, the medical team or hospital cannot legally reverse this order, regardless of the consequences. All a medical team can do is to question the patient again in response to changing medical circumstances, and if the patient changes his or her mind, we can provide as much treatment as possible. Otherwise, if the DNR/DNI order remains in place, the patient goes in peace with the help of sedation.

But in practice, a patient normally chooses a DNR/DNI status and sticks to that decision regardless of the consequences, although if a patient needs help breathing through a tube or mechanical ventilator, such as if they have an emergency like an acute appendicitis, they can legally reverse the order to permit the surgery and postoperative care. After that, the patient can revert back to the DNR/DNI order, since they have recovered. In other words, in real life, the DNR/DNI status can be very fluid, where the patient or the relatives, if involved, can go back and forth in opting for the status or not at a moment's notice, even if there is no rational reason to do so, because this is a very emotional time for everyone.

Unfortunately, by the next day, Jenny had still not recovered. As soon as we took her off the tube connected to the mechanical ventilator, she was still gasping for breath and begged us: "Please, I can't breathe." Furthermore, now she was complaining of agonizing chest pains as well, perhaps because a growing tumor in her lungs was the underlying cause of the mucus collecting there and interfering with her ability to breathe. Because of her already weakened and terminal condition, it was not possible to do any further surgical procedures to determine if she had a tumor or remove the mucus plug. Any such surgery would simply hasten her death, so it would not be medically ethical to do this.

Since her condition now could be terminal, we considered the option of disconnecting her permanently from the tube and ventilator. Or maybe we should give her one last shot by keeping her intubated, so the lung specialist could come the next day to remove the latest plug of mucus in her lungs. Maybe that might return her to baseline and continue the healing process.

It is that kind of "do we or don't we" dilemma that brings up the question of what we can do legally, since the legal determination can be different from what seems medically warranted at the time. This potential for a legal disagreement can occur no matter what we do.

Thus, in Jenny's case, we decided to talk to the patient and determine if she wanted to keep her DNI order in place to bring her battle to breathe to an end. Or did she want to change her status, so we would try as best we could to keep her alive on the chance she might subsequently recover. Unfortunately, we couldn't get a decision from Jenny, since she was already in a state of confusion because gases like carbon dioxide usually accumulate in the lungs if a respiratory failure occurs, which adversely affects mentation, or because the patient has gotten an additional infection on top of the original problem. Whatever the cause, Jenny was in no condition to make any decision.

Therefore I called her son on his cell phone, and he called back about two minutes later.

"I need to ask you what to do about your mother's situation," I explained, and briefly described her condition.

"We have two choices, and we need you to decide now, because your mother can't. Should we try to revive her or let her go?"

Adam replied with the same question at the center of our dilemma. "Is it worth it to try to keep her alive or not?"

I responded with my own indecision and uncertainty. "I'm not really sure myself. On the one hand, it's heartbreaking to connect her up with tubes and put her on a morphine drip to reduce the pain. But it's possible we might have a shot at removing what's plugging up her lungs and give her some more time.

"On the other hand, with Jenny's medical background, all the doors to hope and healing seem to be closing, since her lungs have just about reached an irreversible status. And since she was on dialysis for a while to prevent a buildup of fluid that was settling in her lungs, her kidneys are probably not working anymore either."

"I'm not sure either. So you probably know what' s best," Adam said.

But while his decision to leave the decision up to us might give us a legal reprieve whatever we decided, we were still unsure of the best approach. Thus we decided on the most conservative alternative, which was to intubate her to make her comfortable overnight, rather than letting her breathe on her own as long as possible and then let her go. After that, the lung specialist and the rest of the pulmonary team planned to come in the next morning to remove the excess fluid and clog in her lungs.

Unfortunately, after several hours, the lung specialist and his team found it was not possible to open her airway. It kept filling up with fluid, which clogged up her airway again. Eventually, they returned her to her bed and left her intubated so she could continue to breathe, since she was still unconscious from the anesthesia and could not breathe on her own.

I called Adam at once to tell him the news, explained the situation, and asked him what to do next.

"I'd like to do what's most humane now," he said.

I was glad to hear his decision since I agreed it was futile to keep fighting to keep Jenny alive. Since that's what Adam agreed and we could carry out his wishes, that meant we were doing what is legally required based on following the guidelines originally agreed to by Jenny, and now echoed by her son.

After that, I went to see Jenny, who was now sitting up in bed, a little more awake and comfortable than the last time I saw her, since she was connected to the ventilator by tubes and could breathe more easily.

I explained the situation as diplomatically as I could.

"We can' t do anything more," I concluded.

"I understand, " she wrote back on a pad by her bed, since she couldn't talk while hooked up to a tube. "I know it will be over soon."

Soon after that the medical team removed the tubes connecting her to the ventilator, with instructions to the other nurses or doctors who might see her on their rounds not to reintubate her. Also, they put Jenny on a morphine drip for care and comfort, and a few hours later, she peacefully expired.

Finally it was over. It had been a complicated case, which showed the various legal issues we had to confront in making our medical decisions about how to handle the patient. Fortunately, we were able to maneuver in keeping with the law, so we could both do what seemed best for the patient while remaining within the bounds of the law. In turn, getting the decision from the patient about their DNR/DNI status helped, as did the later decision from her son once she could no longer make any decisions, to go along with whatever the medical team decided was best for the patient. So while we could do nothing medically to help Jenny, at least we could make her as comfortable as possible at the end, which was what she wanted according to the DNR/DNI document she signed several weeks earlier when she still was able to do so.

HOW MUCH IS TOO MUCH?

Since doctors are not permitted to assist in suicides in any way—at least in most states, with five exceptions (Oregon, New Mexico, Montana, Washington, and California), one legal issue that comes up is how much of a drug one can give to prevent the pain and suffering of a patient who is going to die very soon. The legal restrictions and penalties for anything a doctor does to hasten death prevent us from doing anything that might speed up the process. Yet medically, doctors may want to help a patient experiencing severe pain. But that uncertain line between providing pain relief and assisting suicide can be hard to distinguish sometimes, and doctors fear crossing it. Sometimes we can feel wretched that a patient is writhing and yelling in agony because the medicine provided is not enough to quell the pain. Yet to give the patient more medicine might contribute to his or her coming death. As much as a patient may seek more relief, doctors may feel they can do no more or risk being prosecuted for providing excessive medications and even be charged with murder, though the patient given the additional drugs was soon going to die.

This issue came up in dealing with Maria, a patient in her nineties, who had multiple organs that were failing and was going to die very soon. She had lived in a nursing home for the last five years, since Andrea, her older daughter she lived with, felt she could no longer provide sufficient home care. Andrea's two daughters were away at college and had no interest in returning to care for grandma. So Maria went to a nursing home, where she mostly whiled away her days sitting in a chair in the room knitting sweaters for her daughters and grandchildren, watching TV, or observing other patients and medical staff in the dayroom. She said almost nothing to anyone, since due to a brain tumor she had difficulty communicating apart from saying some basic words and concepts such as: "Hello . . . . How are you? . . . . What time is it? . . . I'm getting hot . . . or . . . . It's too cold."

When Maria first arrived in the hospital, accompanied by Andrea, a stylish woman in her mid-sixties who worked as a management consultant, she was experiencing septic shock from an infection that started with a small cut. The infection spread through her body very quickly due to her weakened immune system, which is common in many elderly people. As a result, Maria soon experienced inflammation throughout her body, which led to the sepsis syndrome, resulting in the tissues receiving insufficient oxygen and nutrients, since these are blocked from reaching the brain and other vital organs. This blockage causes many organs to fail, resulting in even more intense septic shock, and if untreated, this condition causes blood pressure to drop and may result in death.

Thus, I knew I had to act quickly to overcome the inflammation that was taking over Maria's body and internal organs, though I couldn't directly speak to her to learn exactly what was wrong because of her brain tumor. After I arranged for her to be placed in a semiprivate room, I spoke with Andrea, who was acting as a proxy for her mother. Andrea provided a brief overview of the situation.

"My mother can't function very well because of the tumor. So she can't talk about and remember things like she used to. Sometimes she has good days, when she knows who I am and seems to understand when I say something simple to her. She can still remember how to do simple things, too, like knitting and crocheting. But otherwise, she is in a near vegetative state."

"We'll do what we can about her septic condition," I said. I immediately arranged for Maria to be put on dialysis to get rid of the toxins that had accumulated in her system, and I gave her some drugs to prevent blood clotting and to raise her blood pressure. Additionally, I arranged for her to get intravenous antibiotics to fight the bacteria that had started the infection.

"I can't promise anything because of your mother's age and her medical problems apart from the sepsis. But at least today's treatment should be a chance to get rid of the sepsis."

Several days later, Andrea realized her mother was doing well when she saw her mother sitting up in the dayroom and starting to knit again.

Unfortunately, the sepsis was the least of Maria's problems, since three days later, she starting having seizures. I called Andrea, now at home, to tell her about her mother's changed condition.

"She's now experiencing a few seizures every hour. She suddenly goes spastic, curls up in a ball, and starts shaking for about a minute before the seizure stops. And they seem to be increasing in number and severity. This is a serious emergency, and I don't think there's much more we can do for her," I said.

At that point Andrea agreed on behalf of the whole family that Maria's condition was now terminal.

A little later that day, I met with Andrea to determine the level of care to be given in Maria's last days. After I explained about the different possibilities, including the DNR/DNI and modified DNR status, Andrea opted for comfort measures only as part of a DNR status. So I wrote up Maria's status accordingly. To this end, we stopped all diagnosis, therapy, and intervention options, including monitoring the vital signs. We also provided Maria and her family with a hospital room with a single bed so she could spend her last days surrounded by her family and friends. She could also have her own minister or other religious leaders, if desired, perform an end-of-life religious ritual without any interruption by medical professionals.

Then I put her on a morphine drip to ease her pain. To do so, the nurse set up a plastic bag with morphine, connected to a machine programmed to dispense a certain amount of morphine every hour or two through a long tube connected to a vein in her arm. The amount depends on the patient's condition, weight, and other factors, with a goal of keeping the patient free of pain or at least reducing the pain, while not providing enough morphine to kill the patient or hasten his or her death.

Determining the amount of painkiller to give to maintain this balance between reducing pain and not killing the patient can be a fine line to stay on the right side of the law. This dilemma is starkly illustrated when the amount given isn't enough to eliminate or reduce the pain, so the patient ends up suffering in agony. Or even if a patient is in a semicomatose or vegetative condition, the patient's body may still respond to pain, and the body's writhing and jerking as the patient goes through hours and days of the drip can speak volumes about the agony he or she is experiencing. Yet as much as we may want to end the patient's pain medically, we are held back from doing so by the legal requirements—at least in most states— because we are not allowed to "kill" the patient, even though that patient is destined to die over the next hours or days without any improvement in his or her condition.

In Maria's case, in administering the morphine drip, the nurse as usual removed any other means of supporting the patient, such as providing fluids or nutrition, so the patient's only comfort was from a combination of drugs. This included a morphine drip to reduce pain, along with three other drugs—Ativan and Haldol to help sedate or relax the patient, and Levsin to stop respiratory tract secretions.

But the big problem for Maria was that during the eight days it took her to die, she was clearly uncomfortable with the level of morphine we could give her without causing her to die from a morphine "overdose," except if a medical team member saw her experience distress, such as if her body began writhing, shaking, or jerking in pain, he or she could up the level of painkillers. When the nurse on duty saw this happen, she gave Maria a small dose to increase her comfort level. Even so, Maria was soon writhing, shaking and jerking again without anyone there to observe or stem the pain.

Thus, this situation was horrible for me and the rest of the medical team, because legally we were not allowed to increase the level of morphine beyond her comfort level without seeing evidence of her distress. Yet it was difficult to determine this balance point, since Maria was now unable to communicate anything about her situation, so we had to rely on any cues from her body, such as her sudden fits that indicated she was experiencing pain and suffering. But someone couldn't be at her side at all times, so often after a slight increase in the morphine level to stop the pain, followed by a short period of relaxation, Maria would go into another spasm of writhing, shaking, and jerking when the pain came back. But our hands were tied from setting the morphine drip at a higher level that would take her life prematurely, so no one upped her dosage because the risk of doing so is considered to hasten the patient's inevitable death. Unfortunately, this likely increase in pain and suffering for a patient who cannot be given more morphine results in increased pain and suffering for the patient's family members who come to the hospital to be with the patient before he or she dies. Though the patient may not be aware they are there, the family members feel better being by his or her side. But as they see the patient suffer, they suffer too, especially when they can't get the medical team to act to alleviate the pain because of the legal restrictions.

In short, as Maria's case illustrates, it is unfortunate that the medical team cannot do anything to break the "barrier of comfort" level which is designed to keep the patient as comfortable as possible without causing death. Medically, we might like to break through this barrier to get dying patients to their destination of death more quickly and painlessly, which would be more humane, since recovery is no longer possible. But unfortunately, the present law in most US states deems otherwise. Legally, the morphine drip can only provide physical comfort to the living; it cannot provide comfort to help the dying patient die more quickly, peacefully, and painlessly, which is what most patients and their families want.

DEALING WITH POTENTIAL LAWSUITS WHEN PATIENTS CAN'T DECIDE WHAT TO DO

Another time legal considerations come into play is when patients are at the end of their life since all systems are failing, but they haven't filled out the DNR/DNI legal document that indicates that they don't want to be resuscitated or intubated. At this time, the medical team may have to decide based on what the patient, when lucid, said he or she wants to do, such as to maintain life as long as possible, even though the medical team doesn't agree this is the best thing to do under the circumstances, which is to reduce pain and suffering and let the patient go naturally. The one exception is where the hospital ethics committee, composed of doctors, social workers, nurses, religious personnel, and administrators, can intervene and advise the medical team not to provide certain treatments to prolong life in order to achieve a more humane end of life, even when relatives are involved. Then the institution would make the decision that the DNR approach should be used after all.

However, barring that exception, matters can become complicated when family members claim the hospital is not doing the best it can for the patient; has mismanaged the patient's care, thereby contributing to his terminal condition; or insist that the hospital should do more or face a lawsuit for poor care. Then the legal dispute can get ugly, even if the hospital ultimately prevails in court or in the settlement procedures.

Normally though, what usually happens is that the legal fate of the doctor and hospital run in tandem. Usually, the family members sue the doctor personally and try to sue as many doctors as they can to increase the potential for a higher legal settlement, since the hospital's liability cap is about $20,000 per case. Then the lawyers of the family members try to obtain as much as they can from the insurance policy of the doctors and hospital. Conversely, the lawyers for the insurance company seek to keep the payout as low as possible.

This kind of legal battle is what happened in the case of Joe, a man in his early fifties who worked as a construction worker and had a long medical history because of his diabetes. Unfortunately, he loved to eat and often forgot to take his insulin to reduce his glucose count, which was higher due to his diabetes. So frequently he ended up in the hospital due to the buildup of glucose in his blood. In the early stages, he suffered from some of the classic symptoms of diabetes, such as urinating often, feeling very thirsty or hungry even after eating, and experiencing extreme fatigue, blurry vision, slow-to-heal cuts and bruises, and a tingling pain or numbness in his hands and feet. Sometimes these symptoms led him to take excessive absences from work, which resulted in him getting laid off from a number of construction jobs.

Then, since he didn't take care of himself, such as by staying up late at parties and by drinking heavily, his diabetes progressed to kidney failure and nerve damage. The disease also contributed to the hardening and narrowing of his arteries—a disease called "atherosclerosis," which made him a prime candidate for strokes and coronary heart disease. Yet despite the risks, Joe repeatedly ignored the advice of the doctors he saw and continued to overeat and indulge in his fondness for chocolate, candy, and cake.

Thus, by his forties, he was spending his last years in the hospital with over fifteen admissions a year for different complications due to his diabetes and heavy drinking. Ironically, the biggest bright spot in his life is that he met his significant other, Sally, on one of his hospital visits when she was the nurse assigned to care for him. When he got out, she moved in with him and continued to help and care for him.

Finally, as Joe's condition continued to deteriorate, so his end of life was likely within the next few months, he ended up back in the hospital, where I first met him. He was already in the ICU unit on a mechanical ventilator as I sat by his bedside. I first looked at his record, which was like a medical version of a rap sheet, listing all the things which had gone wrong for him for fifteen years. Among other things, he had been on dialysis for many years, whereby he came to the hospital every day or two to be hooked up to the dialysis machine. This procedure removed his accumulation of fluids, which would normally be eliminated through normal urine production, but he couldn't eliminate them in this way, since his kidneys weren't functioning. Then he went on his way.

But after he returned home, instead of following the doctor's orders to abstain from drinking and high-fructose soft drinks and snacks to give his kidneys a chance to heal, he did not. So soon he was back in the hospital. Finally his kidneys gave out for good. Though he had multiple kidney transplants, the new kidneys failed because he didn't give up his bad eating habits. Therefore he ended up with a permanent dialysis arrangement due to his diabetes and failure to treat it properly.

When he weakly lifted his hands to greet me, I noticed that he had very few fingers left. As his record indicated, they had been amputated because they got ulcerated due to the reduced blood flow resulting from his diabetes. So eventually gangrene set in, and there was no way to help him heal.

Finally, I asked him to tell me a little about himself and what kind of end-of-life care he wanted.

"I guess this really is the end of the line for me," he acknowledged. "I know my situation has been getting worse."

"Yes, I can see it in your record," I said, and again I glanced through his medical history. As it indicated, he had been in the ICU many times before and needed a machine to breathe because his lungs had become so damaged. Also, he was on dialysis because of the damage from his diabetes on top of having cirrhosis of his liver due to drinking too much. Sometimes he had come to the hospital because he experienced congestive heart failure, which led him to feel shortness of breath, a rapid or irregular heartbeat, and a pulmonary edema, resulting in fluid accumulating in the air sacs in his lungs, making it difficult to breathe.

"So I guess you can see I'm really a mess now," Joe added. "So I think enough is enough. I just want to end it all."

I told him about the DNR and DNI alternatives, and he immediately agreed.

"That's what I want, doc. I think it's time to check out, and if you can ' t assist me in doing it, the 'do not resuscitate, do not intubate' arrangement sounds like the next best thing. Just let me go, and don't try to bring me back."

However, before I could return with the necessary paperwork, his significant other, Sally, now a nursing-home nurse who had lived with him for the past three years, came to the hospital with his long-estranged daughter Betty and son Johnnie, who both lived in other parts of the state. His children had stopped communicating with him about three years before because they were frustrated by his heavy drinking and his drunken angry rants about losing his job and not being given a chance to get it back. But Joe didn't do anything to change. Instead, he kept drinking to forget all of that pain, and he refused to stop because the liquor comforted him, even as it caused his continued medical breakdown and inability to get paid work again, so he had to rely on the support of Sally and social security checks to survive. Since his son and daughter didn't want to enable his continued self-destructive behavior, their checks to him and communication stopped.

But now here they were, along with Sally, demanding that the hospital do all these additional procedures to help Joe, as if this was his chance to regain his health and they felt guilty for not helping him in the past few years.

Sally summed up their viewpoint when she commented, "Joe's just too far gone to make any sense now, so that's why you have to do everything you can now to bring him back."

"That's right," Johnnie agreed firmly. "The hospital probably thinks it's cheaper to stop treating him so he doesn't come back. But if he doesn't come back this time, we'll be coming after the hospital for mal-practice, and it'll be much more expensive for you that way."

After that diatribe by Sally and his son, the hospital called for an emergency ethics meeting to decide what to do. We met that afternoon in one of the hospital's conference rooms and sat around a long table. Be-sides me, the other participants included several administrators, social workers, and doctors, and a priest, minister, and rabbi who visited many of the patients of their religious faith to discuss any last issues or perform any final rituals, so the patient could pass away in peace.

What should we do in Joe's case? The main consideration was what Joe wanted and the medical consensus that his "end it all" choice was the best thing to do despite the lack of any signed paperwork giving us this authority versus the demanding relatives who didn't understand or want to accept the terminal nature of Joe's multiple organ failures. Joe hadn't signed any paperwork because of his foggy mental condition brought about by his heavy drinking, as well as his repeated statements when asked to sign that he wanted to talk to his family first, though he wanted to do what the doctors said was best, too. His relatives seemed to think the problem wasn't as bad as the hospital claimed or expected the hospi-tal's medical team to perform some corrective action from providing drugs to surgery to make everything right. But even if any lawsuit they brought might be misguided and ultimately fail, the hospital still had the expense and aggravation of fighting them. Meanwhile, something had to be decided quickly about Joe before he died, although his death was surely coming within a week or two or even in a few days or hours.

The participants at the conference expressed various positions in how the hospital should react to the threat of a potential lawsuit and what the most ethical posture would be in such a case.

"The relatives really don't understand the seriousness of Joe's condi-tion," one of the doctors said. "They are expecting miracles, when noth-ing we can do will overcome all the damage to Joe's different organ systems."

"So it doesn't make sense medically to resuscitate or intubate Joe," said a second doctor. "It will just cause him unnecessary pain and suffer-ing."

"And Joe told me personally that he wants this," I offered.

"So ethically, that could be the right thing to do," said the priest.

"That's in keeping with the medical oath of do no harm," said the rabbi.

"But they could be bluffing," said the social worker. "And once they see it is futile to try to keep Joe alive, they will realize they have no case."

"Besides," said the administrator, "any lawsuit against the hospital will be expensive for them to bring, and they may not find a law firm to take such a case on contingency. They could also be subject to high expenses if they lose, which they probably will, to cover our expenses for defending against a frivolous suit."

"Yet even if they lose, they may not have the costs to cover any penalty," said the third doctor.

"Still, any lawsuit will be bad publicity for the hospital," the administrator pointed out.

"Let's pray about what we should do," said the minister.

"And whatever we decide, we need to act quickly given Joe's condition on whether to attempt to resuscitate him or not," I said.

The meeting went on and on to decide on the right thing to do or not do both legally and ethically, since there were multiple interpretations and opinions. In essence, the hospital faced the decision of whether to honor the patient's expressed wishes, which were stated verbally to me shortly before he became unable to communicate further. His DNR choice also had the support of several doctors, including myself, since nothing more could be done to help him. So we all believed that the medically sound and ethical thing to do was to stop any further treatment that was only causing Joe to suffer more. But opposed to that view was the threat of a lawsuit by family members who wanted doctors to do the impossible by restoring the patient to a state of health. Yet we knew medically that couldn't be done, and he would certainly die over the next days or weeks as his organs shut down.

Then one of the social workers raised the question of whether the family had the legal position to make this claim.

"Joe has been living with a partner for several years and has been out of touch with his family members. So can they suddenly appear and make any claims on his behalf, when Joe has clearly stated the opposite position?"

Thus, in the end, the hospital decided to take the threat of a lawsuit by the family as a threat that might not materialize, since the family might not have the funds to bring it or would lose. Plus they might not get a lawyer to represent them. As a result, with the potential threat of a lawsuit considered only a small possibility, the hospital chose to do what was most medically feasible and ethically defensible, as well as what the patient told me he wanted.

With that decision made, the nurses made Joe as comfortable as possible with a morphine drip for his last few hours, and he passed away shortly after that. Sally made the arrangements for his funeral service and memorial, and ironically, his son and daughter didn't even stay around for that. They left town and had no further communication with the hospital, just as they had stopped communicating with their dad a few years before.

Perhaps in another situation, the hospital's determination might have been different. But the incident with Joe illustrates the way doctors and hospitals can get caught in a legal and ethical bind when the patient and medical team feel that there should be no special resuscitation or intubation arrangements in the absence of a written DNR or DNI order, and other family members disagree. It seems like such a legal and ethical quandary needs to be determined on a case-by-case basis, based on a medical assessment of the patient's condition; the ethical considerations; the patient's agreement to end his or her life in a natural, peaceful way; and the standing and claim of family members to want a different end. While it might seem that the patient's wishes and medical determination should take priority, legally there could be other constraints and priorities. Joe's story shows the legal and ethical issues that can come up and the need to develop a plan for how to proceed under the different scenarios that might arise when patients, doctors, other medical team members, and members of the patient's family have different views on what to do when the patient is dying and a decision must be made quickly on how to best to treat that patient at the end of his or her life.

DEALING WITH AN EMERGENCY

Legal issues can also come into play when an emergency occurs, so there is no time to determine what the patient actually wants or get any legal agreement in place. Under such circumstances, the medical team generally has to make the best call in deciding whether or not to resuscitate or intubate the patient. The decision has to be made within seconds to minutes, because in a clear life-or-death situation the team has to consider the possibility of reviving the patient to resume a productive life or the inevitability that the patient cannot recover and will be dead very shortly. Such considerations can later be used in explaining the reasons for the decision, and if necessary, this rationale may play a part in any ligation brought by the surviving relatives, although normally they recognize what has been done and why and they accept this choice as the best possible medical response under the circumstances.

That situation occurred in the case of Mrs. Chase, an eighty-six-year old woman who lived on her own with the assistance of a home care worker who came each day to help with regular chores like making her bed, washing dishes, and doing errands. Mrs. Chase had two granddaughters in the area who came to visit every week or two, although she had become estranged from her son, who lived in another state across the country, and they only spoke on the phone a few times a year. He had become busy with his own family, so they drifted apart.

I had once seen Mrs. Chase as a regular patient; we had had time to discuss end-of-life decisions and she was never conclusive about any final statements. I hadn't seen her for a few years when she called my office, so it was unclear if she had made up her mind one way or another as she stated she had been thinking about her coming death for a while.

"I'm short of breath," she told me. "I went for my usual walk around my neighborhood today, and suddenly I found it hard to breathe. I had to sit down and felt my heart suddenly beating very quickly. Then I felt like I was going to faint for a minute or two before I recovered. I've been using an oxygen tank to help me breathe for a few minutes every hour and when I go to bed at night. So I'm scared about what could be happening."

I told her, "You should go immediately to the emergency room, and I can meet you there. We don't have the equipment and tests we need to do at my office, so we can do them at the hospital."

"Okay," she agreed, although instead of meeting me right away, it took her a day to show up at the nearest emergency room across from my office. I got the call she was there from the emergency room nurse, who added: "It seems like she might have pneumonia."

Mrs. Chase was propped up in bed in one of the outpatient rooms, connected to a cardiac monitor, and the nurse handed me her chest X-ray to review. As I looked at it, I saw a dark gray cast on her left side, which was a sign she had the tell-tale lesions of the lung caused by pneumonia.

As I turned toward her, ready to report on my observations, I saw her heart rate zoom within seconds to 212 beats per minute, which is normally a life-threatening emergency. Yet Mrs. Chase didn't have any symptoms of this overly fast heart rate, which normally does not allow enough time for the heart to fill before it contracts, so it reduces blood flow to the rest of the body. The result is that the patient commonly experiences feelings of dizziness, light-headedness, a rapid heartbeat or palpitations, chest pains, and a shortness of breath. So far, Mrs. Chase was not experiencing any of these symptoms, perhaps because the rapid heartbeat came on so suddenly. Still, the sudden increase in her heartbeat to a life-threatening speed was a sign that something was seriously wrong.

But rather than alert Mrs. Chase immediately, since that might increase her stress and heartbeat, I turned to one of her granddaughters, Julia, who had come with her on previous visits to my office years before, and pointed to the monitor.

"This is an extremely high heart rate," I explained. "It could be the sign of an impending heart attack or cardiac arrest, which would be life-threatening. Do you know if your grandmother has decided to be resuscitated or not if either situation occurs?"

"I don't know anything about this," Julia said. "So ask her."

Thus, I reluctantly turned to Mrs. Chase and asked my question.

At once, she became anxious as I had feared.

"Why do you want to know now?" she said.

"We could wait," I said.

I felt I needed to back off, since making a choice under this life-or-death situation might be even more stressful for her. Instead, I asked a nurse to give Mrs. Chase some medication to slow down her racing heart rate, and called a trusted cardiologist friend on his cell phone to ask what I should do.

"I'll be there in a few minutes," he said. Two minutes later he was there.

Since I had to decide quickly without any decision by the patient or her two granddaughters, I felt it important to have an expert in the area to help me decide. I knew we would not only be making the decision for medical reasons, but we had to consider the legal ramifications of deciding for a patient or family members who couldn't or wouldn't make a choice in the face of a critical life-threatening situation. The issue was whether to resuscitate or intubate on the grounds that this life was medically worth saving to return to a relatively healthy life, or not to do so since the individual had no chance of surviving for more than a few hours to a day or two. In this latter case, it would be better to let the patient go, rather than suffer needlessly while kept alive.

"What do you recommend we do if her heart stops or she stops breathing?" I asked my cardiologist friend.

He looked at the monitor and at Mrs. Chase, trying to decide. But before he could make a determination, Mrs. Chase's heartbeat began to slow down. Within a few minutes it was back to an acceptable heart rhythm, about 125 beats per minute, and she no longer seemed to have any major arrhythmia or out-of-order beats.

"It looks like I don't have to recommend anything," the cardiologist said. "It looks like she's going to recover on her own."

So now the emergency was over. But it raised the issue of how to decide in an emergency, when the patient or family members haven't left clear instructions on what to do in a sudden life-or-death situation. At the time, we made our decision based on what was medically recommended, as well as on the legal considerations. Certainly, it is best if the patient and family members can make a DNR/DNI status determination early on under a no-pressure situation, and afterward they can change their decision however they want. But barring these written directives, guidelines to follow in an emergency would help so that the medical team faces no legal consequences for responding based on their assessment of the best medical outcome under the circumstances or on what the patient or family members have verbally indicated that they want. As this emergency situation made clear, having a determination early on is important, because any emergency creates a high-stress situation when it is not always possible for patients, family members, or medical professionals to make the best decisions. Moreover, an emergency can occur at any time because the ordinary vagaries of life can affect everyone, not just those with extensive medical problems.

DEALING WITH THE ASSISTED-SUICIDE ISSUE

One legal issue that has been drawing increased national attention is assisted suicide. Already five states have legalized the ability of a patient to get a physician to provide advice and a prescription for life-ending pills, although each law includes many provisions to prevent abuse. The guiding principle of these laws is that a patient with a terminal condition and less than six months to live should be able to end his or her life with the assistance of a doctor. Commonly, the law provides that he or she needs the agreement of two doctors to get a life-ending prescription for pills and has to wait seventy-two hours after getting permission before filling a prescription. The particular details differ from state to state, but the basic idea is that a patient facing the end of life and experiencing increasing pain and suffering should be able to voluntarily end his or her life. Some of these provisions for getting a second opinion and needing to wait before obtaining life-ending pills are designed to prevent a patient from being forced or enticed into making this decision by others.

The issue has become increasingly part of the national consciousness and debate as the result of two key cases. One was Brittany Maynard's decision to move to Oregon to terminate her life there since it was legal to do so—a choice she made on November 1, 2014. A more recent case occurred in late June 2015, when Christy O'Donnell, suffering from terminal cancer that had spread throughout her body, announced that she was leading the fight for a change in the law in California. Since then, the California legislature passed a law which permitted ending a life for compassionate care, and Governor Brown signed the California's End of Life Option Act in law on October 5, 2015.[2] Besides California and Oregon, the other three states with a law permitting medical aid to dying as of this writing are Washington, Oregon, Vermont with a death by dignity statute; and Montana, with death by dignity provided by a court decision. Another sixteen states as of this writing are considering death with dignity laws, among them New York, Michigan, Wisconsin, Missouri, and Nevada.[3]

Since the issue has become part of the national debate, I am sometimes asked about what a doctor should do if asked about providing such help. My answer now would be that it depends on what is legal in a particular state. Doctors can use that as a guide to their own decision as to whether to assist a patient or not, taking into consideration their own religious and ethical feelings about what to do.

Where assisted suicide isn't yet legal, the traditional guide is to do what is necessary to preserve life, while avoiding unnecessary pain and suffering. So the response here in Massachusetts has been to use the DNR/DNI or modified DNR status as the determining factor. In this way, a doctor or medical practitioner will not assist a patient in ending his or her life, but will let it end naturally by not providing resuscitation or intubation where the patient is clearly dying, while providing comfort through medication to reduce or eliminate the pain and suffering at the end.

13

A QUESTION OF WHEN

The question of when a patient is actually considered terminal is another big issue in end-of-life care. Whether a person has been in an accident, has a fast-acting illness, or is in the last stages of a chronic disease, the big question is whether that person can recover. The other key question is whether a recovery leads to a renewed chance at life, even if the person will have to go through an extensive rehabilitation process or suffer from a continuing disability, such as the loss of a limb or paralysis.

For doctors and other medical practitioners, the general guideline to follow is the preservation of all life. So if there is any hope for a recovery, the doctor and medical team will try to preserve life.

But at other times, if the patient's condition is terminal, the previously discussed end-of-life procedures kick in, such as applying a DNR/DNI (do not resuscitate or do not intubate) status or going full code.

Yet, somewhere between a patient showing all the signs of making a full recovery to one who is already DOA (dead on arrival), there is a time when doctors, other medical practitioners, and the patient and his or her family can be uncertain whether the patient's condition is terminal or if a partial or full recovery is possible.

DETERMINING WHEN A PATIENT IS TERMINAL

This question of when a patient is terminal can be quite complex based on a number of factors: the current condition of the patient, the patient's medical history that indicates past medical problems and treatment results, the medications used now and in the past with what results, and the determination of one or more doctors about the patient's chances of recovery.

Sometimes medical records will show the patient's past history and responses to different medications, but sometimes this information will not be available. In that case, the doctor or other medical professionals assessing the patient's condition will have to get this information from the patient, if he or she is coherent and articulate enough to provide it. Alternatively, it may be possible to get this information from the family or from the hospital, if this information is on file.

But sometimes this information is not available to aid in the terminal diagnosis. Then a doctor or medical team have to decide based on what they know about the patient from what they can observe and what any monitors hooked up to the patient show. For example, doctors might use images from a CAT scan, since these can show large hidden tumors, internal bleeding, very large blood vessels that are stretched thin and about to explode, or an aneurism, which is a weak section of a blood vessel in the brain that could crack. Still other images from scans might show abscesses, dead tissues, and tumors in vital organs. Doctors can then assess how serious the patient's condition is based on the degree of damage to one or more vital organs.

However, any determination can be further complicated by the unpredictability of the patient's healing in any situation. While doctors and medical practitioners can generally predict what is likely to happen given the patient's condition, past history, and other factors, an unexpected change for the better or worse is always possible. As a result, a patient considered terminal might suddenly rally and improve. Conversely, a patient who seems to be recovering might take a turn for the worse and become terminal.

Therefore, while in the vast majority of cases a doctor's prognosis is likely to be correct, and in most cases two or more doctors may agree on the outcome, there can always be some cases where the patient responds in an unexpected way—either favorably or unfavorably—to treatment.

Aside from this potential uncertainty in determining whether a patient is terminal or not, another complication is what the patient and his or her family believe is terminal, since this belief can affect how they respond to a doctor's recommendation of what to do. Generally when a disagreement occurs, the patient or family believe there is a hope for recovery and insist on continued treatment against the advice of their doctor or medical team, until treatment efforts fail and the patient is clearly terminal. In the meantime, the result of such a disagreement is generally more futile treatment, while the patient suffers more pain until the very end.

Thus, as this chapter illustrates, it can not only be difficult in some cases to determine when a patient is terminal, but that assessment can change. Moreover, doctors and other medical professionals can disagree with patients and family members about whether the patient is terminal and what to do about it.

WHEN A HOPE FOR RECOVERY TURNS INTO A TERMINAL CASE

Sometimes a terminal condition develops or is discovered after a patient has been admitted to the hospital and is expected to recover. An example might be when a doctor opens a patient's abdomen to remove the gallbladder, but finds cancer throughout his body. In such a case, the surgical treatment would fail because the doctor has discovered an underlying problem, such as a hidden tumor or series of tumors. Due to this discovery, the patient can now be classified as terminal, but the patient or family may or may not agree with the new determination.

This change of status is what happened in the case of Mr. Alexopoulos, a seventy-something man of Greek origin, who appeared to be very strong and proud when he came to my office with his two daughters, both in their forties. Over fifty years before, as a teenager, he had come to America as an immigrant with almost no money. But a distant cousin took him in and provided a place to stay. Soon he found a talent for entrepreneurship, and he began creating small companies to sell products to Greek immigrants in several suburban communities in New York. Eventually, he gained great success as an importer of trendy Greek goods. No wonder he appeared very powerful and confident.

Everything changed when he fell while trying to get lab work his doctor ordered at the local hospital. His doctor referred him there, since Mr. Alexopoulos had been eating too many rich foods at conventions and business luncheons. But rather than exercise his willpower or enter into a diet program to change his lifestyle, he found it easier to keep up his bad eating behavior and go for a relaxing walk once or twice a week. But after several months, his condition began to deteriorate because his regular treatments didn't alleviate the underlying condition, due to his high blood pressure and high level of cholesterol caused by his heavy weight and high-sugar and starch diet. These were still too high despite any drugs he was prescribed and which he often didn't take. The result was that his condition was causing his organs to slow down because he needed to get rid of excess fluids and waste. He also had some other problems, largely due to overeating and his high-fats-and-cholesterol diet of too much meat, cheese, eggs, and other animal protein. Among other things, he had high blood pressure, extra fluid in the lungs, and low energy and stamina. For example, if he took short walks around the neighborhood, he soon got very tired and had to find a bench to sit down or else he felt like he was going to faint if he didn't rest for a few minutes.

Adding to his problems, after Mr. Alexopoulos fell at the hospital, as he got up from his chair to leave and tried to stand, he felt agonizing pain through his leg and left side, and discovered he had broken his left hip. He was wheeled to the emergency department, where I met with him.

Initially, I had no reason to think about whether he was terminal or not, since his presenting problem was the broken hip. But I wanted him to at least determine his code status in event of an unexpected cardiac arrest, since the hospital policy was for a patient to decide that in advance. This way the hospital could know how to deal with a sudden emergency, such a cardiac arrest, in order to respect the patient's wishes. Once I explained what the hospital needed, he immediately chose the DNR/DNI status.

"I don't want any heroic measures or invasive procedures if my heart stops or I stop breathing," he told me.

Then, since Mr. Alexopoulos was there for his broken hip, I suggested he start with hip surgery.

Iinitially it seemed like a fairly cut-and-dried case, where a DNR/DNI decision is like creating a life-insurance plan for the future. As far as I could tell, Mr. Alexopoulos seemed to be still healthy, although he needed to continue a regular treatment to clear his system of toxic wastes.

Another favorable sign of healing is that he seemed to bounce back after he had a short cardiac arrest when the surgeon cut into his hip to reposition the broken bones. At once the surgical team sprang into action, massaged and pressed up and down on his chest, and in about a minute, they were able to restart his heart. They then hooked him back up to a ventilator to ease his breathing. But rather than further operate on his broken hip, they moved him back to his private room and postponed the surgery for three days.

This time, the surgery was fine. The surgeon repaired his hip, and the plan was for him to spend three or four days in the hospital, go to a rehab program, and afterward return to his everyday life, much as before his fall, by having his regular dialysis once or twice a week.

But that plan didn't happen, for after a series of efforts to treat him, it was clear to me that his condition was now terminal. The multiple conditions came together so there would be no healing this time. He had too many problems.

The first problem to show up was that Mr. Alexopoulos now had an increasingly high blood pressure of over 150/95, then 160/98, then 170/105. Clearly, some problem with his system was driving the spiking numbers. After the results came back for the urine specimen he sent to the lab, these indicated he had a urinary tract infection, and the next day, his blood pressure began to drop and he had difficulty breathing.

At this point, I examined him and told him about his growing list of problems.

"You need extra fluids, so drink a lot of water or soup," I recommended. "That should help build your blood pressure back up, as well as help you breathe. You're also dehydrated, possibly due in part to the infection, so that's causing some of your organs to stop functioning."

Mr. Alexopoulos nodded, and perhaps because my diagnosis helped him trust me, he opened up about his past medical problems. It was as if he had been hiding the truth about his condition, perhaps to prevent others in the business world from finding out and not buying his products. But now he felt safe to reveal what he had kept bottled up.

"I had some problems with my lungs before, and the doctors found some fluid in my lungs, which were drained. I thought that was in the past, so I didn't say anything about it. But I thought I should mention this, since I started having trouble breathing."

To check, I took a chest X-ray and saw some dark grayish spots that didn't look normal. They suggested he might have a small tumor in his chest that led to the past buildup of fluid, which was now causing his breathing problems.

Thus, now I realized that Mr. Alexopoulos was facing the end of life, and my diagnosis was reaffirmed over the next few days, as he remained in the hospital recovering from his hip surgery while I prepared him and his family for his last days.

One indication that the end of life was near was his growing pain due to his surgery and breathing difficulties. After I told the nurse to give him a couple of extra doses of morphine to ease the pain and help him sleep better, he felt nauseous and began vomiting. So instead of the morphine, the nurse placed an NG tube through his nose to drain the extra contents from his stomach. At least that stopped the vomiting, though Mr. Alexopoulos experienced the pain of the tube for a few days until he could resume eating again.

Worse, he still had the original problems with his organs. Then he got an infection in his urinary tract, and his blood pressure continued to rocket up and drop down, so he strangely alternated between extremely high and very low blood pressure. His system seemed to be out of control, and I was certain his condition was terminal.

Thus, I spoke to him again about his original decision to be listed as a DNR/DNI status. At the time I arranged this with him, it was to plan for the future. But now his end of life was coming very soon.

I sat down beside him and explained the current situation.

"Of course, I understand," he replied. "I'll talk to my family. I have a large Greek family, so I may not be able to reach everyone. But I'll let everyone I can know, and they can pass this information on."

Two days later, he spoke on the phone to his two daughters, Julie and Anna, and about a dozen other relatives.

"I told everyone I want to let go quickly," he explained to me. "Since the day of my fall, my life essentially ended. There was no way for me to heal from that, and it made all my other conditions, which I thought I were over with, worse."

The morning before his death, as I came to his bedside where his two daughters sat on either side, he told me about the terrible pain he was experiencing.

"It's excruciating," he gasped, wincing as he spoke. "The narcotics you gave me aren't enough. Since the fall, the toll of this fracture on my life has been totally devastating. You know I'm a proud man, and I have been able to overcome many things, from losses in building my business to losses of people very dear to me. Now I feel helpless and in so much pain, way beyond anything I could otherwise stand if I could see a bright future ahead. But I don't see any real light at the end of the tunnel, and I know my life has essentially ended."

As he finished speaking, Julie burst out crying.

"Can we have a family meeting?" she asked.

I left Mr. Alexopoulos with his daughters, who were sitting on either side of his bed, holding his hand and crying.

A couple of hours later, a nurse called me from the floor to tell me: "The family wants to meet with you today."

"Certainly," I agreed, and about 7 p.m. I met briefly with a dozen family members—Julie and Anna, their husbands, and several other brothers, sisters, and grandchildren.

I began by asking Mr. Alexopoulos, "How do you feel about what you decided?"

"Fine. I know it's my time now, and I want to go peacefully. I feel I am surrounded by all this love from my family, and this has helped me feel ready to go. So I'm ready to let go, as I have been for the last couple of days."

With that, Julie squeezed his hand and looked up at me, with a similar show of determination.

"Everyone here understands what my father wants to do. And we agree. Whatever he wants, we are prepared for that."

With that, I wrote up the final orders to carry out his "care and comfort wishes," and a nurse came in and started a morphine drip to ease his pain. At the same time, his relatives continued to sit around him, as if they wanted to be there to the very end.

Later that night, at about three in the morning, I got a call from the nurse on duty.

"Mr. Alexopoulos peacefully passed tonight."

I hung up feeling a bittersweet satisfaction. It is always sad when someone's life ends, but at least he ended his life as he wanted, with his loving relatives gathered around him, as if they were there to send him off with their final good-byes and love so he could pass peacefully into the dark night.

DECIDING WHEN A PROGRESSIVE ILLNESS BECOMES TERMINAL

With some illnesses, most notably cancer, the big question is when does the illness become terminal. When is there no going back? In such cases, different types of treatment may offer some promising results, and while these treatments may work for some patients, they may not work for others. On the other hand, even when the disease seems so far progressed that its course cannot be reversed, a seeming miracle cure sometimes happens, though it is not clear why this occurred. The possible reasons may be that the person's immune system suddenly responded, an incorrect diagnosis, or even a healing by a spiritual leader. But no one really knows.

So a key question is when should the patient and doctor decide it is time to give up because there is no hope for a cure? Ideally, the patient and doctor have already agreed on what treatment should be provided after the disease has progressed to where further treatment is expected to be medically futile; now the goal now should be to provide the patient with compassionate comfort and care to the end. If the agreement isn't already in place, it should be worked out now, since the patient's condition could worsen at any time, and the patient may not be able to make any further decisions about his or her future treatment. Any agreement should therefore indicate who will be called upon to act as a proxy for the patient, once the patient can no longer make these decisions. However, as previously described, where there is no agreement, the medical team or doctor currently seeing the patient will make that decision. But unfortunately, for the patient, the default will be taking an aggressive action to do everything possible to prolong the patient's life, despite all the pain and suffering that effort entails.

One of the most common progressive illnesses where it is necessary to determine when the patient's condition has become terminal is cancer. That was the situation for Mrs. Blanchet and Mrs. Sutton, both in their seventies, who were struck down with cancer that was spreading through their bodies when I saw them, although for several years they had been living with and trying to fight off their cancer. Following are their stories.

A NICE LADY WITH KIDNEY CANCER

For Mrs. Blanchet, the problem with kidney cancer started about three years earlier. At the time, she was an elementary-school teacher with a husband who worked as an engineer for a scientific lab, and she had three sons in their early twenties, one a salesman for a major corporation, another an IT manager for a small company, and a third working as a retail sales clerk. The family was living the suburban good life, and besides teaching, Mrs. Blanchet was a volunteer docent for a local art museum, a supporter of a local theater troop, and active in other community organizations.

Then she noticed a growing pain in her back. After she discovered blood in her urine, she decided it was time to see a doctor. His assessment was that she was in the early stages of kidney cancer, and he recommended that she arrange to have the one kidney removed, which she did with a surgeon at the community hospital. After two weeks of rest, relaxation, and healing, she returned to her everyday community activities, thinking everything was fine.

But two years later, she experienced back pains again and discovered the cancer was in the other kidney. But instead of having it removed, leaving her with no kidney and a daily dialysis arrangement, she submitted to radiation. Again, it seemed the strategy worked, and she and her husband celebrated by going to a neighborhood street party. She even gave talks at community civic clubs and her local library about her experience. Everyone was particularly impressed when she talked about how she had beaten cancer twice and won.

However, the cancer remained lurking in her body like a hundred-year plant that seems to be dead for a century, but it is only waiting for a time when its body releases the hormones that lead it to flower. As a result, when I saw her after another year, she was not only complaining about more intense back pains but had other problems.

"I started feeling the pains in my back a few days ago, and I thought it was just a sprain from some heavy lifting in moving boxes," she told me "But the pain kept getting worse, and I saw some blood in my urine again. Plus my hips are really sore, so I'm having trouble walking. It even hurts to move my legs."

I glanced over her medical record, noting that she had had some treatment for kidney cancer before. When I examined her, I found that her cancer had not only remerged as a tumor in her kidney, but it had spread to a couple of other sites. She even had some line fractures in her hip bones, so no wonder she had trouble walking.

"But I didn't fall or break any bones," Mrs. Blanchet complained, when I told her about her hip bones rfractures.

"That doesn't matter," I told her. "In this case, the cancer is eating away at the bone, so that's why the bone is broken in those areas."

Since the cancer might be terminal now, I recommended radiation therapy.

"The radiation caused your cancer to go into remission before," I told her. "So it maybe helpful again, though this time it is much less likely to be permanent."

She returned home and went for weekly radiation treatments for the next few weeks. At the same time, she joined a rehabilitation program, so she could heal and strengthen her hip bones through a series of exercises, after which she could start walking again. The rehab program was like attending a yoga class with an instructor who led the class in body stretches, leg waves, and other exercises. A few weeks later, Mrs. Blanchet called to say she was thrilled.

"I'm making so much progress in the classes I'm taking, and I hope to get involved in some of my volunteer activities again soon."

I hung up feeling uplifted and inspired, since normally in an end-of-life situation, many of my patients are in their last stages of deterioration, so there is little cheer in any diagnosis. Mainly I just experience the satisfaction of making the patient's last days as comfortable as possible. But now it seemed like Mrs. Blanchet was making such great progress that I could list her as a great temporary success.

But two months later, Mrs. Blanchet called to say she was miserable again.

"I think the cancer is back, and now everything's even worse. I'm feeling excruciating pain in my back and I can barely walk. Though I've been seeing doctors at the pain clinic and they prescribed some tablets and pills to ease the pain, as soon as I take a few steps, I feel huge pains through my hips. So mostly I've been lying in bed for the last week. I even got an inflatable bed to make it easier to sleep, but that didn't stop the pain at night either."

"Then come to the hospital, and I'll see you right away," I said.

About an hour later Mrs. Blanchet arrived, driven by her husband and accompanied by their older son, who took off from his sales job for a day to see her.

Minutes later, she was lying on my examination table, and a nurse was beside me to help with the examination. When I turned Mrs. Blanchet over to examine her back area, where she reported the excruciating pain, I discovered a wound covered with pus from an infection. The smell from the wound was overwhelming. So I stepped back, as did the nurse, and we both put on surgical masks to continue the examination, which included taking more X-rays of her back and hips area.

As I suspected, the cancer was back and was even more ravaging, so I felt her condition had become terminal. To reaffirm my diagnosis, I asked the oncology doctor in the hospital who handles cancer cases to examine Mrs. Blanchet to see if she agreed with my end-of-life plans for the patient, which eventually would include putting her on a morphine drip.

"Of course, I agree with your assessment," the oncology doctor said.

I told Mrs. Blanchet the prognosis, along with my recommendation for a compassionate, peaceful end without any special effort to get her heart or breathing going again once it stopped.

"Let me think about this for a couple of days," she said.

Two days later she was back, accompanied by her husband, who helped her walk into the hospital by leaning on his shoulder.

Carefully, she eased herself into a chair across from me, obviously in great pain.

"I agree with what you suggested," Mrs. Blanchet said. "I just want to go to sleep and not wake up. Every time I wake up, I'm in great pain."

The following day, I had a meeting at her bedside, which included her husband and three children.

I explained the purpose of the meeting to everyone. "This is our final meeting to determine what Mrs. Blanchet wants, so we can carry out her wishes."

"Of course," said her husband. "That's what we want to do."

Then, her eldest son, who was closest to her, spoke up. "I'm the one who is supposed to make decisions for my mother if necessary, and I agree to do that. I think what my mother wants is the best thing for her, so that's what we'd all like to do."

Thus, unlike some meetings with family members that bring out the worst in people, as family members form cliques supporting different positions, which may or may not be what the patient wants, everyone here was in agreement. As a result, the half-hour meeting was relatively short and sweet.

Then, as everyone agreed, I asked the nurse to set up a morphine drip to make Mrs. Blanchet as comfortable as possible. "And change the dosage based on what's most comfortable for her. Don't worry about any kind of time schedule. What's most important is to reduce any pain and suffering while nature takes its course."

Two days later, Mrs. Blanchet did pass away. As I came into her room after the alert went out that she had died, I saw the smile on her face, showing that she had died in peace.

A PATIENT WITH CANCER AND DIABETES

Mrs. Sutton is another example of a patient who was living with cancer, as well as diabetes, for over two years. At any time, the cancer could go into remission, while the diabetes could be controlled, so initially her case wasn't terminal. Rather, it was an example of setting up a DNR/DNI agreement in two steps, as her two diseases progressed from being treatable to being terminal.

When I first met Mrs. Sutton as one of my private patients, she was in her early seventies and had three living children in their forties—one son and two daughters, though her husband had passed away. Since her family could afford it, they were helping to support her living in a private apartment at a retirement community that could provide assisted care as needed, and eventually the center could provide round-the-clock nursing assistance. It also provided a place where she could socialize with other residents age sixty or older in an environment that encouraged patients to do whatever they could at their level of health and mental agility. As Mrs. Sutton wished, she could go to movie nights, participate in improv skits with other residents, eat with other patients or by herself in the dining room, and have guests over to visit. It was a little like living in an adult camp for the elderly, so Mrs. Sutton was in an ideal, comfortable setting for responding to her needs as her diseases progressed.

At our first meeting, I found she had colon cancer in addition to a recurrence of a cancer she had several years before. Now she had developed throat cancer as well, perhaps due to her heavy smoking, and she had had diabetes for several years. After I told her what I found in my examination, she was apologetic, though in a humorous way, like a little kid caught taking cookies from the cookie jar who says "I'm sorry," but is also saying in an unspoken message: "Not really." As Mrs. Sutton told me:

"I guess I haven't been very good, and now you caught me. I know you told me to stop smoking, but I couldn't, so I didn't. I guess this is God's way of punishing me for being bad. But I wasn't able to stay away from the sweets, which you recommended, and I didn't take the medicines either to control my diabetes. My bad."

She laughed, but I didn't laugh with her.

"Look," I said. "It's your choice. We can try again, and there's still a chance to reverse the cancer and get your diabetes under control."

"Okay, I'll try," she said, and I repeated my advice about reducing the sweets and taking her medications.

However, she only followed my advice sporadically, and a few weeks later, she came to my office with a cough. Since she had no other symptoms, I prescribed a cough syrup to take several times a day. When she called for a refill a month later, I asked her to come into my office.

"I'd like to take a chest X-ray to see what's going on in light of your history of throat cancer and now a cough that won't go away."

"And don't forget I still smoke," she said, trying to inject a note of levity into what I thought was a serious matter.

"Yes, that, too," I said.

The next day, I first took a chest X-ray, which showed a dark grayish mass in her chest. To look more closely at was going on, I arranged for her to have a medical radiation technologist perform a CAT scan, which provides more detailed information than an ordinary X-ray.

"This CAT scan will help us learn more about what this dark grayish mass is, since we can see it in 3-D," I explained.

To conduct the scan, I led her to a room where the CAT scanner was located. Once there, as a technologist observed from a nearby control room, I asked her to lie on a narrow examination table that slides in and out of a large, box-like machine with a hole or short tunnel, in the center. Once she slid in, an X-ray tube and two electronic X-ray detectors opposite each other took a series of photographs. Meanwhile, the technologist at a computer workstation in the control room monitored the examination and could hear and talk to Mrs. Sutton as she moved through the machine.

The process was a little like a patient going through an MRI machine for a brain scan, but in this case, her whole body was scanned.

As before, Mrs. Sutton tried to make light of the experience.

"Wow! This is like going through a fun house!" she exclaimed, laughing as the slider pushed her further and further into the machine.

But this was no laughing matter. When I looked at the CAT scan, it showed a very large mass at the right side of her trachea, which is the main breathing pipe.

After explaining what we found, I told her: "This is very serious. The tumor could quickly block your breathing through the trachea. No wonder you have been coughing for the past few weeks."

Then I moved quickly to process her transfer to the cancer center within four days. I provided the medical team there with all the appropriate workups, including the CAT scan of her chest and additional PET scan, which stands for positron emission tomography and is done with the same CT machine. But the PET scan additionally measures important body functions, such as blood flow, oxygen use, and glucose metabolism, to indicate how well the organs and tissues are functioning. Importantly, the scan enables doctors to distinguish good tissues from cancer tissues.

"This is a matter of life or death" I told her. "There could still be hope, but you need to follow our medical directives for your treatment if you want to get better."

"Sure," Mrs. Sutton agreed. And this time she didn't try to crack a joke. Instead she looked very somber and thoughtful.

But would she really follow our directives? And whether she did or not, would the additional radiation and surgery work to stem the cancer? Could she get her diabetes under control again?

It was like a medical murder mystery case, and it was up to the patient to follow the directions, like clues, to favorably resolve the case. But would she? And could she still get better whether she followed the directions or not? I still wasn't ready to declare her condition terminal, though I didn't hold out much hope.

About two weeks later, Mrs. Sutton ended up in the emergency room with a hemoptysis, which involves coughing up blood or blood-stained mucus from the bronchi, larynx, trachea, or lungs. She had been undergoing her regular radiation treatment for her cancer of the throat and trachea when she began spitting up blood.

I rushed there to see her, and it didn't look good. Her breathing was very shallow, and the right side of her chest seemed to be not moving at all, so I thought that the tumor in her trachea might be obstructing her bronchia, the small tubes that branch out from the trachea into the lungs. I also noticed that the veins in her neck seemed to be distended and purple, whereas normally the neck veins collapse when we breathe in and expand when we exhale. This problem with her veins suggested that the growth of the tumor was holding back the return of the blood to her heart.

At least Mrs. Sutton was still conscious, and I explained the situation to her.

"It looks very grim," I concluded. "But to be sure, we need another CAT scan of your chest, so we can see how large the tumor is in three dimensions."

"What about code status?" she asked.

"We can review that, too," I said.

"Then resuscitate me," she said. "I know I haven't followed your directives for treatment in the past. But this time, I will. This has been like a wake-up call for me."

I hesitated for a moment, feeling bad about telling her that there was no hope of redemption now, and any change in her behavior in the future would be too late, because as far as I could tell from her condition, the death sentence was already in. Now it was only a matter of time, maybe days, until the sentence would be carried out.

"Unfortunately, it's too late for that," I finally told her. "There are too many problems in too many systems. I'll respect your wishes, but I recommend that we stop any further treatment should you experience a cardiac arrest or stop breathing."

As Mrs. Sutton thought over her options, I invited her family members—her son and two daughters—who were nervously waiting outside the emergency room to come in. As they stepped inside, I provided a brief update on Mrs. Sutton's situation.

"She is at a disadvantage compared to the average person having a cardiac arrest because of the tumor in her airway," I concluded. "So I don't recommend she be resuscitated if her heart stops because I believe the damage will be beyond repair, and she's agreeable to that."

Briefly, the family members discussed the situation among themselves. Finally, her son told me:

"Okay. That's fine with us, too."

Then I led her family members in to see her, and stepped away so they could have what was likely to be a final family gathering in private.

Given all of Mrs. Sutton's other problems, I didn't want to complicate her last time with her family with any "what if" medical scenarios that were unlikely to happen. I thought it better to let them have their last happy moments together; then she could be better able to go in peace, and the family would feel more peace, too.

IT'S AN EMERGENCY—AND A CHANGE OF HEART

What do you do when there's a life threatening emergency and the patient suddenly has a change of heart and wants to be resuscitated, no matter what? The big problem is that the patient has already given written assent to the medically recommended DNR/DNI status to go peacefully. But in the heat of an emergency, everything changes, and suddenly the patient is screaming "Save me, save me." It's a scene worthy of a TV show like *Grey's Anatomy* or *ER*, where everyone is rushing around in the operating room in a state of complete chaos and no one is sure what to do. Should the medical team follow the written procedures already in place, or shift midstream to attempt a dramatic rescue that could prove fatal in the end because the patient is already so far gone?

That's the situation I and the medical team faced with Ralph Thompson, a ninety-five-year old man, who had been in a nursing home for over a decade, when he contracted pneumonia and was struggling to breathe. By now, he had lost contact with his family members. His siblings had died years before, and so had his son and daughter in their seventies, while his grandchildren had gone their separate ways. So he was very much on his own, though still quite alert. He continued to play bridge and other card games with several players, raised a few plants in the nursing home garden, and took daily walks around the grounds when it wasn't raining, using his walker to get around. Then pneumonia struck and left him feeling very weak and fragile.

At first it seemed he would recover, and as he rested in his semiprivate room, I discussed his DNR/DNI status with him. He quickly agreed: "That's what I want to do. I want to go quickly and peacefully this way."

But then he had a rough night, during which he tossed and turned and woke up repeatedly, since he had trouble breathing.

I got a call from the hospital in the morning to see him. As he pulled himself up in bed, he told me: "I've been struggling to breathe all night." He gasped for air several times. "Please, please help me, doc," he begged. "I'll see what I can do," I told him.

After I explained the situation to the nurse on duty, I called for the rapid response team to come help. Within minutes, several nurses from the ICU arrived, along with a nursing supervisor, the nurses from the floor, and a respiratory therapist. They rushed into his room, and moments later, one of the nurses began giving him medications to help him breathe again.

But he continued to gasp for breath even more frequently, so his condition was clearly deteriorating.

I pulled out my phone and called the anesthesia department. "Send someone over to intubate a patient who's having trouble breathing."

A few minutes later an anesthesiologist and an assistant arrived with a ventilator to help Ralph breathe.

As they rushed to set up the machine, Ralph gasped and screamed: "Please hurry. Help me breathe. I can't breathe on my own now."

Meanwhile, Gina, who used to be his daughter-in-law before his son divorced her, arrived at this chaotic scene at his room and explained: "I've been appointed Mr. Thompson's proxy, so the hospital called me to tell me about his condition."

Since Gina was now his proxy, and Ralph could no longer convey his wishes, the medical team turned to her for guidance.

"Don't intubate him," Gina said. "That's what he originally said he wanted. And that makes the most sense, given his age and the way things have been getting worse and worse."

But inside his room, Ralph kept screaming. "Please, please. You have to help me breathe to stay alive."

The scene, like out of a movie, starkly showed the dilemma of having a DNR agreement on file, but now the patient in the throes of a life-threatening emergency was screaming for help, while his former daughter-in-law proxy had joined in the decision-making process. A day ago, I wasn't sure Ralph's condition was terminal, but after a difficult night, it clearly was, and the big question the proxy and medical team faced was whether to stop the lifesaving measures in exchange for giving Ralph some comfort at the end.

To ask for advice, Gina made a phone call to her current husband. But cell phone problems kept interrupting the call. Meanwhile, as the minutes ticked by, the anesthesiologist sought to attach the tube to intubate Ralph, assuming the order was to do so.

Finally, Gina gave up trying to get her husband's advice.

"Okay, I think we need to stop all of this," she said. "As Ralph's proxy, that's what I think we should do. He's not going to get any better. He'll just suffer. So stop."

With her decision made, I rushed back into the room and told the anesthesiologist, "You've got to stop what you are doing. We're not going to intubate the patient after all."

Fortunately, Ralph was now barely conscious and no longer screaming, so we all felt comfortable stopping the procedure, though the medical team continued to use other possible measures to help save Ralph's life. One was using the BiPAP machine to pump air in and out of his lungs. The team also used a morphine drip, an injection of Ativan to calm him, and a bronchodilator to relax the bronchial muscles to the airways, so they became larger, allowing more air to pass through the lungs.

The result is that Ralph began to breathe deeply again. So we all agreed we had done the smart thing in not trying to revive him by connecting him to tubes or using compressions, electrical shocks, or other full-code measures that could leave him in an even worse condition and suffering more.

Even so, none of these procedures helped to change the fact that after Ralph's difficult night, his condition had gone from recovery possible to definitely terminal. And a few days later, Ralph did pass away. He simply stopped breathing, and this time, there was no bringing him back.

GETTING PREPARED AFTER A CANCER DIAGNOSIS

One of the problems with a cancer diagnosis for determining an end-of-life treatment plan is knowing when the cancer becomes terminal. Part of the confusion is due to the scare that comes from any cancer diagnosis, though the most common cancers are treatable skin cancers, except for melanoma, the most dangerous form of skin cancer. A melanoma occurs when unrepaired DNA damage to skin cells, usually caused by ultraviolet radiation from sunshine or tanning beds, triggers mutations that lead skin cells to multiply rapidly and form malignant tumors, which usually look like or develop from moles. Usually, these are black or brown, but they can be skin-colored, pink, red, purple, blue, or white. If melanoma is recognized and treated early, it is almost always curable, but if it is not, the cancer can grow and spread to other parts of the body, where it becomes hard to treat and can be fatal.

In contrast to skin cancers, the cancers which cause the most problems are those in the large internal organs, such as the colon and lungs, and in the breasts, and often these cancers spread to the liver, lungs, bones, or spread even further to other organs, disabling them or pushing them away, so they interfere with a normal physiological function. For instance, they can make eating more difficult, when they push against the esophagus, or disrupt movement, when they push against the spinal cord. Or they may take up space in the abdomen and generate excess fluids that interfere with normal digestion.

However, because of the progressive nature of the disease, it can sometimes be difficult to know when a cancer becomes terminal, because sometimes a treatment will work and a patient will go into remission at almost any stage before a patient's condition is deemed terminal—and sometimes even after that. But other times, the treatment won't work and the disease will continue to progress.

Since the progress of any cancer is uncertain, it is important to address the patient's code or resuscitation status early on in the event of a cardiac or respiratory arrest, though it can be hard to bring up these issues. Patients often don't want to have these conversations, since they don't want to think about their own mortality or they hope the cancer will recede, so the conversation won't be necessary. Furthermore, there is no clear triggering point until the cancer is well progressed as to when such a conversation about a terminal cancer should occur.

As a result, many patients with cancer go through the painful progression of a tumor or multiple tumors while denying the seriousness of their condition, until it is clear their condition is terminal. Unfortunately, by the time this conclusion is made, some patients are no longer in a position to make a determination themselves about what to do after their death, so family members or doctors make that decision for them, whether or not that is what the patient would have wanted in making these plans early on.

The other issue that often comes up is the fluidity of the patient's DNR/DNI code status, since patients and their relatives often waiver in the decision they have made. As a result, they can opt in our out of the code status they have chosen for any reason. The patient's choice is the determining factor, but if a patient can no longer make this choice, the relative in line to become a proxy takes over, much like succession passes when a king dies or becomes incapacitated.

That's the situation that occurred for Barry, a man in his late seventies, who had retired from being the CEO of a successful start-up tech company and was enjoying the perks of retiring with a big nest egg in cash, stocks, bonds, and investments. Finally, he could lead the life of a gentleman of leisure, and he was enjoying it to the hilt—going on trips around the world, playing golf at world-renowned clubs, and attending art gallery receptions and auctions. It was truly the good life, and he didn't want it to end.

As a result, when the first sign of cancer showed up—a dark brown mole indicating melanoma, due to his overexposure to the ultraviolet rays of the sun—he ignored. It didn't hurt and it was on his shoulder, so he covered it up, and when it got bigger, he added a little more ointment to treat skin blemishes, and continued his jet-setting lifestyle.

Perhaps with treatment, he could have stopped the melanoma in its tracks, such as by having a localized operation to remove it. But since he ignored it, it continued to grow. Then, gradually, as the cancer spread to other organs, it began to interfere with his lifestyle, though initially, he didn't connect the new symptoms to the small but growing mole on his shoulder. Among these symptoms were a growing shortness of breath as he walked around the golf course, an upset stomach after a big meal, and a cough that began while he was giving a speech at an art opening to praise the artist. At first, he attributed these problems to other causes, such as overexerting himself, eating too much, and the beginnings of a cold.

Yet after these symptoms persisted for a month and got worse, he went to the hospital for a check-up, where I first met him. When I broached the subject of options for the future, he was only interested in talking about the treatments that could deal with his present problems.

"Just do what is necessary to fix what's wrong," he told me. "I live a pretty active life since I retired, and I want to get back to it. I don't want to think about what might happen in the future; I just want to enjoy what's happening now."

So I dropped the subject of future treatment possibilities and spoke to the hospital oncologist about what to do to fix up Barry for now. But I suspected any remission would be only temporary; the cancer had spread too far to be contained for long.

Yet, for a while, all seemed fine, and Barry was soon back to the life of a retired gentleman with plenty of discretionary funds—playing golf, going to resorts, attending art openings and auctions. He also began going to sporting events, such as quarterback racing and polo matches, and watching from ringside seats and private boxes. So he thought he was fine.

But then the symptoms started up again and they were worse than ever, when he found himself gasping for breath and spitting up blood with each breath in the bathroom of a high-priced charity event. Finally, as he was wheeled into the operating room for an emergency operation, he acknowledged the reality of his situation.

"I'm going to be dying now, doctor," he gasped to me.

"It's hard to tell. But maybe," I said.

"Well, I'm ready to talk about the treatment options you wanted to talk about now," he said.

So I explained the DNR/DNI and full-code options, as the medical team joined the surgeon in the nearby operating room. He quickly agreed.

"It really has been a good life, especially in these last few years since I retired. But now I understand it could all come to an end, because I'm too sick to keep doing what I've been doing. Now I realize the alternative even if you can revive me—days of living at home or in assisted care, in a nursing home, or in a hospice. And I don't want any of that. So doctor, if you need my signature to keep all that from happening, I'm ready to let go."

Thus, before the operation, Barry agreed. No heroic measures. No resuscitation. He had lived his life as actively as he could on his own terms. Now he wanted to go out on his own terms, too.

That's what happened. A few days after the operation, while he was in his private room, still resting in a semiconscious state, his breathing and then his heart stopped. Since the nurse on the floor knew he was DNR/DNI, she did nothing, and a few minutes later, he passed away, exactly as he wanted to go.

This story illustrates the importance of working out a future treatment plan for a progressive illness, like cancer, as early as possible with the patient and his or her family once it appears the disease is irreversible. Even if some chance of a reversal exists, it is still a good idea to have a future treatment plan in place, because the course of the disease is so unpredictable. Moreover, at this final stage of the illness, complications are increasingly likely, such as infections or unexpected clots in the lungs or legs, which could be life threatening. Thus, it is best to have a written document in place, so the medical team has a clear idea going forward of what to do should a life-threatening incident occur.

In Barry's case, it was fortunate that he was still alert and conscious enough that I could get an agreement when he was being wheeled in for his final operation after a sudden life-threatening episode. But often a patient in this situation will not be conscious, so if no agreement is in place, that can result in a great deal of uncertainty about what to do when time is of the essence. Generally, what would happen is the most medically conservative approach of giving the patient the full-code treatment, as previously discussed.

But most patients and their families don't want that barely alive but painful end, so it is important to get an early agreement as soon as possible. As much as a patient like Barry might not want to talk about making arrangements before an emergency occurs, it is ideal to get this conversation going and obtain an agreement once a patient's condition is considered terminal. The problem with cancer and other progressive diseases is that it is not always easy to determine at what point the disease becomes terminal, because of all the chances for recovery and remissions. Yet, as possible, it is best to have the discussion early on, so the patient understands the options and can make an early choice in case a life-threatening event leads to a cardiac arrest or cessation of breathing—the triggering events for giving the patient the full-code revival treatment or letting him or her go in peace.

14

DENIAL, DISAGREEMENT, AND A CHANGE OF HEART

Once a doctor or medical team have deemed a patient's condition terminal, the patient and other doctors can sometimes disagree with this determination. Patients may do so because they want to deny that they are at the end of their life and hope that the diagnosis is wrong or can change. Both patients and other doctors may also believe there is a greater hope of recovery. Or even if patients accept a terminal diagnosis, they may sometimes have difficulty deciding or change their minds about what to do. Another consideration in treating the terminal patient is how aggressive the treatment should be, or what to do in the case of an unexpected emergency. This chapter deals with these various issues.

DENIAL OF WHEN THE END IS INEVITABLE

In some cases, patients want to deny their condition is terminal, despite all evidence to the contrary that has been presented to them. As a result, they want all kinds of treatments, thinking they can change the verdict about their terminal condition. However, while they may delay the inevitable outcome a short time, ultimately their efforts will fail.

That's what happened for Mrs. Moskowitz, a jewelry and boutique shop owner in her sixties who lived in an upscale community. She was used to doing things her way, and she supervised a half-dozen employees who did what she wanted. She had two sons, Matt and Kevin, in their forties, who were very close to her. Usually they responded to her demands by outwardly following them, even if they personally disagreed, such as when she insisted on them coming to family gatherings by themselves without their wives. Rather than battle it out with her to permit their wives to attend, they came alone.

Now Mrs. Moskowitz was in the final stages of lung cancer, after having been admitted and discharged three times over a two-year period. She had been given every possible treatment each time, from medications to surgery to removing the diseased section of her lung. Afterward, doctors warned her to stop smoking yet she ignored their admonitions, as if the laws of nature didn't apply to her. Perhaps she thought she could outwit these laws because of her success in her store, so she could afford to pay for whatever treatments she wanted even if the doctors advised these wouldn't do any good because of the seriousness of her case. Yet still she persevered, thinking that this time the surgeons could cut out the remaining cancer from her lung. But it was already too late, since the surgeons couldn't cut anymore without removing essential parts of her lung needed to keep her breathing. Furthermore, by her third visit, the cancer had spread to other parts of her body. Thus it was only a matter of time, perhaps a few weeks to a few months, until the end.

Despite this grim prognosis, now she was back, seated across from me, her two sons seated next to her, asking me to arrange for still more treatments. Yet as she spoke, she looked frail, tired, and uncomfortable while sitting upright, as if she was forcing herself to sit up straight so she seemed in charge.

"I'm sure another operation will remove the diseased tissue, so I can begin healing again," she said.

However, I was certain that no further healing was possible. All the signs showed that she was actively dying, though she didn't want to believe it, and she continued to insist on getting further treatment.

"There is nothing we can do anymore," I told her firmly.

"Why not?" she asked. "Why can't the surgeons take out the remaining cancer cells in my lungs and anywhere else in my body? Or why not use radiation again to kill the cells?"

"Because the cancer is too pervasive," I told her. "Any operation or radiation will destroy the organ's ability to function, which is certain death, so there is no reason to do either procedure. And drugs will have no effect now in reducing the effects of the cancer. We tried them before, and they weren't effective."

"Well, maybe these techniques might work now. I've been much more careful about my diet, and I've been resting more to keep my stress level down."

But no matter what Mrs. Moskowitz did to turn things around, the lab work didn't lie.

I handed over a copy of the report I received on her blood work.

"Look, your bone marrow is at the end of the line. It isn't producing enough new blood cells that you need for healing. You have almost no blood platelets, which are the small circular elements in the blood that come from the bone marrow which assist in blood clotting. In a normal person, there are about 150,000 platelets in the blood, but you have only about 30,000 units, which is extremely low. It's not enough for them to stick together to repair any small bleeds. That means if there is any break on the skin or in any organ in the body, the blood vessels are likely to bleed into that injury or organ. It's like what happens when a hemophiliac has an injury, except this is even worse."

"Then what about a blood transfusion?" Mrs. Moskowitz suggested.

"A transfusion won't work because we can't provide a lasting supply of enough blood when your count is so low. Plus your blood pressure has dropped way down, along with your growing weight loss and weakness, and your blood platelet count has been dropping fast. So that suggests the ability of your bone marrow to produce blood platelets is shutting down."

Mrs. Moskowitz looked thoughtful, perhaps bewildered by all the medical terminology I had thrown at her to convince her that her situation was terminal and any further treatment would be futile.

Yet, as much as I regretted being so direct with the bad news, I continued explaining my final verdict, so she and her sons could properly prepare for the end.

"You need to understand that any treatment now will be medically futile. At most any treatment, such as a blood transfusion, might give you a few days more, but otherwise, there is nothing we can do. So I recommend we just leave you be and let nature take its course."

"But I still want the treatment," Mrs. Moskowitz insisted. "As long as there's life, there's hope."

Her sons tried to dissuade her.

"Why don't you just let nature take its course," said one of her sons.

But Mrs. Moskowitz remained firm. "No, I want the transfusion."

"Okay, I'll make the arrangements, if that's what you want," I said.

After she and her sons left, I discussed the case with the two nurses who had been caring for Mrs. Moskowitz, as well as with the palliative care team and two social workers.

"Why don't we call on the ethics committee at the hospital?" a doctor on the palliative care team suggested. "They might help to 'certify' that treating a patient with a certainly terminal disease at the end of the line is most likely completely futile."

However, it was impossible to get the committee together on such short notice the same day. So we had to go forward with plans for the transfusion, even though I was concerned that there could be an immediate emergency if Mrs. Moskowitz started bleeding, since it might be impossible to stop it given her low platelet count.

Yet Mrs. Moskowitz had been insistent that she wanted the transfusion, and she was full code in the event of a cardiac arrest, meaning we had to be ready to do everything to bring her back.

Thus, later that week, Mrs. Moskowitz and her sons returned to the hospital, and I transfused her with both blood and platelets since her count was so critically low. It was a fairly simple procedure, though futile, where a nurse set up a bag of blood with a tube that was inserted into a vein in her arm. About two hours later, it was done.

"Thank you for doing this," Mrs. Moskowitz said. Later, as she rested in my office before going home with her sons, she told me, "I feel more comfortable."

So briefly her conditioned stabilized, though there was no possible long-term positive outcome in sight. Her condition was still terminal—she just had prolonged the process for a short time. That turned out to be just a few more days. I got a call from one of her sons; their mother had died that day. At least she had passed away peacefully and with little pain, when her breathing simply stopped and there was no time to revive her, since she was already dead for some time when the nurse on duty found her during her regular rounds.

In essence, the determination that Mrs. Moskowitz had a terminal condition had begun when she came to my office with her two sons. Perhaps if I had seen her on a previous admission, I might have assessed her condition as terminal at an earlier date. But while the exact date her condition might be judged terminal might be hard to pin down, she prolonged the dying process for several more weeks or days. But regardless of the specific date of changing her condition from nonterminal to terminal, the basic facts didn't change; her condition was terminal since there was no possible cure—and she died within a few days or weeks of that determination.

ANOTHER END-OF-LIFE DENIAL

The effort to deny the inevitable unfortunately occurs in a number of patients, though sometimes, unlike Mrs. Moskowitz, patients may refuse recommended treatments because they want to believe their condition is not as serious as it really is. That was the case with Mrs. Roberts, a seventy-one-year-old woman who had end-stage kidney disease and multiple myeloma, a form of blood cancer that develops in the bone marrow. In myeloma, the normal plasma cells turn into malignant cells that produce large quantities of an abnormal immunoglobulin called "monoclonal protein" or "M protein," resulting in bone pain, anemia, weakness, and an inability to fight off other diseases.

Before the disease struck, Mrs. Roberts had been living a fairly active life as a member of a retirement community and had little contact with most of her family members, since three of her children who lived across the country had their own problems. One daughter suffered from cancer, another daughter was bipolar, and a son was schizophrenic. Though another son was a professional in a management job, she only saw him occasionally for holiday dinners with his family. Thus, after she left her job as a bookkeeper in a large company, the members of the retirement community became like a surrogate family, and she developed a few strong friendships with some of the women she met in the group's activities, such as movie and game nights.

About three months earlier, I had met her when she came to the hospital complaining about a pain in her lower back. After examining her and doing some blood tests, I quickly diagnosed her as having kidney disease and some early signs of cancer of the bone marrow. I then invited two cancer doctors to examine her and look at the blood-test results in order to confirm my diagnosis. Once they did, I gave her my recommendation:

"I think you are fine to go home now. But I'd like you to come back so I can do a further treatment, which includes chemotherapy. And I'd like you to closely follow up with us at the cancer center so we can monitor your progress. Then, if we see any problems, we can refer you to a hospital, since we can't do any additional types of treatments for an outpatient."

However, she never came back for the recommended treatment, and she didn't follow our advice to let us follow up on her progress and get lab work and chemotherapy for the myeloma.

As a result, when she came in because of bleeding from large hemorrhoids in her rectum, the two problems she had before were further advanced, for she now had worsening kidney failure and her cancer of the bone marrow was much worse. Before I would not have considered her condition terminal, since she could have possibly reversed her kidney disease with the proper treatment and her multiple myeloma could have gone into remission. But now both conditions were too far along, so I now considered them terminal.

"What can you do for me now?" she asked me. "What about a transfusion to increase my blood count? Or what can you do about my heart, since it suddenly starts beating rapidly and irregularly. Then, I feel dizzy, weak, and tired, and sometimes find it hard to breathe for a while."

I realized she was describing the symptoms for atrial fibrillation, a condition characterized by rapid and irregular heartbeats. I had previously prescribed medications for her to take for this problem, though she had never taken the pills consistently. No wonder her condition had gotten worse. And now there was no going back.

I tried to explain the situation to Mrs. Roberts as gently as possible.

"There isn't any cure for your conditions," I concluded. "The diseases have progressed too far now. So the best thing is to make care and comfort arrangements for the end of life."

She hesitated for a few moments, as if she was finally coming to terms with her condition, since it was no longer possible to deny it. The bleeding that had brought her in, along with her repeated shortness of breath, weakness, dizziness, and faintness, helped her recognize that she had come to a point where she had to face the inevitable.

"Would you like to ask your son who lives nearby to help you with the decision-making process?" I asked, since she seemed to be stuck in deciding what to do.

She snapped back to attention. "No. I'd like to decide on my own destiny. I guess your suggestion seems like the reasonable thing to do."

So that's what I arranged—for some morphine to ease the pain and Ativan, a drug commonly used for anxiety, to help her feel calmer by sedating her. Fortunately, she could still eat a regular diet based on what she liked, so she could at least enjoy her last meals.

After that, Mrs. Roberts and her son, who had come to help her, left my office, and they both appeared very calm and peaceful, as if they had both accepted that this was the final end. It had been a long struggle to get her to accept the reality, and to some extent, she had contributed to her terminal condition by denying its seriousness three months earlier. At that point, her condition could have gone either way—to healing or to death. But now that no further denying was possible, she was able to come to terms with what was, as had her son. As a result, to the extent it is possible to feel good about giving a patient a terminal verdict and telling her what to do to make the end as comfortable as possible, I felt good. I also felt heartened that I could leave her with the one bright silver lining—her choice of whatever she wanted to eat until the end.

THE DIFFICULTY OF DECIDING WHAT TO DO

The question of when a person can or can't make a decision can come up when patients change their minds over the course of treatment. Either they are competent to make it for themselves, or if they are no longer able to do so, a relative or the medical team takes over as their proxy in deciding what to do. Unless they have instructions to the contrary, the medical team's default will be to do everything possible regardless of any pain or suffering, unless their actions would harm the patient.

While a patient might have a change of mind at any time, even before his or her condition is considered terminal, sometimes the patient wants to make a change after deteriorating so much that it is clear there is no reversing the dying process. But suddenly the patient may feel a change is possible due to renewed hopes for recovery; thus leading to a change of mind.

That's what happened in the case of Mrs. Miriam Zapata, a fifty-seven-year-old Hispanic female, who had a history of using multiple drugs. In her early fifties, she had ended up in a methadone clinic, where she and other drug abusers obtained their methadone legally so they could go about their daily activities rather than undergoing withdrawal or going back onto the streets to seek illegal drugs to feed their habit. For Miriam, these daily activities meant hanging out in a substandard rat-infested hotel where she had a small room, chatting with hotel and street people in the lobby and on the street, seeing people in the street pass by, and watching TV in the lobby or in her room. Occasionally, she went to visit her children and elderly parents, who lived in the suburbs. They were willing to help her turn her life around if she could get the training to get a regular job, such as a receptionist, file clerk, or administrative assistant. But Miriam had trouble staying focused or committing to any regular program to help herself. So she ended up out of work, out of money, and back on the street again and again. At least the methadone program helped her stop the injections of heroin and speed, so that was a first step in getting her life back together.

I first saw her when she came to our community hospital complaining about abdominal pain.

"It hurts so much, I can't eat anything," she said.

I began my assessment by reviewing a hospital file with her medical history, and Miriam briefly gave me a summary of what was in the file.

"I recently saw some physicians in Boston after I suddenly experienced pain in my stomach. At the time, they said I had some sort of tumor or cancer in my pancreas. But they couldn't prove anything, even after they sent me to get a biopsy in a nearby care center. So they told me I most likely had some kind of cancer and sent me home."

"Any medications?"

"Just a few painkillers. Something like aspirin or Tylenol, I think. I don't really remember, but after a day or two the pain went away. So I didn't think much more about this. Until now."

At this point, I wasn't sure of the seriousness of her condition, though I wanted to discuss her DNR/DNI status while she was still rational and sanguine about her condition. At once she agreed to a "do no resuscitate/do not intubate status" if things got really bad.

"I just want to go quickly and quietly," she said very firmly, though within a week, she would change her mind.

After sending her home, since the painkiller seemed to alleviate her presenting problem, I discussed the case with the gastroenterologist specialist to obtain his prognosis for Miriam's condition.

"She has a three-inch tumor in the head of the pancreas," he replied. "Also, she has kidney failure, because she has been unable to eat for some time. She also has liver issues; that's probably why she developed acute jaundice. And she has liver cirrhosis and hepatitis C, which are common for patients with a history of alcohol and drug abuse of multiple drugs."

Thus, beyond what I observed from my initial meeting, I realized that Miriam was suffering from multiple organs failing at the same time, making her prognosis even worse. It's like in a business, where a number of systems fail, not just one, making it harder and harder to make repairs, especially when more and more repairs have to be made over time, which can eventually lead to business failure.

When I met with Miriam a few days later to tell her the results of my meeting with the specialist, she at first seemed very clear headed, understanding, and agreeable to what I felt she should do now.

"Yes, I understand the prognosis is very poor," she said. "And I agree to the DNR/DNI status you recommend. I just want to be comfortable if the situation is irreversible."

I assured her it was. "There are so many things going wrong now. It's what called a 'multisystem organ involvement.'"

"I wish I could have been able to control my use of drugs and alcohol when I was younger," she said wistfully. "Then maybe all this wouldn't have happened."

I simply nodded, feeling she had reached a level of understanding, tinged with regret, and there was nothing more I could say.

But shortly after our conversation was over, on her way back to her flophouse hotel she had a mild panic attack, coupled with a brief shortness-of-breath episode. She shakily staggered off the bus at the next stop, and as she stood in the doorway of another flophouse hotel a few blocks from her own, she had a hallucination. She saw a figure in a long white robe who came to her, saying: "You can still turn your life around. There's still time." Then the figure dissolved in a burst of white light. To her, this was a sign from God that she still had hope. She just had to determine she could do better, and then she would be healed.

As a result, she called me and said, "I want to reverse my DNR/DNI status. I'm certain I can get better now, and I want to set up a meeting with my family to tell them this."

Ironically, Miriam was actually worse, and her hallucination was a sign of this. Moreover, on top of the tumor in her pancreas, her kidney failure, and her liver cirrhosis, she came down with a severe cold.

The next day, we had the meeting, and besides a few family members she hadn't seen in years—her parents, son, and two daughters—I had invited a representative from social services and from pastoral services, along with two members of the continuity-of-care team to discuss her palliative care in the future. I began by describing Miriam's case, pointing up the failure of her multiple organ systems, and concluding with her original decision for a DNR/DNI status.

"Miriam originally agreed that she just wanted comfort and care, once it was clear that her condition was terminal and not irreversible."

"That's right," her father said, speaking on behalf of the family members who were present.

The social service worker and minister agreed.

But Miriam was determined to change everything. "I want to live and be treated for everything. Because I know it is possible for me to change now. I know I will be all right."

Yet as much as Miriam might want to believe in her vision of recovery, her situation was medically futile. The cancer, which had attacked her major organs, along with her other organ failures, was no longer curable. Perhaps in the news and in films, stories about miraculous recoveries help to fuel a belief that anything in possible. However, these are the very rare exceptions—perhaps one in a million—that help to convince others that they will be gifted with a medical breakthrough due to spiritual, religious, or other powers. But in almost all cases, these are misplaced visions. The patient's focus should be on making the last days as comfortable and painless as possible, not going through agonizing treatments in the hope of illusory cures.

But there was no convincing Miriam. Her mind was made up, even after the results came in from a test which one of the cancer doctors did by removing some of the fluid in her belly, which often accumulates in people with cirrhosis of the liver. When the test came back, it showed her liver was clearly infected. Additionally, a pneumonia diagnosis showed her lungs were infected and inflamed, resulting in a decision that it was time for Miriam to go to the hospital for her many conditions.

Still, Miriam didn't believe the direct prognosis. Even as she lay in her hospital bed, she was convinced that she would soon be healed. So we continued to evaluate her situation over the next days, which only confirmed that everything was terminal and medically futile. Yet, on the basis of that vision of a miraculous healing, she had reversed her long-time decision on what to do about the end of life.

What should the medical team do now that she had reversed herself, wanting the full treatment rather than a calm and peaceful end? At the same time, her family still supported her original choice of a comfortable, graceful exit. Initially, the team planned to proceed with the patient's new wishes, thinking this the legal and ethical thing to do, so if Miriam experienced a heart stoppage or an inability to breathe, the team would do everything possible for her, even knowing it was medically futile, until she was declared dead. Then all efforts would stop.

Ironically, Miriam did experience a cardiac arrest, and after all the electric shocks, needles, and chest compressions, she actually survived a first round of CPR and the full-code treatment. However, afterward, she was in a much deteriorated site, where she had to remain attached to a mechanical ventilator to support her failing systems to keep her heart pumping and her breathing going. So she was still alive, but barely, and perhaps she was still feeling pain and suffering in a semiconscious state, although there was no way to know what kind of brain damage had occurred and how permanent it would be.

It was the worst possible outcome resulting from Miriam's change of heart, and the inability of the medical team or her family to dissuade her. Yet she had been mentally competent at the point where she had changed her mind, so we felt legally and ethically we had to go with her current wishes, despite knowing she was making a huge mistake, since whatever we did would be medically useless. In this case, she ended up in a kind of half-alive zombie state, a little like a case of the living dead in a horror movie.

Given our uncertainty about what to do, I called for an ethics committee meeting and to demonstrate Miriam's current condition, I invited the committee members to join me and the nurse caring for her in Miriam's room. Then I questioned her with some "yes-no" questions, to which she couldn't respond. So the committee members could readily see that Miriam no longer had the mental ability to understand or decide anything about her condition.

For the next hour in the hospital's conference room we hashed out what to do. I explained what happened after we performed the full-code treatment procedures Miriam wanted, concluding with my assessment of the situation.

"At this point, her mental ability has significantly decreased as a result of the cardiac and respiratory arrest. Now she has lost the ability to any longer make any meaningful decisions about anything, including her own health."

"If that's the case," the head of the ethics committee advised, "her proxy has to take over and make the decisions for her, since she can no longer make decisions for herself. It is also clear that any further interventions will be medically futile and that her loved ones want us to be very conservative and as humane as possible in approaching her end of life. So any conflict about this option is unlikely."

I was relieved to hear that determination that Miriam's wishes were no longer dictating our behavior and treatment options, since she was no longer competent and had succumbed to the very circumstances we foresaw based on our experience and expertise. So her proxy could now take over and act for her. I also felt this was the best option, since even though Miriam had drifted away from her family over the years, the family members still loved and cared for her very much, so they were in the perfect position to decide on her behalf.

As soon as the meeting ended, I called her parents, who were having a family meeting with her son and daughters awaiting my latest update on Miriam's condition. Her father answered, and I explained what would occur next.

"You're in charge of what happens to her now as her proxy," I said. "Medically, we had to intubate her and put her on a mechanical ventilator in the ICU as part of her request for CPR and resuscitation. So the question we are facing now is whether to extubate her and disconnect her from the breathing machine. Or we can just let her be, and she will expire very soon. In either case, she will die. There is no hope of recovery. She is already almost completely brain dead, except for a limited control of some bodily functions. So it is just a matter of days or maybe a little longer."

For a moment, her father left me hanging on the line as he conferred with the other family members at the meeting. Then, he returned and gave me the answer I had been hoping for:

"We're agreed. She should be DNR/DNI, as we all agreed originally."

I quickly wrote up that order, and a few minutes later, the family members arrived at the hospital for one last visit to Miriam's hospital room to say goodbye. As they walked down the corridor to her room, her father stopped by my office and signed the DNR/DNI agreement.

I told him: "We'll now move her to the care and comfort level. We'll do the minimum needed to keep her comfortable so there's no pain."

I joined the family in Miriam's room to explain the plan, as the nurse stopped the tube conveying regular medications to her body through her arm and started the morphine drip, so Miriam would experience a complete nothingness, free of all pain.

Despite their tears, the family members looked calm and peaceful, glad for this final resolution, and a few minutes later, Miriam peacefully passed away. Thus, in the end, despite Miriam changing her mind in the face of medical advice that any full-code treatment was medically futile and in the face of her family's opposition, her order was changed back to what it was originally. So eventually, she did meet a caring and compassionate end with her family around her, and she went in peace.

A CHANGE IN PLANS

Change is another factor that sometimes comes up in end-of-life cases, either because circumstances change or because a patient continually changes what he or she wants, sometimes in response to changing circumstances. It can help when patients have alternate scenarios for what to do under different circumstances, such as if a sudden emergency occurs due to a relapse. However, many patients don't engage in such advance planning, resulting in a scramble at the end to decide what to do, and sometimes the family, doctor, or medical team have to step in to determine the final end-of-life treatment, since the patient is no longer capable of doing so.

Such a situation occurred for Mr. Montgomery, a one-time bus driver now in his late sixties, who wasn't used to planning anything. He was used to taking orders and carrying them out, not in deciding what those orders should be, and he had little contact with family members, who lived out of state. For a few years he had a steady girlfriend, but they had broken up about a year earlier so now he was largely on his own. Mostly, he spent his time in solitary pursuits, such as going to baseball and football games and seeing popular movies from Redbox to keep down his expenses.

Then he got lung cancer, and for a time he tried to beat it by having radiation, which seemed to work for a while. He would go into his treatments coughing and having shortness of breath, but a few days after the radiation, his cough went away and he no longer had trouble breathing. But a few weeks later, his cough started up again as did the shortness of breath, so he had another radiation treatment. For a time, he hoped to find a cure for his cancer, for which he was being treated, so his condition could not yet be termed "terminal."

But after about four months of these treatments, when he walked into the hospital for a radiation appointment, his condition was deemed terminal. What happened is that as the nurse weighed him, he complained he was experiencing an "intense shooting pain" in his left hip. So the nurse noted that and asked the radiologist to come look at the patient as he lay on his back on the table of the machine. After looking at Mr. Montgomery's X-rays and poking and prodding his left hip, the radiologist determined that he had some metastatic lesions to his hip where the cancer in his lung had spread. As a result, the pain in his hip had become so great that it interfered with his walking, since with each step he felt a searing pain.

Now his cancer had become terminal, and at this point, he was referred to me. My first step in treating him was to ask a nurse to administer a large amount of narcotics through his veins. As I reviewed his case, I thought about how he might have had a terminal cancer condition for some time before he came to the hospital, except it wasn't diagnosed. As a result, apart from the radiation treatment directed at his lungs, his cancer wasn't treated, and the possibility of the cancer metastasizing to other parts of his body wasn't considered. So for a time, he acted as if he was healing, going about his life normally apart from the radiation treatments each week. Then everything changed once he developed the acute pain in his hips, which made it difficult for him to walk. Now he needed the very high doses of narcotics that I gave him to keep his pain under control.

Once his pain was controlled, I asked him, "Do you have any plans in place for what to do now?"

Mr. Montgomery looked at me blankly, like he didn't know what I was talking about.

"It's about end-of-life planning," I said. "Besides any medical decisions about treatment, it includes all the legal and financial arrangements you want to set up in advance."

Although I would only be involved in working out a treatment plan, I wanted to point out, as with other patients who haven't engaged in planning, that they should create such plans when they can still think clearly about what they want. However, now that Mr. Montgomery's thinking was a little fuzzy from the medication needed to control his pain, I wasn't sure how well he could make such plans.

"I don't know what you mean," Mr. Montgomery said finally.

"I know this may be difficult for you to think about now, but you should talk to a lawyer and family members about what you want to do about your estate and any memorial and funeral arrangements, so they can plan these. We can talk about your treatment arrangements, too, or if you can't decide what to do yourself, we can work things out with your closest family member."

"Yes, do that," Mr. Montgomery said, groggy from the narcotics needed to dull the pain. I could tell that he could no longer do any planning himself, because of the unforeseen acute event that led him to come to the hospital for radiation.

Eventually the medical team, radiation consulting doctor, and myself had to make the decision to start the radiation treatment and increase the narcotic doses to keep him both awake and minimally pain free, though after a while it was clear the radiation treatment wasn't working. The cancer in both his lungs and hips was too far advanced to do anything, except make him weaker and sicker. So finally we kept increasing the doses of narcotics to over 30 mg per hour, the most I have ever seen. But while he felt less pain, he became increasingly unaware of anything around him, until he slipped from a state of semiconsciousness to being completely unconscious. Meanwhile, to prevent any pain, the nurse placed him on the morphine drip and increasingly upped the amount from 30 mg to over 50 mg an hour, which exhausted the hospital reserve for morphine. So we had to switch the medication to Dilaudid, which is seven times stronger than morphine on a milligram per milligram bases. Then he finally passed away.

In short, in Mr. Montgomery's case, once I determined that his condition was terminal after he reported his intense hip pain and other areas of pain, triggered by the tumor, the medical team shifted from trying to help him recover to doing everything possible to relieve his pain and suffering, which required much more painkillers than usual because his pain was so intense.

WHEN THE PATIENT ISN'T REALLY TERMINAL—AND DOCTORS DISAGREE

Another situation that comes up from time to time, though more rarely than the case where the patient's terminal status is unclear or the patient may not want to acknowledge it, is the case where the determination of a "terminal status" is possibly applied too soon. This may occur because the patient's condition isn't terminal at that time, based on the patient seeming to rally after the "terminal" determination. But if the patient wasn't really terminal, this is an error in diagnosis, rather than the patient suddenly recovering from a terminal condition.

While it may seem like no harm is done by working out an early treatment plan with a patient, it can be psychologically upsetting to a patient to think that a treatable medical problem is a sign of a terminal condition when it may not be at that time. Such a presumptive diagnosis could actually trigger a series of negative events and experiences for the patient, who thinks his or her condition is terminal, when it really may not be. This shows the need for an accurate assessment and sensitive discussion with the patient about the results and the meaning of these findings about the seriousness of his or her condition, because any finding of a terminal illness can be a very unnerving, upsetting experience. So doctors and other medical professionals need to be both understanding and diplomatic in conveying this information to the patient and then providing guidance on what to do.

Certainly, any incorrect diagnosis can be a problem. However, while a patient with a terminal condition who gets a wrong diagnosis may feel a sense of temporary relief or even take some time to participate in enjoyable activities if able to do so, it's worse to advise a patient his or her situation is terminal when it is not. While some patients may accept what they think is their fate and simply feel sad until they are correctly diagnosed, others may respond to the initial incorrect diagnosis by going into a downward spiral marked by depression and other negative emotions and behaviors, showing the need to get it right. This potential for error is the reason why a medical team or doctor will not normally tell a patient his or her situation is terminal; rather the doctor or team will commonly let the facts of the patient's illness speak for themselves, allowing the patients come to recognize that their condition is terminal. However, on an individual basis, I sometimes advise patients to make end-of-life preparations, such as preparing legal papers, when I think the patient can handle this information.

Part of the problem in telling patients or family members that their condition is terminal is that there is some confusion about the meaning of a "terminal" diagnosis, given that what may seem terminal under some conditions might not be terminal under others, where other treatment possibilities could lead to a remission or cure. For example, if a patient is advised that he or she has a Stage IV cancer, this would likely be considered a terminal diagnosis, since the cancer has spread far beyond its origins in the body and has reached other areas, such as distant bones, the brain, and the liver. The patient's situation would likely be terminal, since short of a miraculous recovery, the patient's death would normally occur within a few days or weeks.

However, the condition might prove not to be terminal if the patient seeks an alternate type of care, such as going to a research institute like the National Institute of Health where trials of a new cancer treatment are being conducted. In this situation, the patient might have new hope, and in a few cases, patients who seek the latest innovations in medical care do thrive, though these results are usually only temporary and occur only in a small percentage of patients. Such a patient might not actually be terminal at that time under those changed conditions, although at the time the likely outcome of the treatment might not be known, so a condition might be terminal for some patients but not for others.

Given these qualifications, the real terminal status occurs when the patient reaches the point of no return and the medical team concludes this at the same time. Usually, at this point, the patient, or his or her relatives, agrees to a DNR/DNI code status, so arrangements can be made for a comfortable end of life with as little pain as possible. Often, the medical team or a doctor will call on the hospice team and they will make the final arrangements as to whether the patient will die in the hospice, nursing home, hospital, or even at home under the care of relatives or a visiting nurse or doctor. These arrangements are typically made as quickly as possible, since the patient's time is clearly short. This is quite different from the situation where a terminal condition is assessed, but the end is weeks or months away, so there is the possibility that the terminal diagnosis is not really correct after all.

Under this short-term scenario based on medical certainty, usually the patient will accept this determination based on trusting the credibility of the primary care doctor or medical team who have made this determination, as a result of their long-time knowledge and expertise in confronting hundreds of such cases. Even with this terminal assessment, some patients may still have a slight chance for short-term survival if something heroic is done for them, such as using CPR, chest compressions, or rescue chemotherapy to try to bring them back from the brink. However, such efforts generally come at a high price, such as suffering from the horrible well-known side efforts of chemotherapy, which include hair loss, severe nausea, and vomiting. Also, some patients suffering from the final stage of lung cancer who are revived may spit blood almost continuously or cough almost nonstop, while patients suffering from extreme damage to their gastrointestinal track may have a lack of control of their elimination functions, so they can't have a bowel movement and nurses have to clean and bathe them until the end. Still other patients may find a tumor growing that increasingly blocks their airway, causing a continuing sense of choking and drowning, as well as sometimes continuously spitting up blood. And these are just some of the end-of-life sources of pain and indignity that occur when patients and their family members seek to prolong life in the face of a terminal condition that can't be reversed. However, at other times, these experiences may lead patients and their families to want an end to further treatment; they have acquiesced to the inevitability of death, and they just want the painful process of dying to end.

HOW AGGRESSIVE SHOULD THE TREATMENT BE?

The question of how far one should go in treating the illness comes up as it becomes increasingly more serious, such as the case of an aggressive cancer. Should one be more conservative in selecting individual remedies from a repertoire of possible treatments, such as using medications, radiation, or diet? Or should one do everything possible at once, hoping at least one strategy might work when there isn't much time to try out different approaches in sequence? While one treatment may work in some cases, a combination of treatments may work in others. But it is not always clear in advance which remedy is the most effective—or which one is pulling the most weight in the mix of remedies. Then again, too many remedies at the same time may prove counterproductive with some patients, so the treatment may seem worse than the cure, such as when a blitz against cancer not only destroys the cancer but damages surrounding healthy cells. Yet this seemingly damaging treatment may in the long run prove the best, since it is what eliminates the disease.

The problem is that medicine is called the "art of medicine" for a reason, because different combinations work in different patients—and they work at different times as a disease gets worse, until a treatment works and the patient gets better—or it doesn't work and the patient dies. Thus, it is not always certain what is best to do in any given case, though drawing on past experience and the accumulated knowledge of medical practice can help to make a more effective diagnosis and provide a more effective treatment.

Yet there are always probabilities, much like in any scientific or social science experiment. One can generally predict an outcome with a certain chance of success. Commonly, the 95 percent success level is used in drawing conclusions, though a lower percentage is often used. Making choices of treatment plans for a patient is like that—there is no certainty, only a certain likelihood that a given approach will work or not, reflected in the figures commonly cited for curing a disease—such as a 50, 60, or 70 percent chance of recovering from a particular type of cancer. But what often isn't provided is the stage of the illness when different treatments are used, because it can be complicated to try to determine and compare stages for different patients, since different doctors may determine these stages in different ways.

This question of what combination of treatments to apply when came up in the case of Ida Walsh, a woman in her mid-sixties, who was suffering from lung cancer along with pneumonia and bronchitis. She also had a recurring skin cancer that had been the original site of her cancer. It had been treated with surgery and radiation and seemed to be gone, but then it returned and metastasized to her lung.

In deciding how aggressive a treatment to apply, I looked at religious, emotional, social, cultural, and personal variables, which vary from patient to patient, since they affect the strategy chosen. For example, when a patient is a teen or young adult, especially if they are in the early stages of an illness like cancer, I would recommend a more aggressive strategy, because there is a chance of curing the disease by getting rid of the cancer. Additionally, a younger patient has more of a future to look forward to and they are more likely to be resilient to any side effects of the treatment than older patients. By contrast, with older patients of sixty or over, if they have a more advanced state of the disease, I might suggest doing less, because the chances of a cure are less likely. So the strategy would shift to helping such patients enjoy as long a life as possible and then obtain care and comfort as they become more and more incapacitated by the disease.

In Ida's case, the situation was more complicated, since before her illness, Ida had been a very active woman, though now she was bedridden. She had recently retired from her job as an educational administrator, and she had put her time into community volunteer efforts to help the disabled and homeless find care facilities and receive contributions for their care. Also, she was active in several sports, including golf and tennis, and she had a daughter and son who had their own families in other states, though they spoke by phone each week to keep each other updated on what they were doing. Thus, she didn't want to give up without a fight, and I agreed that we at the hospital should do whatever we could to aggressively treat her multiple conditions. In fact, Ida initially urged us to do something, rather than us suggesting this approach.

"Please try any treatment you want," Ida told us. "Even if you think it's experimental, try it. I'd like to have a fighting chance to get through this. I don't want to give up now."

As a result, while Ida quickly agreed to a DNR/DNI approach should the treatment fail, we decided to not give up on her by opting for a care-and-comfort approach, which means no interventions. Given her many problems, this care-and-comfort approach to help her to a peaceful end would have been quite reasonable and humane. But Ida insisted and I agreed that it would be worth it for our medical team to more aggressively use a number of treatment approaches to fight for a cure or remission. Though she would experience some discomfort in the short run, in the long run I thought she had a good chance of overcoming the diseases, since she had a history of good health along with an active, healthy lifestyle before she suddenly found herself fighting several illnesses.

Thus, after I consulted with the medical team, we agreed to treat her pneumonia with appropriate antibiotics, and we decided to give her intravenous fluids to help her stay hydrated and keep her electrolytes in balance. Maintaining this balance is important, since these minerals in the blood and other body fluids carry an electric charge that can easily become imbalanced when a patient gets a variety of medications for different illnesses. In addition, we gave Ida bronchodilators to relax the bronchial muscles and thereby enlarge her airways to better enable air to pass through the lungs, since these were constricted by her chronic pulmonary disease. Finally, we gave her medications to prevent clot formation, since these could easily occur because of the extended time she was bedridden. Though we weren't sure what the outcome would be, we felt that Ida would now have a good chance of getting better on her own, once her system rallied due to the cocktail of treatments we put together for her.

Then we watched and waited, feeling like we needed this all-or-nothing approach to enable her to rally, since without any one of these treatment strategies she might not make it, although we didn't know enough yet about how she would respond to these treatments to know which one or ones were primarily responsible for her healing.

Fortunately, Ida said that she was fully supportive of our approach when I or a doctor from the medical team stopped by to see how she was doing, which largely confirmed the progress we were seeing on the monitor. But it was good to hear the input from her. It made her treatment more personal, which is a good thing, because with all the medical technology, there is a growing tendency to treat the patient like an object giving us progress readings on the monitor. But only the patient can describe how he or she is feeling about the way the treatment is going; and the patient's attitude can make a big difference in how he or she continues to respond to the treatment, since a positive attitude can further healing, while a negative attitude can interfere with or slow down the healing process. Then, too, getting input from the patient can help to humanize the profession of medicine by keeping the patient involved, and a positive cheerful patient like Ida can help brighten one's day.

For example, one day, a few days into our more aggressive treatment, Ida called out to me cheerily, as I stopped by her bedside to check on her progress and sought information both from her and the machine.

"Hey, doc," she called out. "I think you'll be pleased to hear I'm already feeling some progress. I can breathe a little more easily now. I think that means my lungs are healing from the pneumonia and bronchitis."

When I sat down on her bedside and looked at the machine, I could see the line for her breathing was going up and down more regularly, rather than the more irregular spurts I noticed before that suggested she was gasping for breath and the air was rushing in.

"That's good, and that's what the machine shows, too. So if you're healing from that, that's a good sign. It means you are responding positively to the medications we are giving you, so your air passages are clearer. Now we still have to knock out the underlying cancer, and that can be a little harder to treat."

"I'll try to stay positive. Maybe that'll help. "

However, while it looked like the attacks on her lung would eventually be turned back, the cancer was still there, obstructing part of her lung, and she still had lesions from the original skin cancer.

"We may have to operate to get those lesions out," I said. "They aren't responding to the radiation. It's just killing cells around the cancer, but the cancer is still growing."

"Then, do what you have to do, doctor," Ida said.

The next day, using localized anesthesia, the surgeon removed a large patch of cancerous flesh from her upper arm. When I saw her that afternoon, her arm was swathed in bandages. She held it up like a trophy won in a battle, and when I asked about the cancer, she acknowledged what I suspected.

"Yes, I am feeling some spreading pain from my arm," she said.

Her report reflected one of the potential drawbacks of this more aggressive approach, since the agony might go on for some time, although it can be relieved somewhat with morphine and other painkillers. However, these drugs can interfere with the patient's alertness, when a patient like Ida wants to stay alert and communicate with the medical staff and any visitors.

Another problem with this more aggressive approach is that there is no way to predict with certainty what the outcome will be. Even so, it might be helpful to create a time line with the patient and any close family members who are following the patient's progress. This time line can be set up by mutual agreement with the patient so that as of a certain time, if the patient shows insufficient signs of recovery, still is in frequent pain, and the patient's condition is now deemed terminal, then a patient's previously discussed DRN/DNI status can be activated, if the patient has agreed to this status. Then the patient can receive complete care and comfort, but no further treatment to defeat the disease.

"Please do that," Ida agreed. "If the fight is over and there's no way to win, I'd like the end to be short and sweet. I've had a really good life, but if it's time to check out, I'd like to go through a fast check-out line and get through it as quickly as possible."

With that agreement, I began making the arrangements with the nurses for the type of medication to keep Ida as comfortable as possible. To do so, it was necessary to determine, based on the characteristics of the patient, such as her weight, body mass, type of disease, and other factors, what medications to use, in what doses, and in what order to keep her as comfortable as possible. Normally, the medication of choice is morphine, and I spoke to the supervising nurse about what dosage to give, as well as the pros and cons of having a patient go into a coma while still breathing, since during that time the patient would experience no pain. But how long could or should this coma last? As I explained to the nurse:

"Ida understands that we will be putting her on a care and comfort arrangement now for her final days. I'd suggest we start with a morphine dosage of 2 mg an hour, though feel free to increase it up to 10 mg, so she can remain in a relaxed, peaceful state. If she starts losing that state of peace, you can increase the medication."

"What if the patient experiences a coma?" the nurse asked.

"Then it might be good to up the dosage so the patient reaches the desired level of comfort even if she is still in a coma, while she is still breathing on her own and maintaining a stable blood flow. Normally, this coma state will go on for a couple of days, but in some cases, it can last for as long as seven to ten days, before the patient comes to a natural end."

Finally, I asked the nurse to arrange a family meeting. Though family members lived in other states with only a weekly phone call connecting them over the years, I felt they would be able to at least visit Ida one last time before the end. This visit could also be a time for the family members to come together and support each other in the grieving process.

While sometimes family gatherings can turn into a source of conflict, when different family members have different ideas of how the patient's life should end—or if they push for further treatment, regardless of the medical prognosis or the patient's wishes to end things quickly, it still is important to let these differences surface and get resolved. This way, the family and relatives can better bond together and support each other in this time of sorrow.

In this case, I didn't foresee any areas of disagreement coming up for discussion, and when Ida's son and daughter arrived with their children, everything went smoothly. Even when one grandchild asked the whole group, "Can we go see grandma now? Why can't we go see grandma?" her mother explained why they couldn't.

"Grandma's resting now. We can see her later if she wakes up, or at the service we'll be holding for her to honor and remember her."

I thought that was a nice sentiment with which to remember Ida's journey. Along the way, we had done what we could to try to cure her different diseases, and we were successful in curing two of them. But the third one, the cancer, proved impossible to treat. It had spread too far and gone too deep. Once we realized it was not possible to heal her and that her condition had become terminal, Ida and I agreed it was time to bring about a quick and comfortable end. That's what we did, and now her family was gathered like a coda to support that ending and be present when Ida was finally ready to go in peace.

NOTES

INTRODUCTION

1. Catherine E. Shoichet, "Brittany Maynard, Advocate for 'Death with Dignity' Dies," CNN.com, November 3, 2014, http://www.cnn.com/2014/11/02/health/oregon-brittany-maynard.
2. "The California End of Life Option Act and Death with Dignity," *Death with Dignity*, January 22, 2016, https://www.deathwithdignity.org/news/2016/01/california-end-of-life-option-act; Sounmya Karlamangla, "How California's Aid-in-Dying Law Will Work," *Los Angeles Times*, May 12, 2016.

2. CORRECTING COMMON MISCONCEPTIONS

1. Josh Hafner, "Jahi McMath, Pronounced Dead Years Ago, Is 'Healthy,' New Photo Claims," *USA Today*, March 21, 2016, http://www.usatoday.com/story/news/nation-now/2016/03/21/jahi-mcmath-pronounced-dead-years-ago-healthy-new-photo-claims/82082798/.
2. Faith Karimi and Jason Hanna, "Drugs, Near-Drowning Led to Bobbi Kristen's Death," CNN.com, March 4, 2016, http://www.cnn.com/2016/03/04/us/bobbi-kristina-autopsy-unsealed.
3. David McNamee, "Heart Attack Survival Rates Influenced by Time of Arrival in Hospital," *Medical News Today*, July 30, 2014, http://www.medicalnewstoday.com/articles/280292.php.
4. "Sudden Cardiac Arrest: A Health-Care Crisis," Sudden Cardiac Arrest Foundation, About Sudden Cardiac Arrest, http://www.sca-aware.org/about-sca.

5. "Heart Disease and Lowering Cholesterol," WebMD.com, http://www.webmd.com/heart-disease/guide/heart-disease-lower-cholesterol-risk.

6. Ali S. Raja, MD, "Survival from Out-of-Hospital Cardiac Arrest: Good News," *NEJM Journal Watch*, December 4, 2014, http://www.jwatch.org/na36298/2014/12/04/survival-out-hospital-cardiac-arrest-good-news.

7. "King County Has World's Highest Survival Rate for Cardiac Arrest," *Public Health News*, Seattle and King County, May 19, 2014, http://www.kingcounty.gov/depts/health/news/2014/May/19-cardiac-survival.aspx.

8. Resuscitation Central, "Early Defibrillation Programs," Resuscitation Central.com, http://www.resuscitationcentral.com/defibrillation/early-defibrillation-sca-chain-of-survival/.

9. Peter Meaney et al., "Cardiopulmonary Resuscitation Quality: Improving Cardiac Resuscitation Both Inside and Outside the Hospital," *Circulation*, July 13, 2014, http://circ.ahajournals.org/content/128/4/417.

10. Z. D. Goldberger et al., "Duration of Resuscitation Efforts and Survival After In-Hospital Cardiac Arrest: An Observational Study," *Lancet* 380, no. 9852 (October 27, 2012): 1473–81, http://www.ncbi.nlm.nih.gov/pubmed/22958912.

9. DEALING WITH DEMENTIA

1. Richard Glatzer and Wash Westmoreland, *Still Alice*, directed by Richard Glatzer, Sony Pictures Classics, December 5, 2014.

12. LEGAL CONSIDERATIONS

1. Patrick McGreevy, "Aid-in-Dying Bill to Take Effect June 9 in California," *Los Angeles Times*, March 10, 2016, http://www.latimes.com/politics/la-pol-sac-assisted-suicide-law-can-take-effect-20160310-story.html.

2. Ibid.

3. Death with Dignity, August 7, 2016, https://www.deathwithdignity.org/take-action/.

INDEX

advice and support, from hospitalists, 5
AED. *See* automated external defibrillator
aggressive treatment possibilities, 9–10,
   252–258
aging patients: hospital-doctor relationship,
   6–7; palliative care services for, 10
AIDS. *See* HIV/AIDS
alcoholism, 147, 202–203, 203
alternative care, for terminal patient, 251
Alzheimer's disease, 108, 113, 122, 125
aneurism, 214
aneurysm of brain, 19–20
antiarrhytmics, 168
antihypotensive agents, 168–169
anxiety: Ativan for, 182, 200, 230, 241;
   families experience of, 159; heart attack
   from, 44
appendicitis, 194
arrhythmogenic condition, 18, 188–189
arsenic poisoning, 78
assisted-living facility, 22, 27
assisted suicide, 3, 51, 52, 197, 210–211;
   DNR comparison to, 83; life-ending
   medication, 210–211; Maynard, 2, 211;
   O'Donnell, 191, 211; provisions for,
   211
atherosclerosis, 202
Ativan, for anxiety, 182, 200, 230, 241
atrial fibrillation, 168, 240; patient
   example, 143–146

attorney: dementia involvement of, 108,
   120, 126, 127–128; lawsuits and, 202,
   207; power of, 125
automated external defibrillator (AED), 42
automatic responses, in brain death, 103

balance point, for morphine administration,
   199–201
Bilevel Positive Airway Pressure (BiPAP)
   machine, 16, 74–75, 79, 147, 148, 186,
   193, 230; for CO_2 accumulation, 74;
   CPAP compared to, 186
blame deflection to doctors, 118
blood: coagulation test, 178–179; flow
   blockage, in strokes, 130; platelets,
   177–178, 179, 237, 238; transfusion,
   237, 238. *See also* high blood pressure
blood clots, 99–100, 166, 179, 199; cardiac
   arrest and lung embolism from, 179; in
   lungs, 183
blood pressure, 175; antihypotensive
   agents for, 168–169; cuff, 187
bodily functions: brain death and, 14, 40,
   159, 246; machines control of, 31–32,
   95, 99, 104; shutdown in ICU, 98,
   102–103; terminal diagnosis and, 33,
   96; tumors shutting down of, 22
bone: cancer spread to, 222; marrow
   cancer example, 239–241
brain: aneurysm, 19–20; CT scan for injury
   to, 102–103; tumor, 198, 198–199

ABOUT THE AUTHORS

Sebastian Sepulveda, MD, is a nephrologist in Chelmsford, Massachusetts. He is affiliated with Lowell General Hospital and has nearly thirty years of experience as a doctor and professor of medicine, specializing in emergency medicine and end-of-life care. He has also worked as an associate professor of medicine at the Medical College of Georgia, now known as Georgia Regents University in Augusta, Georgia. He has been a member of several professional organizations that deal with terminal patients, including the Society of Critical Care Medicine, the American Society of Nephrology, and the American College of Chest Physicians. He conducts workshops and seminars for patients with serious illnesses and their family members to help them better understand and make arrangements for end-of-life care.

Gini Graham Scott is a nationally known writer, consultant, speaker, and seminar leader, specializing in business and work relationships, professional and personal development, social trends, lifestyles, and criminal justice. She has published over fifty books with major publishers and has published over sixty books under her own publishing label. She is a *Huffington Post* regular columnist, commenting on social trends, new technology, and everyday life. Recent books include *The New Middle Ages*, *Scammed: Learn from the Biggest Consumer and Money Frauds Not to Be a Victim*, and *Lies and Liars: How and Why Sociopaths Lie and How You Can Detect and Deal with Them*. She has received national media exposure for her books, including appearances on Good Morning America, Oprah, and CNN.